LOCKED

DOWN

BUT NOT

OUT

A COVID DIARY BY
GILLIAN JONES-WILLIAMS

This book is in honour of the heroes of the NHS who fought so hard to save us during Covid-19. All proceeds go to the fund for families of NHS workers who lost their lives during the pandemic.

Quotations from real people were written down verbatim whilst listening to a live television broadcast.

The opinions expressed herein are solely those of the author.

Photos courtesy of Spiros Kurtidis.

Published by Goldcrest Books International Ltd
www.goldcrestbooks.com
publish@goldcrestbooks.com

ISBN: 978-1-913719-28-9
eISBN: 978-1-913719-29-6

This book is dedicated to all of the NHS workers who put their lives at risk on a daily basis to save us from coronavirus, but, particularly, those who lost their lives in service.

It is also to remember all the other essential workers who kept our country running whilst putting themselves at risk.

Personal Dedications

To my wonderful husband Keith, for not only getting me through lockdown but being my rock!

To my children, Lawrence and Elly who I missed desperately during lockdown.

To my granddaughter, our very own lockdown baby, who I cannot wait to meet in February 2021.

To my amazing team at Emerge who worked tirelessly to keep the business afloat.

In loving memory of the inspirational legend
Captain Sir Tom Moore

1920 - 2021

Song for Now

Our world changed so quickly, the lights went out one day.
Everything we knew was gone; our freedom taken away.

The streets so empty and quiet, the world is so very still.
Our lives have changed forever, indoors against our will.

Only time will show, only time will tell.
What we will call this, heaven or hell?

But to learn important lessons, to open wide our eyes.
The pain was so horribly real, we lost so many lives.

What can we learn, what will we do?
What will this mean for me and for you?
And if this makes our world a safer place.
And if our lives enter a better space.
Then the universe has spoken.
And we have heard.

To live in peace, to savour our time.
Being close to loved ones, that piece felt so fine.
The world has changed before our eyes.
We won't ever return.
But we can make the future work.
If we love, we care, we learn.

INTRODUCTION

Why would you write a book about the worst year that many people have ever experienced in their lives? Would anyone want to read it? Or would everyone just want to bury the memory of the five months deep inside the hidden vaults of their brain, instead, remembering it as one of the hottest springs recorded in history? I am already picturing the amount of people, who, on 31st December 2020, will fill their Insta and Facebook feed with: 'Can't wait to see the end of 2020' or one of many variations on that. However, I do not feel that way. I really do not want people to forget this year.

For me, this year has been the richest journey of my life, filled with fear, sadness, desperation, hope, joy and learning; lots of learning. More than probably in the entire sixty years I have been on this Earth. And believe me, I like to reflect and learn. But, never ever, have I experienced the depth of introspection 2020 threw at me. The need to throw away my internal rule book, rethink my entire approach to life, both personally and professionally, and to accept the challenge to truly step-up as a leader and business owner.

But that is not why I wrote the book. I started recording the events surrounding coronavirus the week before lockdown, when everything started to get serious. I wrote every single day; in the morning about how I was feeling personally and my struggle to hang on to my business, and in the evening when the Downing Street briefing happened, but also throughout the day when things pinged up on the news. And I could not believe what I was writing; it felt like I was writing a fiction novel and now, when I read it back, I still am shocked at some of the things that happened.

At first, I did not know why I was so obsessed with writing it every day, as I thought it was just to be a record for my children and friends, but then things changed. Suddenly, I was not just recording deaths of people in hospitals but watching the very people who were dedicating their lives to saving us all, going to work, contracting the virus and losing their lives, and this is when I started to realise that I wanted to publish the book to support those workers. This was a battle and they were our front-line troops. In the armed forces, people are thoroughly aware of what they are signing up for when they join. From day one they know that they face the possibility that they will be in a life-threatening situation. And they are given the equipment to ensure that it is as fair a fight as can be anticipated. But doctors and nurses sign up to their role believing that they will go to work and save people's lives, not to go to war. This is particularly true for those who are still at medical school. And yet, we sent them in to war, in fact we begged them to go into war for us. And they did it, willingly, diving deep into the front line, often without the equipment that they needed, and with little knowledge of the enemy. And all we could do was clap. Then, as they continued to battle, working long hours every day, often sacrificing their home life with their own family in order to protect them, and whilst they worked in terrifying conditions, helplessly watching people die, over worked and overwhelmed, they had to contain their anger as the public refused to stay at home and flocked to beaches and street parties.

Suddenly, the playing field was levelled – the rich were as much at risk as the poorer communities; it did not matter how much money you had, it afforded you no protection at all. It did not matter how clever you were, or how important you were at work; there was no value you could add to saving lives. The only people who could save us were the NHS workers. And meanwhile, as we locked down, we suddenly realised that all of those people who you might not have noticed as important in your life, the shop assistant, the bus driver, the delivery driver, the post person, and many others were suddenly elevated to lifesaving status. But for how long? Once the pandemic started to ease would we still celebrate them and thank them? Or would we quickly forget?

2020
Sunday, 8th March
The calm before the quiet

I turn and glance around the house for one last time. Everything has been cleaned, the beds changed, laundry washed, ironing completed, and stray items put tidily in place. I feel stupidly smug and satisfied. Often when we go on holiday, we rush out of the door leaving chaos behind, but this time we have had time to get organised and my sad, borderline OCD tendencies tell me that I will relax more on holiday knowing I am coming back to this orderly and pristine existence. My crazy life takes me travelling around the world with not a moment to relax and my routine is pretty much run to a military schedule. Knowing that when I returned, I would only have half a day to pack and unpack before I hit the ground running, meant organising another case ready to pack and unpack before I left. My crazy life – everyone commented about it. If only I had known that the rest of my life would not exist in any recognisable format when I returned....

It is the 8th March. We are heading for the slopes for our annual skiing holiday. A holiday that we look forward to from the time we return each year, and our excitement is palpable. For the past few weeks we have seen the news about the coronavirus in China, and then the spread to

Italy, but it isn't really affecting us yet. In February people had started to take notice of it but it was so far away in China, South Korea, Iran and Italy. There were still more headlines about Harry and Meghan and Brexit rather than coronavirus, but what we didn't know is, that behind the scenes in the last week of February, 442,675 phone calls were made to the non-emergency NHS line, 111. There was a ripple of anxiety around but no one in the UK was really scared. By the 1st March, the virus had reached the UK with cases in England, Northern Ireland, Scotland and Wales and we had wondered if we would actually be able to go skiing. But the majority of cases were in Italy and not the area of France we were going to. If you had been to Northern Italy you had to come back and isolate, but that was all we heard. The Prime Minister did a briefing and launched the Government's coronavirus action plan, declaring it a level-four incident. He mentioned that schools might need to close and large-scale gatherings be reduced, but it was hard to truly visualise this happening. The next day a woman in her seventies became the first victim. The press reported the words that we were soon to become so familiar with – underlying conditions. Reports started to filter through of hand sanitiser selling out in supermarkets.

After that, the numbers of cases crept up – 115 by the 5th March, and on the day we left, 273 cases, which still felt small – only 4 in our local area.

In the weeks before we flew to Geneva the business events that I had attended had been concerned about the potential spread of the virus and anti-bacterial handwash was becoming a pre-requisite in many reception areas, but nobody really thought it would seriously affect the UK. My year had started so well that my mind was very focused on my business – the business that I founded twenty-five years ago and had built into an international training company.

In January I had turned sixty and amongst my busy work schedule I had been showered with surprises for a month, so it had passed in a blur.

To add to the excitement in January I had been named as one of the f;Entrepreneur #ialso, top 100, 2020 female entrepreneurs. The f:Entrepreneur campaign celebrates talented female entrepreneurs from all over the UK in order to recognise the powerful women who run so many businesses in the UK and you become part of the #Ialso community so I felt really honoured and to celebrate we had been invited to a reception at the House of Lords on the 4th March. The day before the event, we were asked not to kiss or hug the other women, which was a shame as we were all connecting on Facebook and were excited (and I am definitely a hugger!) but we were just glad the event wasn't cancelled. It was a wonderful day of Mimosa, deep conversations, connections, laughter and potential joint ventures, and we left feeling full of hope and excitement for the future. The week after that was International Women's Day and I toured around making presentations to raise money for my charity for abused women. The feedback was intensely positive, the women inspired, and I felt on top of my game. Business was looking good for the year, despite Brexit, my team was working hard and were the best they ever had been, and I felt confident enough to take on a new person from the 1st April. Little did I know that I was about to potentially lose everything within a week.

Our taxi picks us up and we meet one of our skiing party, Sally, at the airport. Sally is renowned for being a bit of a drama queen and looks like a parody of the invisible man with sunglasses on (despite the gloomy conditions) and a white scarf covering most of her face. Keith tells her that the flimsy cloth will do nothing to protect her, but she remains like that for the whole flight. Sally is obsessed with the virus and talks of nothing else. It is like living with the Grim Reaper. She spends all day scrolling through her phone telling us how many deaths there have been. Each morning she comes out of her room and shouts the body count over the wooden balcony into the kitchen to us whilst we have breakfast. After three days we ask her to stop. She is bringing everyone down and ruining our holiday – we all know the virus is happening and that we will have to face the news when we return, but for this week we just wanted to be in our skiing bubble. She is surprised when I mention the impact she is having on everyone and tells me she is just curious about it. I ask her to be more quietly curious. My heart tells me the situation is getting serious, but I don't want to face it yet.

We dress for our first day's skiing – the cumbersome and boring part of the sport – layers, salopettes, gloves, skiing boots (that have my feet wincing with pain within seconds of doing them up), and head for the slopes. Our ski guide, Alex, is Italian, young, floppy-haired, charming and as mad as a box of frogs. He greets us with a big smile, tells us the weather conditions are rubbish and that there is coronavirus everywhere. We agree not to ski with him that day but to just do a couple of lower runs and try out the conditions. He is right – the conditions are pretty sticky with low visibility, so we ski till lunchtime and then come home. The slopes are near deserted and I know it is not the conditions that are keeping people away. There is a very strange feel to the resort.

The next day we get ready to go out again. The night off seems to have done nothing to reduce Alex's crazy tendencies and he refuses to allow anyone else in the bubble lift with us, shouting at them that he has coronavirus! They back out looking terrified. He is petrified about it, but we are not surprised as he is Italian and they seem to be hit hard. Thankfully, the good thing about skiing is that you cannot talk too much when you are on the slopes, just when you stop and when you are in the bubble lifts. Sally, who is single, is highly amused by Alex and takes to him immediately, despite his incoherent ramblings. We get to the top of Courcheval and start the run down. The first slope is good even though visibility isn't great. At the top of the next slope we stop and wait whilst Alex discusses our technique. Sally scrambles to get closer to Alex knocking my husband, Keith, out of the way, sending him flying and they both tumble into the snow. She screams in pain. She has hurt her wrist. We stand around clinging to the side of the steep slope whilst Alex looks at it. He decides to call Mountain Rescue as she clearly can't hold a pole to ski down. She objects loudly and we have a twenty-minute debate whilst she refuses to go down in the blood wagon. Alex eventually persuades her that there is no choice and she reluctantly gets in. We ski quickly behind her down into the medical centre at Courcheval. I send Keith and the others off to have lunch whilst I stay with her in the medical centre and the verdict comes through – it is broken. I then discover the French have a crazy system where they put on a cast and give you a sling but you cannot leave the clinic until you go to the pharmacy and replace the resin and sling. It takes thirty minutes of my broken French, and the very irritated clinic receptionist's broken English, for us to determine this. The outcome is I have to go to the pharmacy, which is right through the shopping mall and down the road. Walking in ski boots is never easy but walking distances on pavements and up stairs in ski boots is incredibly challenging. I quickly twist my knee on the steps. So that was it, no more skiing for me and my role for the week became nursemaid to a very needy Sally as we become chalet-bound with our injuries.

Thank goodness for the rest of the group and the fun we had in the evenings playing games after dinner and relaxing. As the week progresses the news starts to filter through from the UK – things are escalating quickly and looking worrying. The death rate was still low, but it was concerning. The World Health Organisation declared a pandemic on the 11th March. Sports were being affected and all football matches were starting to be played behind closed doors. Italy was now on full lockdown. I worried that might happen in the UK. I email my team to say we should prepare for a potential lockdown and look at what we can do from home and prepare any materials we need. The reply is quite a surprising one – they said that whilst they didn't really know what lockdown would mean and were pretty sure it wouldn't happen, and if it did, then we would probably be able to go to work as it was such a small office. If only we could have known then that less than two weeks later we would be in lockdown.

The news keeps coming, telling us that apparently, stockpiling is happening – videos of people fighting over toilet rolls in supermarkets are appearing online – I find it hard to believe it has got this crazy so quickly, and selfishly feel glad I have booked a Sainsbury's delivery for Sunday afternoon. I wonder if my toilet rolls will arrive?

Each day I check my emails. My accounts manager wants to have a meeting to go through some projections and my stomach flips as I know it will be bad. We have more information from our clients postponing courses. Our business is delivering face-to-face training courses and, at first, we thought they were being super cautious in cancelling but as the rest of the week goes by, and each day brings more cancellations, I realise the business is in trouble. Bookings had fallen off a cliff, and as a training company if we don't have any training courses to run, we are not earning any money.

On 13th March in the US, President Trump declares a state of national emergency. Later that day news comes through that the London Marathon is cancelled along with the Premier League and English Football League, and Theresa May's elections. Ironically, the week before we left I had been asked to join the Marathon as a tail walker – the shock of realising I had only five weeks to train had galvanised me into action but now I have plenty of time.

On the 14th of March, the last day of the holiday, I wake up feeling inexplicably low and for the first time in a long time I can't control my emotions. I am tearful and fed up. Keith goes out skiing and I have a meltdown – sobbing uncontrollably in my bedroom. I don't want anyone to know, so I tell the others I am going for a walk and to take my skis back to the shop in the hope I can shake it off. One of the party, my good friend Stephen, messages me and comes to meet me in La Tania for a coffee. We sit in the outdoor coffee shop and watch the sparse line of skiers zig zagging down the piste – it really is bizarre how empty the slopes are. I feel jealous and angry that I haven't been able to ski, but I also feel scared and depressed. I have hit rock bottom.

I blurt it all out whilst Stephen listens, my fear of making my team redundant after they have been so loyal to me, but at the same time I have financial reserves in the business that are my pension, and If I use the reserves to keep the business going then I stand to lose the whole pension. It is like playing roulette with the highest stakes ever. I know that I could easily find work for myself if I did close the business, but we are doing so well, we started the year on such a high, can I do that to the team? Stephen orders coffee and brandy, and as the smooth liquid burns my throat I start to feel marginally better. He is in the same business as me and has had exactly the same thing happen – all bookings cancelled for two months.

On the 14th, which is our last night, we go out for our traditional last night Pizza in La Tania. We are just finishing dinner when the news comes in that President Macron has declared all pubs, bars and restaurants to be closed, and they have four hours to do it. The rest of the resort is also closing and we listen sympathetically to a group of people who have arrived that afternoon to the news that the resort is shutting down – nothing will be open tomorrow including the ski lifts.

The next morning, we wake and leave the chalet for the airport. The arrivals hall is chaotic with queues winding around for miles to check in. There is an eerie feeling of evacuation in the air, people look nervous and jittery. We join the queue and settle in for a long wait, but Sally has other ideas. She requests special assistance and they immediately take us to the front of the queue. I don't resist – the sooner I get away from being in close proximity with all of these people the better. Sally is still doing her Invisible Man impression with her scarf around her face. We check in and she leaves us to go to the assistance area. We wait for the plane and it is on time – the scene on the aircraft is very much like the final scene from the film *Argo*, tense silence whilst we wait on the tarmac desperate to take off in case they change their minds; convinced someone will board and tell us that the borders are shut and we cannot leave. But we do take off and the flight is uneventful.

The house is peaceful and tidy and the cat is delighted to see us. All so normal. We unpack but we both are feeling unwell. I am really hot and Keith has chills. We are exhausted and achy. Is that the effect of skiing or do we have the virus? We have no cough so concede that we don't. I cancel my personal training session the next morning as I am not feeling great. We agree we should self-isolate for a week just in case we have symptoms.

The Sainsbury's order arrives on time that afternoon – including the toilet roll! All so normal.

We watch the news – the US bans gatherings of 50 or more; I wonder if that will happen here?

Around the world people start to look to Italy, France and Spain, which have already gone into lockdown, and wonder if it could happen in their countries or even here. Still, there are many people who are blasé and complain about why there was is so much fuss – isn't it just flu?

Boris Johnson appears on television and tells us he will seek to shore up people's confidence in the Government's handling of the coronavirus pandemic for as long as necessary. The idea of Boris Johnson giving people confidence is so absurd that I can't take him seriously. I was an avid Brexit Remainer, so I have no time for Boris – or any of them really any more for that matter. In December I completely lost interest in politics.

We watch a lot of news and a feeling of impending doom starts to hit me.

Monday, 16th March

I get up at 6.00 a.m. and go for a long walk to clear my head and think through the implications of what is going on. I know that I can't go to work but there are things I have to pick up, so I phone them and warn them. Only my office manager, Dawn, and accounts manager, Gemma, are in this morning. I tell them that I will come in and get the things from my office and they must stay away from me. It all feels a bit over the top but I don't want to put them at risk.

I drive in to the office and stand at the door whilst we have a brief catch-up. I feel cross that I can't stay and spend time with them after being away for two weeks already. I pick up my box of files and tell them to disinfect the door handles after I leave. It feels strange saying goodbye – although I say it is for a week, in my heart, I know it is going to be longer.

I look in my diary and today is a busy one – a coaching briefing with a client at 11.00 a.m., an accounts update followed by a webinar at 1.00 p.m. and then another coaching call for two hours in the afternoon, so I barely have time to get settled at my desk at home before the first call.

A client messages me to ask how I am doing and I am touched. They tell me that they have put a hold on spend, but if there is anything that they can get they will call us. It gives me hope to receive the email.

At 12.30 p.m. I have a call with Barry and Gemma. Barry is my ex-husband and the father of my two children. When we were married he was the financial director of the company, but when we divorced it became acrimonious for a while and he stepped away. Fortunately, now we are best of friends and I retain him to advise me on our financial situation and also to support our highly capable accounts manager, Gemma.

They deliver the news factually and gently. We have lost what amounts to £100,000 in cancelled bookings. It stops you in your tracks when you hear figures like that even though I was pretty sure it was something in that region. We have a very business-like discussion – even though Gemma is the accounts manager she needs to understand where my head is. What do I do? Do I take my money and shut down, knowing that I will always be able to work and that I already had lost a massive chunk of my pension pot? Or do I stick with it and pray that we will survive and recoup the money? Gemma is understanding and they both know that it is one of the most difficult decisions of my career.

I tell them I want to think about it and get on with my afternoon's calls. I am heartened by messages from some of my clients offering us pieces of work if they can get purchase orders.

I complete the day in a daze – still shell-shocked as to what is happening and not quite comprehending what it is going to mean to isolate for a week. I speak to my daughter Elly who is due to go to Barcelona for her birthday on Wednesday and is horribly disappointed. I hate to hear her so down and not to be able to do anything for her.

The Prime Minister hosts the first daily update with UK Chief Medical Officer, Professor Chris Witty, and Sir Patrick Vallance, the UK's chief scientific adviser, to give us some guidelines.

Boris Johnson says that we should all avoid non-essential travel and contact with others to try and curb the virus and that people should work from home where possible as part of a range of stringent new measures.

Advice is also given that pregnant women, people over the age of 70 and those with certain health conditions should consider staying at home for twelve weeks. I have a lung condition – borderline COPD, so I realise I am at risk, but I am certainly not staying at home for twelve weeks!

Boris also announces some more measures including asking people to avoid social gatherings and crowded places, i.e. pubs, clubs and theatres. He adds that all unnecessary visits to friends and relatives in care homes should stop. I think of my best friend, Sarah, whose mother has rapid onset of dementia and is in a home and gets very agitated without visits. If she can't visit it will be devastating for both of them.

This is followed by a plea from Boris to only use the NHS when we really need it. Apparently, we are only three weeks behind Italy – the worst-hit country in Europe. But I feel certain that it will never get to that point here; everyone is saying that they have a high population of elderly and that is why they have been so badly hit.

Further advice states that anyone with a persistent cough and fever should stay at home for fourteen days and not go out at all. Those people should, if possible, avoid leaving the house even to buy food or essentials – but they may leave the house for exercise, and in that case, at a safe distance from others. This is absolutely surreal.

Boris adds that drastic action is needed as we approach the fast growth part of the upward curve of cases, and Londoners should really take heed as this is where it is spreading most. My heart goes cold; my son, Lawrence, is in London with his fiancée. I rationalise that he is not in any at-risk category, or vulnerable, and try and relax.

I make my decision about work. I can't let them all down now and if I let twenty-five years go down the drain due to a virus then I will always look back and wish I had fought. I need to be strong and determined. However, I also need to tell them the truth. I can't fight this alone and they need to understand the odds. I write an email to the team but don't send it – I want to re-read it in the morning and be sure it is what I want to say.

We are due to have Keith's son Sam for the weekend, but just in case we have got the virus Keith decides to message Sam's mum and say that we are in isolation for a week.

We watch the news. All NYC schools close. Wow, schools closing, that is serious stuff. Latin America starts to apply restrictions on their citizens with Columbia and Costa Rica closing their borders

I sit on the sofa with my laptop intending to work and am asleep again in seconds. I don't understand why I am so exhausted and achy – I also then go to bed and sleep for eight hours.

TOTAL DEATHS – 55

Tuesday, 17th March

It feels strange when I wake up today. It is nice in some ways that I don't have to travel but weird that I am not delivering my Women's Development training programme at the ECB; I always enjoy going to Lord's but yesterday we cancelled it. I still wake early and go to the gym. I am incredibly lucky that a few years ago my husband built me a gym in the garden as it was so hard for me to go to one due to my strange working hours, and even though it is small, I have managed to pack enough equipment in it to have a really good session. Although today it is half-hearted as I still don't feel great.

I'm at my desk by 7.30 a.m. I get started on my proposals as I have no appointments now. I think of the team all in the office and feel quite nostalgic. Before going on holiday I hadn't been in the office for two weeks and I miss them all a lot.

The news plays on my iPad whilst I work – France goes on lockdown with Europe's most stringent measures. They have 6,500 infections with more than 140 deaths. The EU bans most travellers from outside for thirty days and the EU has voted to close at least 26 countries. However, our borders are staying open.

I send the email to the team. My heart still fells heavy, but I feel it is the right thing to do. I am not sure how they will respond.

Lucy, our co-ordinator, replies immediately to thank me and say she completely understands. Rob my designer tells me, in his own inimitable style, that was a bit of an 'oh shit' moment first thing this morning, but thanks me for having faith in them. My gut tells me I am making the right decision.

My team are all at work and I stupidly feel a bit jealous and left out. Normally I would love to have a day working at home but now that I have to if feels different. I have no appointments, so I start to work through my long list of tasks but calls and emails keep pinging in interrupting my flow and I don't make the progress I hoped.

Keith is home too and I suddenly realise that we are going to have to set some ground rules if we are going to be able to survive the week spending twenty-four hours a day together. We have only been married for five years this year and due to my travelling, we are apart for a significant part of the week – in fact, if you really sat down and calculated it, probably it would equate to less than a year! When I met Keith in 2011 some people thought it wouldn't last. They expected me to be with someone who was a big businessman and Keith was a teacher. But I loved the fact that he wasn't a businessman and didn't have a corporate job where he bought home his work, and what had struck other people as ordinary, to me was stable and added simplicity to my chaotic life. Keith is strong and very comfortable in his own skin, a man of simple tastes, but he is kind and loving and highly practical. After we met, he never went back to teaching and started a property company, and now we have nine properties that are rented out that he manages. So, he is used to managing his own day, arranging his appointments and tasks in his own time, and having the house to himself. This was going to be a real test of our relationship.

He is banging about loudly in the kitchen and I am grumpy; I can't concentrate so I put my earphones in. Why is it that when he does a task he does everything so loudly – is this a man thing? Well, this is going to be fun for a week trying to concentrate whilst he slams around. Keith is highly efficient when he does jobs but that translates into a lot of noise. At times it feels like he is throwing the plates like Frisbees from the other side of the kitchen, and as I try to work all I can think about is the chips in my china! However, I am grateful that he does help and is good around the house; without him I wouldn't be able to do my job. As well as running our property business he keeps the house running and the garden maintained, and looks after me above and beyond the call of duty.

News comes through that a further 14 people who tested positive for coronavirus have now died. Briton's are advised against non-essential travel to anywhere in the world as experts admit the UK could already have up to 55,000 cases of the virus.

Euro 2020 is postponed until 2021 – well at least that news makes me happy!

Before I know it, the day has gone and it is time for the Prime Minister's briefing. He states his plan for beating coronavirus and stopping it spreading starting with shielding vulnerable groups. He hints that whilst the measures announced are already extreme the Government may have to go further. He gives an overview of what they are doing. He then makes a strange comment, that we must act like any wartime government and do whatever it takes to support our economy. Wartime? Is that how they see this? However, he does start talking about the impact it might have on businesses and how the Government will support them, which sounds hopeful.

Rishi Sunak, Chancellor of the Exchequer, starts to speak and unveils a £350 billion bailout, promising to do whatever it takes to help keep businesses and households afloat.

He states that the government will pay 80% of people's salaries to avoid redundancies – I am not entirely clear if this will help us but it sounds good and I am sure that many people will be relieved.

His presentation is powerful and he is sincere and dynamic. I wonder if we might have just found our next Prime Minister. His promises are extreme and the way that he describes his offering is almost as if he was paying it out of his own pocket.

He says he is extending the Business Interruption Loan Scheme so that they can now offer loans of up to £5 million, which were previously capped at £1.2 million, with no interest due for the first six months.

He also offers an additional cash grant of up to £25,000 to help businesses through this period. Additionally, he tells the camera, he is extending the business rates holiday to all businesses, irrespective of their rateable value.

All this is coming on top of the multi-billion-pound package he set out at the budget. Where on earth is he suddenly getting all of this money from? At the budget he had announced that he was providing £3,000 cash grants to 700,000 small businesses – he now announces that he is increasing this to £10,000. He really has deep pockets.

Finally, he announces that mortgage lenders will offer at least a three-month mortgage holiday.

He finishes with a rousing statement delivered impeccably:

"Let no one doubt our resolve. When I said in the Budget that we will do everything we can to keep

this country, and our people, healthy and financially secure – I meant it."

"The measures I have announced today are part of a comprehensive, coordinated and coherent response to what is a serious and evolving economic situation."

"These are only the first steps – I will set out the next stage of our response in the coming days."

"We have never faced an economic fight like this one. But we are well prepared. We will get through this. And we will do whatever it takes."

'The boy done good,' as my old dad used to say!

TOTAL DEATHS – 71

Wednesday, 18th March

Today reality really hit. The trigger is such a ridiculous one, I was idly watching *Good Morning Britain*, as Susanna Reid presented an article, and admiring her dress. I thought of my wardrobes that were packed full of clothes – a necessity for my job, standing up in front of people and training – and wondered when I would ever wear them again. I miss dressing up every day, even though when I had the opportunity it felt like a chore, when I had to choose an outfit every morning at 6.00 a.m. and yearned to just throw on some jeans and a sweatshirt. I also hate packing, which I did most nights, and should really feel great that I didn't have to do that for a few weeks. But I don't.

I feel my head swimming with thoughts and I look around at my house. We had recently remodelled the ground floor as I felt our dining room was too small and my study was even smaller. We had decided that if we built out behind the current lounge, we would have a wonderful, massive, open dining room with bi-folding doors onto the decking, and the current dining room would become a huge study. I didn't work from home very often, but I was thinking forward – maybe one day in the future I would work more from home. Little did I know how important this space was going to be for me. The house remodelling became a wonderful project for my daughter and me – she has a talent for home design and meticulously instructed me on how to make the space work with her beach house theme. It was a manic time leading up to Christmas and I barely had time to even look at the new items being delivered, but it was completed and I moved into my new study. I loved the study but the only downside was that it had no doors and opened out onto the kitchen area. Keith said he would put the doors up later and I nagged him regularly. He seemed reluctant – I think it was one of those fiddly jobs that was worthy of procrastination, and so the rest of the house got finished and still no doors. But I was so delighted with the rest of the house and hugely excited to have dinner parties in my new dining area. Ironically, apart from one casual supper the night before we went skiing, they never happened.

But now I look at the house differently. I suddenly realised that clothes and furniture have no worth at all. No one comes to the house, so it doesn't matter how it looks. Our houses are all beautiful prisons, and we all have four walls; we are all equal. My expensive clothes, on holiday in the wardrobe, mean nothing and nobody cares how I look. My lovely convertible car that I worked so hard for and enjoyed so much, sits useless in the drive. All of those things that we used to get so worked up about, marks on jackets, lost earrings, towels on floors, stains on floors and sofas, the trivia that fuelled arguments, was all gone. There was only one thing that was important now and that was survival. And the irony is that the hierarchy is crumbling; those people who thought they were so important in their careers are now finally seeing who the important people are, the ones who make a difference to our lives and are doing the crucial jobs we need. The people who work in the

NHS, the care workers, and the emergency services – these are the people who are now working to save our world, if it can be saved. The playing field is truly being levelled.

But there are more – the shop assistants, the farmers, the people who process our water, provide our electricity and broadband, and the cleaners and refuse workers – the world is feeling a whole new level of respect for these people. If they didn't respect them before then they need to now as they are the ones who are keeping our country ticking over, the core of our daily lives; the people who would not necessarily be noticed until they stopped doing their jobs, ironically are the ones who are on the lowest income and work the longest hours. I hear of retail assistants being abused in shops because the shop did not have stocks and I feel embarrassed and upset for them.

I start work at 8.30 a.m. and I still feel overloaded with tasks. At 10.00 a.m. I have a call with a new client, and it starts differently to other calls with new clients. We immediately discuss the situation and she laughs that she is doing the call in her bedroom as her husband needs to use the study. It is so good to focus on work and we look at ideas for a mentoring programme. She asks for a proposal and I add it to my list. The call is far more collegiate than it might have been if we were face to face. Before even starting the call we had something in common, which helped to connect us.

I begin the proposal, but it is hard to focus. I have a call with one of my clients in Saudi Arabia in an hour or so. They were the first people to cancel two weeks of training early on when the virus news was coming through. At the time I felt it might have been a bit pre-emptive but now I realise they were absolutely right. She wants to look at potential ideas for some webinars for those people who are at home. I have always shied away from online training, my grasp of technology is not as strong as it should be and I always felt I needed the face-to-face connection, but at this point we have to be open to anything.

It is a good call; I have always had a great relationship with her and it is a relief to talk to her. She outlines what she is thinking but is very open to ideas. She knows as much as me about technology and I feel grateful that she is willing to learn with me. She knows that this is not our area of expertise and that we are going to have to navigate this together.

News is coming thick and fast. Supermarkets are starting rationing. I still don't understand this desperate scrabble for toilet paper. The pound has slumped to its lowest level in thirty-five years as the virus pushed traders to ditch Sterling.

Sad news for music lovers – Glastonbury is cancelled. It is the 50th anniversary and was set to be absolutely major this year, but they can't risk spending three months on set up for it to be cancelled.

Not such sad news, the *Eurovision Song Contest* is cancelled. And then a momentous announcement – filming on *EastEnders* and *Casualty* has been suspended. Ironically, I was on set there recently training the new assistant directors – they were so excited about beginning their blocks on the programme, which of course will not happen now. This is soon followed by *Coronation Street* and other soaps. What will most of the nation do without their weekly injection of soaps? I wonder whether eventually the whole of the TV network could start to crumble.

I go back to focusing on my work until the Prime Minister's briefing. He is joined by Jenny Harries, Deputy Chief Medical Officer for England, and Sir Patrick Vallance, Chief Scientific Adviser. I hope for some news on self-employed support, there has been a massive outcry from freelancers and self-employed that nothing has been offered.

The briefing starts and this one is a shocker – shit just got real. Gavin Williamson is making a statement now in House of Commons that schools are due to close on Friday – and will probably stay closed until September. This is shocking and my heart goes out to all parents and children. I am not sure of the implications for Sam, but for the classes of 2020, those who were leaving this year, it was devastating; exams, proms and farewells to classmates and teachers will not happen. He assures us that pupils will still get their qualifications. He also reminds parents that children should not be left with older grandparents, or older relatives, who may be particularly vulnerable or fall into some of the vulnerable groups.

Boris Johnson then tackles the subject of going out. The UK had been told they couldn't go out to pubs and restaurants, but people ignored this. So, he repeats that *everyone* – *everyone* – must follow the advice to protect themselves and their families, but also – more importantly – to protect the wider public. He urges us all to stay at home for seven days if we think we have symptoms.

He also reassures us that he will massively scale up our testing capacity in the weeks ahead so that we hit 25,000 tests a day. There is a call-out for any retired healthcare professionals to come back to support the NHS.

He finishes by saying: "But we will not hesitate to go further, and faster, in the days and weeks ahead. And we will do whatever it takes so that we beat it together."

My friend Lauren talks about how profound it is that Boris Johnson is such a fan of Churchill and in a twisted way the universe has provided him with his Churchill moment. In future years, when they talk about coronavirus, will they speak as they did during the war ('it was a good war') and describe it as a 'good pandemic'? I sincerely hope not.

TOTAL DEATHS – 103

Thursday, 19th March

I wake up early (or at my normal time) before 6.00 a.m. Ironically, I have been sleeping really well this week. I don't know whether it is because I am not having to travel in the morning or whether it is because I have slept in my own bed every night, something I haven't done since we moved in. Generally, I will stay in a hotel at least two nights a week often staying away for weeks at a time. Or am I sick? I am falling asleep every night on the sofa and still sleeping for seven hours a night.

I need to get out, so I go for a walk to the shops with my rucksack. This was a new rucksack that I had ordered before I went skiing, which I have yet to use for work, but I manage to get some supplies and the rucksack can carry quite a lot.

I feel a bit melancholy today and I realise it is because it is Elly's birthday. It's not even because I can't be with her, as I wouldn't always be with her, but I just think of her and miss her so much. I WhatsApp her and sing 'Happy Birthday' badly to her, which makes me feel even more emotional. She has decided to go to Dorset instead for a few days – a family member has a house there that she can stay in near the beach and at least they are getting away. She suggests that I come for dinner on Saturday night as I am only forty minutes away, and that cheers me up temporarily.

I also feel ridiculously irritable today. I know it is because I am emotional, but I find it even harder to cope with Keith banging around. I am really cross that he hasn't put the doors on the study yet. We bicker about it and then suddenly I realise the ridiculousness of this in the bigger context. However, it galvanises Keith into action and he orders the doors – apparently, they will arrive next Tuesday. He counters my excitement by telling me that he probably won't be able to get the wood for the frames as the wood merchants are closed. So close but so far!

I am starting a new coaching assignment with a publisher and we have a great session – coaching on Zoom works really well and we enjoy our first meeting. Towards the end her cat jumps onto her lap and she introduces him. I feel that I should introduce our cat, Maisie, and we sit there on Zoom having cat conversations. It really is a very different world now!

I keep the news on throughout the day. A newsflash comes through that the UK interest rates have been cut to the lowest level ever – well at least that would benefit my son in buying his house. Lawrence (who has been known as LJ all of his life) lives in London and we have been looking at houses for the last six months. I feel glad that we haven't bought one yet as I wonder how stable the housing market would be.

In other news, Australia and New Zealand close borders, with Australia closing it to all but its citizens and residents from 9.00 p.m. on Friday. New Zealand followed suit but from Thursday night. In the US, Donald Trump signs the Coronavirus Act 2020 ordering free virus testing – infections have now passed 9,400.

In London, dozens of tube stations have been closed in an attempt to try and slow the spread, however trains are still busy. People are urged not to travel, if at all possible.

Italy's total deaths approaches China's already – nearly 3,000 people have died as opposed to China's total deaths of 3,245, and it is dreadful to see that the number of fatalities has overwhelmed the funeral industry. Coffins are now being lined up in churches.

Japan's deputy prime minister, Taro Aso, (who has a history of making gaffes) says that the Olympics are cursed as speculation over postponing the event due to the outbreak mounts.

The Prime Minister's briefing begins with profuse thanks to the media and everyone in the country who is complying, and confidently states that he thinks we can turn the tide in the next twelve weeks. He talks about trials for the first vaccine within a month and negotiations to buy a so-called antibody test, which would be as simple as a pregnancy test, and could tell whether you had the disease. He states that whilst it is early days, if it worked then the Government would buy hundreds of thousands of them as soon as practicable because if you knew you have had it you could go back to work.

He promises to ramp up tests from 5,000 a day to 10,000 to 25,000 and then up to 250,000.

A sterling finish from Boris Johnson: "And that is how, by a mixture of determined, collective action and scientific progress, I have absolutely no doubt that we will turn the tide of this disease and beat it together." Is it just me or is he getting rather good at this? No jokes, no gaffes, just some very earnest statements – unlike his counterpart in the US.

TOTAL DEATHS – 144

Friday, 20th March

I wake up this morning finding it hard to believe it is Friday – it is going to be another busy day workwise and I have a long to-do list. I have already done an hour and a half on the laptop before Keith wanders in for breakfast.

He takes a call and tells me that the doors won't be delivered. Apparently, it will be next Tuesday or even Thursday. I say nothing and keep typing.

Today I am feeling in much better health and more positive and tell the team I will be back to work on Tuesday. On Monday I have a hospital check-up and several calls, which it makes more sense to do from home. We discuss the fact that we can all work safely in our building – no problem.

I send Keith out for food, as I start to get really excited about going to Dorset and look forward to cooking a roast dinner for Elly, and Ernie her partner, and seeing her gorgeous cockapoo, Moby. It will be good to have some normality. Keith goes out to the shops and comes back triumphantly with chicken and vegetables. This will be the best Mother's Day present ever, and I think that if only LJ could be there too it would be perfect.

An hour later, Elly messages me and tells me that she thinks I shouldn't come to Dorset. I am disappointed as I feel as if it would probably be safe, but I understand why she feels that way. She says she will come to dinner on the way home on Sunday and I look forward immensely to seeing her. Two messages later she tells me she doesn't think she should come. She has read something that talks about visiting parents and then two weeks later they died of the virus and is terrified that could be me. Sadly, I have to agree with her.

I do a coaching session online and ironically it is one of the best sessions I have had with this client. I wonder if it is the lack of distractions, but we seem to go to a far deeper level. I wonder why we have always insisted on face to face when we coach.

It is incredibly quiet when I go outside mid-afternoon for a cup of tea – no planes flying over and very little traffic. We live close to Southampton Airport, so I am used to hearing planes taking off and landing, but just the sound of birds ring around the garden today.

My children do a group WhatsApp and start to tell me they think it is a really bad idea that I go to work next week. They can be quite strong together and persuade me to do things and they are so concerned about the risk; they beg me to stay at home. I tell them I have to go to the hospital on Monday anyway and I will be fine.

But the big news of the day seems to be about toilet rolls! In Northwich, a queue of 600 pensioners had formed for toilet rolls before the shop opened at 7.00 a.m. Many stores have now started to limit how much people buy. I shake my head in amazement.

The Prime Minister comes out for his briefing; he is looking very sombre and the boyish, affable idiot that we are so used to is replaced by a tired and serious-looking figure.

He is joined by the Chancellor of the Exchequer, Rishi Sunak, and Deputy Chief Medical Officer, Dr Jenny Harries.

The Prime Minister tells the country that we are going to fight the virus with testing, with new medicines, and with new digital technology that will help to track the disease as it is transmitted, and thereby, eliminating it, to stamp it out.

Plus, he says, it will be achieved by the country following the guidance issued on Monday, which was to stay at home for seven days if there were any symptoms, or fourteen days if anyone in your household has a new, continuous cough or a high temperature. He reminds us that we should work from home if possible and keep washing our hands and that these actions would help to take the strain off the NHS. He then continues with a stern speech, some parts of which feel like a rousing war time effort:

> *"Bit by bit, day by day, by your actions, your restraint and your sacrifice, we are putting this country in a better and stronger position, where we will be able to save literally thousands of lives, of people of all ages, people who don't deserve to die now."*

> *"People whose lives can, must, and will be saved."*

> *"And as we take these actions together and as we make these sacrifices; we can see the impact on the real economy."*

> *"Already, fantastic British companies, already under huge strain, big and small."*

> *"Workers who are finding that their jobs are under threat or are going, through no fault of their own. And to all of them, we in government say: We will stand by you."*

> *"And I say that to companies, remember our joint objective: to beat this virus. And we will do everything in our power to help."*

He then sets us a teaser that Rishi Sunak is going to explain how the Government are going to support workers in addition to the packages already set out for businesses, and to reassure us that the UK economy is going to bounce back and that these measures are temporary.

Of course, it is. What does temporary mean? What does in time mean? What does bounce back mean? It wasn't particularly healthy before.

He finishes his speech with a statement that is going to hit people hard.

> *"We are collectively telling cafes, pubs, bars, restaurants to close tonight as soon as they reasonably can, and not to open tomorrow."*
>
> *"Though to be clear, they can continue to provide take-out services."*
>
> *"We're also telling nightclubs, theatres, cinemas, gyms and leisure centres to close on the same timescale."*
>
> *"Now, these are places where people come together, and indeed the whole purpose of these businesses is to bring people together. But the sad thing is that today for now, at least physically, we need to keep people apart.*
>
> *"And I want to stress that we will review the situation each month, to see if we can relax any of these measures."*
>
> *"And listening to what I have just said, some people may of course be tempted to go out tonight. But please don't."*
>
> *"You may think you are invincible, but there is no guarantee you will get mild symptoms, and you*

can still be a carrier of the disease and pass it on to others."

"So that's why, as far as possible, we want you to stay at home, that's how we can protect our NHS and save lives."

"We will get through it together, and we will beat this virus."

Churchill would have been proud.

We are lucky enough to have a hot tub, and we decide to have a dip with a gin and tonic – it feels like such a treat and I congratulate myself for lasting all week without a drink. I think of all the people who don't have a garden and feel very privileged to have a nice one.

I am still exhausted and fall asleep on the sofa – third night in a row.

TOTAL DEATHS – 177

Saturday, 21st March

Today I wake up feeling a little excited. I am going out this morning. I feel pretty sure I don't have the virus and I am willing to take the chance. I have a hair and beauty appointment booked and I want to go to it. Naughty as it feels to go out, I relish driving my car and doing something normal. I have my hair done in the knowledge that this will probably be the last time for a good few months. I then have my pedicure done and enjoy the conversations with my beauty therapist. But as I leave it feels poignant, as if I am saying goodbye forever. No re-booking another appointment as I normally would.

I flick through the news – UK military planners have been drafted in to help feed vulnerable people isolated at home during the crisis, to protect more than a million people who are the most at risk of being hospitalised.

In Italy, their government orders the closure of any activities that are non-essential production activities after the total deaths rose by 793 to 4,825 on Saturday – a horrific jump. The only shops that will stay open are for essential supplies. In Spain, former Real Madrid President, Lorenzo Sanz, dies – no one is immune from the virus.

In other news, there is still the issue of the Britons stranded abroad, including 400 in Peru, but the Foreign and Commonwealth Office say they could be flown home early next week.

Some good news for the homeless – hotels in central London will offer beds to rough sleepers to help protect them against coronavirus. A trial this weekend will offer 300 beds to people known to homelessness charities. I sometimes help to feed the homeless in Southampton, so it is a charity quite close to my heart and I am glad that they will have some respite.

A campaign is announced to 'clap for carers' and shared across social media, urging people to join in applause whether it is from their front garden, window, balcony or even indoors. This is to show everyone involved in the effort our appreciation for their hard work against the virus.

After dinner we play Scrabble – and as always, I lose, although I argue the wine has impaired my ability to think.

TOTAL DEATHS – 233

Sunday, 22nd March

I wake up today feeling normal – yesterday, ironically, was one of the best Saturdays I have had in a long time. I hadn't been obsessing about work, I got out for a day for some normality and Keith and I had a lovely evening. We feel close and I take the time to lie in whilst we watch the news. Snuggled here it could be any Sunday – this is the irony, the world inside is strangely normal, you could easily just forget what is happening outside – until you watch the news. The death rate has taken its biggest leap today and we are apparently two weeks behind Italy. But the sun is shining, and I head for the gym, throwing the doors open and trying to enjoy the fact that I don't have to rush my session. The endorphins start to kick in and I feel pumped, pushing all negative thoughts away. The gym helps me to think clearly and I realise I need to have more of a structured strategy. I need a plan. I always need a plan but today more than ever I need a plan. I put that on my mental to-do list for tonight.

I cook myself my weekend breakfast treat – poached eggs on toast with avocado – and I eat it outside in the sun. The sun feels good on my face despite the slightly cool morning chill. And then I start to cry. It hits me with no warning and I can't decide what I am crying about. Being alone on Mother's Day, being scared of catching the virus, the thought of losing my business, the thought of losing life as we knew it, or the thought of everyone dying. All of it. None of it, I don't know. I just sit in the sun with tears pouring down my cheeks. I open my card from my daughter and read her WhatsApp message and I feel some comfort.

And then suddenly, from nowhere, I see a butterfly. A yellow butterfly carelessly drifting around. I can't remember when I last saw a butterfly and I am fascinated. It somehow feels like a symbol of hope, of freedom. I make that analogy myself – there is no truth in it, but it makes me feel better to consider that this beautiful, delicate creature is reminding me that one day we will again fly free. My sister-in-law had given me the book *Signs* by Laura Lynn Jackson for my birthday, and I guess my eyes had been alerted to ask for, and see, 'signs'. It flutters off into the distance.

I start looking at the garden and decide to attack it today, the earliest we will ever have started spring gardening but I have such a strong desire to have everything in order that this feels the right place to start. I go into the garage to get some tools and the first thing I see is the Christmas pudding that I made last Christmas ready for next year. This triggers me again – the thought of the normality of last Christmas, the fear that we won't ever have another Christmas and the hope that we will, and everything will be the same again.

I check my emails and am delighted and relieved to see an email from Saudi with an order for online training – 10 sessions plus some video sessions. A few more pennies in the coffers; I feel eternally grateful for the support of our clients.

The Prime Minister comes out for his briefing, marching to his podium as dishevelled as usual.

For much of the weekend the sun has been brightly shining, and people have poured outside to take advantage of it. With limited leisure options open to them they crowded into parks and on to the summit of Snowdon, but they were seen and widely condemned. This was not social distancing.

We are now being told that if we are at risk, we have to be on total lockdown for twelve weeks. That is me, I wish I wasn't but due to my lung condition I am at risk. This is it. Three months, twelve weeks, eighty-four days – and we have no guarantee that will be the end. I definitely need a plan. I write to the team advising them that they should prepare to work from home. I then set my goals and my schedule so that I have a clear plan going forward for the next 12 weeks. I set the goals for all aspects of my life; the house, my fitness, work and personal goals.

I feel hugely better now that I have a plan, I always do, I didn't realise how important this was going to be to me in the next couple of months and the impact that the goals would have on me.

TOTAL DEATHS – 281

Monday, 23rd March
Official Lockdown, Week One

I wake up just before 6.00 a.m. today with my normal foggy thoughts – Where am I? Which hotel am I in? Which country am I in? And what am I delivering today? And then quickly the realisation dawns, I am at home, I am in lockdown and will be at home for at least the next eighty-four days. I try to shake off the fear about the implications and then I remember the dream that I had, dark and colourless but all the same so vivid. I was wrapping up my company. I can't picture who I was dealing with but I know it was official and it was so fast – it was taking less than a day. I push it to the back of my mind and go to the gym – my personal trainer and I had decided that we would try a virtual session. I am doubtful, my Wi-Fi never normally stretched that far, and I am still battling with my resistance to virtual learning, but I am pleasantly surprised. I end up doing a far harder workout that I normally would, and my positivity manages to supersede the rising panic that hits me daily.

I get ready for work – time to watch the morning news. I have always watched *Good Morning Britain* and today Piers Morgan is giving a roasting to the Health Minister,

Matt Hancock, who can't get a word in. Piers is relentless – Why are the Government not forcing lockdown? What are the Government doing? He doesn't allow Matt Hancock to answer the question and a fight ensues – I can't quite believe the persistent truculence that Piers Morgan displays in the face of the deeply disgruntled minister. They are like children arguing and not giving in to each other.

The day is busy, and my new schedule works well – I feel positive, creative and enjoy my meetings with my team on Zoom. We start working with our Saudi client and there seems to be a real possibility of working online.

My hair salon and beauty salon announce they are closing – I knew this was coming and had done some preparation, but I can't help feeling concerned for my best friend who runs two hair salons, and my beautician who is self-employed. And, I am embarrassed to say, I mourn the loss of my high-maintenance hair and nails.

At 8.30 p.m. Boris Johnson is going to do a briefing for the nation. Instinctively, I know what he is going to say. He is about to announce some of the most draconian restrictions the country has ever seen. The country is officially going on lockdown, and in this crazy world we now live in, I feel relieved. If this is what it takes to stop it then this is what we need to do. He states the rules: You can only leave home to exercise once a day, travel to and from work when absolutely necessary and only go shopping for essential items. You must stand two metres apart from people you don't live with. You mustn't gather in public in groups bigger than two.

It feels like he is talking to naughty children who wouldn't do as they were told and now we are being punished. The whole country is grounded! His words are stark: "You must stay at home." My children WhatsApp to check I am OK and we all try to take the news in together – this is historic, never has the country ever seen anything like this, and as much as we saw it happening around the world, the reality of it happening feels so different. Police will be used to reinforce the rules; fines will be issued. The newsreader looks shell-shocked as she talks about the 'extraordinary measures' and that coronavirus is the biggest threat this country has faced for decades. Once again, I reflect on how this has happened. Two weeks ago I was on the slopes in France, having fun, although feeling overwhelmed and overloaded with work, and planning for the future, and now we are stuck in this parallel universe, where nothing is the same, nothing will ever be the same and we are probably all losing track of what 'the same' is.

I go to bed and pull the covers tightly over my head.

TOTAL DEATHS – 335

Tuesday, 24th March

I had forgotten to set my alarm, so I wake at 6.30 a.m. after yet another deep sleep. How strange that I am sleeping so well during this period. I open my eyes slowly and then remember that I need to try and get to the shop early – with lockdown being announced I am sure that there will be nothing in the shops. It is my morning for walking anyway, which means I can combine a walk with foraging for food. I put on my rucksack, feeling like an intrepid explorer, and am out of the door by 6.45 a.m. As I walk down the road, I am passed by at least seven or eight cars. The lights of the Co-op shine brightly and welcome me, lulling me into a false sense of security that I will find all the treats that I desire, which, at this point, is fresh fruit and veg. I was wrong, so wrong. The shop looks like it has been ransacked. Apart from the fresh bread they are bringing out of the bakery, the fruit and veg is almost completely empty. I manage to collect a cucumber and tomatoes, four oranges, some pears and some chillies. I feel ridiculously grateful and add some cat food and olive oil to my basket. When I get near the checkout the assistant shouts at me to stand still. It is like being in a US cop show! She tells me that she will step back, I will place my basket on the counter and then step behind the incident tape. She will then check out my food but cannot pack it in my bag, so she will then step away and I will pack it. I am grateful that they are taking it so seriously and as I pack she tells me that her staff had already been abused today for the lack of food. I put on my heavily laden rucksack and decide to walk to the next shop about a mile away.

I return home and after a shower I dress and again the day takes over – I am at my desk before 9.00 a.m. and apart from a break for home-made soup at lunchtime I don't move from my desk all day

At 5.00 p.m. I put on the news as the Health Secretary takes on the briefing today. He's beginning to feel like an old friend now as I have seen so much of him over the last week. Some positives; he announces over 35,000 more staff coming to the NHS including final year medics. They announce that next week a new hospital is opening, NHS Nightingale, at the Excel Centre in London. There will be 2 Wards of 2,000 people. With the help of military and clinicians he optimistically announces he feels they will have the support they need. But we still need to slow the spread of the virus, and he urges us to comply. Then a rallying speech: "A massive thanks to all staff, paramedics, pharmacists, care workers. We salute you and I will strain every sinew to give you everything you need." The words are absolutely apt, but I can't help focusing on the 'straining of the sinew' – not a term I am familiar with.

The questions are random tonight; calls for clarity on rules from people – they are still hazy about allowing some construction workers to work, clarification on whether children can still move between parents and a question he fields to his female colleague: 'Can boyfriends and girlfriends meet in public if they don't co-habit?' Her response is that the principal rule is to stay in household units. Alternatively, she boldly suggests, just test the strength of the relationship and see if one wants to be permanently in another household – ooh err! – but not switching in and out. I can see a lot of boyfriends getting nervous about girls pushing to move in with them! Matt Hancock summarises by saying: "Make your choice and stick with it!" How bizarre.

There have been 8,077 cases – 355 increased to 422 deaths, and 135 people recovered. The biggest jump yet.

The Japanese Olympics are cancelled until next year. Wow, not even postponed.

Keith tells me he has checked our insurance for our dream holiday in July to Mauritius. It was to be a big family celebration for my sixtieth birthday. The idea of it happening is slipping further away now, but the good news is we are insured. If you can call that good news.

India goes on lockdown and we get the news that the first child dies from coronavirus. This is another dimension and my heart breaks for the parents.

TOTAL DEATHS – 422

Chinatown, London

St Pauls Cathedral, London

London Assembly Building and Tower Bridge

Greenwich Market, London

Tate Gallery, London

Lambeth Bridge, London

Wednesday, 25th March

I wake up without the alarm today at 6.45 a.m. It's gym day. Keith is blissfully asleep next to me, so I slip out of bed quietly. I don't know why I am so concerned about waking him as he will only turn over and go back to sleep, but I am considerate and manage to dress, creep down the stairs and feed the cat without waking him. I muse over something my son said last night – since this has happened, I feel our relationship is getting better, we seem to talk to each other with more respect. LJ tells me that he and his girlfriend, Sophie, have discussed this and reckon that the arguments are generally due to work. So that's it then – if I want a loving and calm relationship I give up work? Whatever, I feel it bodes well for our retirement and decide to leave it at that. I text my best friend, Sarah, to book 'virtual' lunch with her, which makes me giggle. We book for 12.30 p.m.

En route to the gym, in the garden (no parking problems here!) I detour to look at plants. The garden has become my obsession lately and I love to watch daily to see which plants have new buds on. I have rescued two Azaleas in pots at the bottom of the garden and bought them up to the decking as they appear to have died, and each day I peer hopefully in to see if they might have survived. Nope!

My gym session is a little half-hearted today – I ache a bit from the last two days and so I settle for doing forty minutes. When I come back in to get ready, I turn on the TV and Piers Morgan is ranting about people not staying home to work – he demands to know: Who are the essential workers? I hate to say it, he is right – but I still don't like him. He is so full of anger and aggression and seems to just want to score points with people. I am all for tough interviewing but not bullying and in my eyes, he is a bully.

I am at my desk ready to work at 8.30 a.m. and at 10.00 a.m. we have our Zoom call. I am finding myself having to really step up as a leader – the team have always been self-directed and often manage without me for weeks, but at the moment I feel they need me to be more decisive and communicate more clearly. So, we have a call to set priorities. Spirits seem high overall, and I try and put lots of energy into the conversation. I remember my teachings to others: 'In the face of uncertainty, create a little certainty,' and we focus on the immediate projects.

At 12.30 p.m. Sarah FaceTimes me. Sarah has been my best friend for nearly thirty-five years. We have been through everything together, births (a boy for her, a girl and a boy for me) deaths, (too many to mention), including both of our dear fathers and my mother, and marriages (three each, the last one in the same year in 2015!). Sarah is one of those people who light up a room when they walk in, a shining bundle of energy, laughter and naughtiness, and she bounces off everyone, leaving them basking in the light that she casts. Everyone loves her and she is the kindest, bravest, funniest and most loving person I have ever met. We get each other. Totally. One word, and we know exactly what we are thinking, and through the most diverse and difficult times, we have been there for each other. But our biggest challenges have been over the last two years when, following her successful recovery from breast cancer, she was diagnosed two years ago with secondary cancer. Incurable. F**!!@g cancer – it was so unfair. Why her, why not me? As if having bastard breast cancer wasn't punishment enough, she now had to wake up every morning knowing that she has incurable cancer. It is in her bones, her ribs and her back; two small growths and we call them Small and Stable as that is what the doctor tells her at her PET scans, and that is what we hope for with the results. Still small and stable. She is on chemotherapy tablets every day and a radiotherapy wash every three weeks, but she deals with it – the way that I would hope I would deal with it but probably wouldn't – with humour and tenacity. The drugs make her tired and achy, but she still somehow looks beautiful all the time and today is no exception. To add to her already overflowing plate her mother developed rapid onset of Alzheimer's last year and she has spent the last year looking after her until she had to have her put into a home, and still she visits daily. The visits are tough as her mother swings between not recognising her, verbally abusing her and being emotional and loving. This was something I was very familiar with. My mother was a chronic manic depressive and I had the most turbulent childhood being abused by her and watching her swing from low to high moods, and being sectioned into hospital for months at a time. And whilst you know it is the illness talking, the abuse is so strong it is hard to accept; she may not mean it. So, I feel Sarah's pain and I could see that she was close to the edge, her voice was shaky, despite her joking and laughing. She tells me her nurse has told her she can no longer visit her mother and has to lockdown for twelve weeks. We don't say it, but we both know that it could mean she never sees her mother again. This situation really is survival of the fittest and the hospital have told her to come off her chemo tablets for two weeks to try and boost her immune system. That scares me but I have faith they know what they are doing. How can life be so unfair? So, her world was already tense and surreal, her normality thrown up into a haze of uncertainty, and then this.

We say goodbye and I carry on working on my webinar scripts. News comes through that Prince Charles has tested positive but seems well.

The afternoon passes quickly, and it is time for the Prime Minister's briefing, this time the PM is joined by the UK's chief scientific officer, Sir Patrick Vallance, and England's chief medical officer, Professor Chris Whitty.

Boris Johnson is looking exhausted and more dishevelled than ever. His starter is the limited numbers of doctors and specialised equipment, and how the concern is that the more people who get sick at any one time, the more risk there is, and the importance of delay. Hence the clear instruction to stay at home unless it is for the reasons he has previously set out. He thanks us all for complying and I feel strangely compassionate towards him. He has almost becoming credible as he sounds really sincere. He talks about the volunteer appeal. When launched, the appeal had hoped for 250,000 volunteers, but they now have 405,000 to drive medicines, bring patients home from hospital, make calls to check on people at home, and will be crucial to people isolating. What an amazing country we live in. Boris comments that is as many volunteers as the population of Coventry – what a strange analogy. Why Coventry?

Still no news for the self-employed, but he promises that Rishi Sunak will tell us tomorrow – it is much more complex to find the right tailored programme. Apart from wanting to hear the help for my son and many of my friends, it is always a pleasure to hear Rishi!

Questions come thick and fast from the journalists: "Can you honestly say the NHS is coping?" "What difference would having the right testing make?" "What about profiteering?" "Will the police start harsher enforcement?" Boris remains relatively self-assured, despite looking as though he hasn't slept for two weeks and definitely left his comb in a hotel somewhere. He manages to sound in control even if he looks hopefully between each of his colleagues for support after each question.

The death rate rises again after 28 people die. It represents the smallest rise in the number of deaths since the 17th March – more than a week ago.

But there is the biggest increase in the number of infections across the UK – up 1,542 to 9,529.

A quarter of the world is now in lockdown – this is almost impossible to comprehend.

TOTAL DEATHS – 465

Thursday, 26th March

I didn't sleep well last night so although I wake at 6.30 a.m. I am a bit foggy. It is ridiculous as I know that I don't have to start work until 9.00 a.m. but I always wake thinking about what I need to do. My schedule dictates walking exercise this morning, so I don my rucksack and head for the Co-op. As I get near, I see a big Co-op delivery truck – I feel excited thinking it might be restocked. As I walk past the window, I see the staff all stocking the shelves with fresh fruit. There is no one around, this is my moment, and as I push on the door I realise it is locked. The sign says: 'Closed for restocking, will be open shortly.' What does shortly mean? Ten minutes? Twenty minutes? Half an hour? The assistant opens the door and tells me they will be an hour. Crestfallen, I thank her – there is no point in giving her any grief. That would take it to 8.15 a.m. and I do have a call at 9.00 a.m. so it will be too late for me to get dressed and ready. I decide to walk to the next Co-op, which will give me a longer walk, and when I get there I am rewarded with a few basics.

The day is massively busy again, checking off content, an email from a client asking for a proposal – it's £5,000 but might get us in front of a wider audience, so we go for it. I stop and reflect on the hard work the team is doing this week, and if all the proposals that we have been working on come in, we will already have recouped some of our cancellation income. However, there are more cancellations from other clients. It feels like plugging my finger in a dam.

I stop briefly at lunchtime for home-made soup with Keith, and he has been to the hardware store to get something essential to fix the toilet. The DIY store next door were giving away trays of pansies. This makes me ridiculously happy – our garden has never looked this good this early in the year – normally we are still tidying in June so I can see that I might actually get some weekends lying out there and reading my stack of books. However, it has been too early to buy annuals so this will give us some colour in the pots. Another positive, and despite everything, I am still managing to feel strong and positive. Before I go back to work, I take a lap around the garden to watch what is growing.

The global economy is looking dismal despite the US declaring their $2 trillion package aimed at supporting businesses, airlines and manufacturers. It seems coronavirus could still kill the economic foundation of the US. Jobless claims have soared.

But just occasionally the news is better, (if like me, you are grasping at straws). In Italy there is the faintest glimmer of hope after Lombardy reported a decline in deaths and new infections, followed by the reality that the overall death rate in Italy has risen from 662 to 8,000. But in South Korea, a ninety-six-year-old woman becomes the oldest person to recover – so it is possible.

I spend the afternoon making fun videos with one of my team on how to survive home working – *Grumpy Rob's Survival Guide to Working from Home*. We are a bit nervous about whether people will expect us to be more serious in these troubled times, but we hope the British humour will embrace it and help us to stand out amongst the myriad of other offerings to help people.

Notification comes through to say the Isle of Wight Festival is being cancelled. This has been a tradition for my girlfriends and me for the last fourteen years – one of the highlights of our year; four days of alcohol, girly chat and good music. The line-up announced had been insane this year and whilst we were expecting it to be cancelled it is still disappointing. We resign ourselves to the fact that we will have to wait for next year.

It is time for the Prime Minister's briefing and Rishi Sunak arrives looking groomed and poised. His presentation is seamless and polished, yet sincere. I think I may be a little bit in love with him; the compassion he shows as he describes what the government has already done in supporting business is mesmerising. His articulation and pronunciation is immaculate.

We all draw a breath; he is just about to announce the package for self-employed people. He lists a variety of them and says: *"To you I say this – you have not been forgotten; we will not leave you behind. We all stand together."*

The package is not dissimilar for employees, but more complicated to administer. They will pay self-employed people a taxable grant of 80% of their salary up to £2,500. He mentions that this is the most comprehensive scheme in the world. I message LJ to see if this might help but it seems it won't be paid until June. But still better than nothing.

It occurs to me how strange it has been that we are in a pandemic, but each country seems to be responding to coronavirus in isolation.

The G7 had a video conference meeting to try and find ways to co-ordinate responses, but once again the US put their big foot in it by drafting a separate statement referring to it as the Wuhan Virus. President Trump and his senior officials have been accused of repeatedly calling it the Chinese Virus, although lately Trump has backed off.

I reflect that today has been a good day at work; the calls and projects we are currently working on give us some hope – we are still a long way from being out of the woods but I cling on to the hope. I almost feel guilty that I am now, in a bizarre kind of way, enjoying my days, and when I focus on the here and now everything feels normal.

And then suddenly there is the clapping. At 8.00 p.m. I go into my front garden and I hear the clap from my next-door neighbour. I can't see them through the trees, but I can hear them, slowly at first and then whole street erupts; loud enthusiastic clapping, followed by cheers and whoops and even fireworks. A car drives up the street hooting at us all and I stand in the darkness, the eeriness of the silence without the cars being sliced through by the rapidly increasing crescendo near and far, and suddenly it all becomes too much for me. I burst into tears and start sobbing, crying for these amazing people who are our only hope. This is the reality; millions of NHS and care workers are out there risking their lives to save our lives and there is nothing we can do apart from clap and pray that they don't give up on us.

Facebook explodes with videos of people's own streets' response to the call for clapping, or condemnation for those roads that didn't turn out to join in.

I spend the rest of the evening wondering what we could do for the NHS when this is all over to thank them. Anything I think of feels trivial. They deserve to be the highest paid people in the country and I seriously hope that the Government are rethinking their wages.

We decide to watch TV and they are scheduling *Contagion*. Like most of the UK, of course, we watch it. Keith questions why it has been scheduled but I can't help feeling it was a deliberate ploy to scare the people who are still refusing to stay in. Who knows?

TOTAL DEATHS – 578

Friday, 27th March

My eyes ping open. I know the answer. My unconscious brain must have been whirring at full pelt during the night. This! This is how I can help the NHS staff. This stream of consciousness that I have been recording each day to keep me sane could potentially be a way to create a fund for families of NHS people who have not survived coronavirus. I feel excited but scared. Was it possible to get a book deal and sell it? Would anyone want to read it? Is my writing good enough?

I go in the gym and fling myself into a session as I work through the possibility of doing this – should I self-publish to get the maximum of money to the people, or should I pull on one of my publishing contacts and the might of their marketing teams?

I feel really pressurised to work and chain myself back to my desk. I am sending emails out to clients to offer them help. At this point we don't want to be pressing anyone for any work but we do want to stay in touch. A client emails to say that they want me to work on a contract but are told they can't spend money now. I tell them I will help them as I trust them to pay me later!

And then the news comes in that Boris Johnson tests positive for coronavirus. Three weeks ago the nasty bitter side of me might not have cared, but today I feel for him and genuinely hope he doesn't get full blown Covid-19. I also worry for the country. He is suffering mild symptoms and is self-isolating but not stepping back from his duties.

I have a conversation with Gemma and Barry and we decide to furlough three members of staff. I call them personally to talk them through. One of them is really struggling working from home alone but there is nothing I can do. I explain the conditions and I think they are OK but make a mental note to keep an eye on them as my intuition tells me they may not be.

More news, Matt Hancock is now also testing positive – not surprising considering how close he and Boris have been.

I continue flicking through the news. There is a headline about ventilators. The Government regrets to announce that a chance to procure ventilators somehow ended up in Boris Johnson's spam folder! What? They say a communications mix-up meant it missed the deadline to join an EU scheme to get extra ventilators for the coronavirus crisis. Really? So why didn't the EU give us a call to see if we had received it?

Emergency plans are activated all over the country turning crematorium car parks into temporary mortuaries using wedding marquees. What a horrible thought.

A client takes up our proposal and asks for an invoice for £5,000. You would have thought it was £50,000 from my excitement, but just the fact that it is possible to do business in this environment is so heartening. We finish the content for our fun videos and even I laugh out loud at *Grumpy Rob's Guide* and then we go to the 'virtual' pub. It feels good to laugh and enjoy a drink together. It is a shame that we can't do it every week.

News comes in that the lockdown in France has been extended by another fifteen days – not unexpected.

Boris Johnson appears; he has developed minor symptoms, a cough and he is self-isolating. He isn't in PJs, although even with his tie on he looks as if he has just got out of bed, but thanks to video communication he can still talk to people. Without Boris taking the briefing Michael Gove is now in the hot seat.

There has been a big rise in deaths – 181 deaths in twenty-four hours taking it up to 759 in three weeks. The rate is doubling every three to four days with London having most cases. Chris Whitty is now also showing symptoms, which is not surprising as he has also been with Boris a lot. We are told that all non-emergency surgery is cancelled for three months. The news includes an interview with a prostate cancer patient who won't be having his operation. I wonder how many deaths there will be that are non-corona but due to the hospitals not being able to help.

We are told that the Cardiff Principality Stadium is being used as a hospital, plus Birmingham's NEC, and the Manchester Conference Centre will be ready next month.

And then Boris is on our screens, speaking from Number 10, where he is self-isolating.

> *"I want to bring you up to speed with something that happening today, which is that I've developed mild symptoms of coronavirus – that's to say, a temperature and a persistent cough."*
>
> *"And on the advice of the Chief Medical Officer, I've taken a test that has come out positive, so I am working from home. I'm self-isolating and that's entirely the right thing to do."*
>
> *"But be in no doubt that I can continue, thanks to the wizardry of modern technology, to communicate*

with all my top team to lead the national fight back against coronavirus."

He goes on to thank all involved and in particular the amazing NHS staff and to say how moving the national clap was last night.

He is careful to also mention the police, social care workers, teachers, everybody who works in schools, DWP staff.

Michael Gove takes some questions. Tonight, he stands further apart from Dominic Raab. In the press, speculation has started over who would take over if the Prime Minister got really ill, and we are told that it would be Dominic Raab. Amazingly, I hope that he doesn't, I somehow feel we need Boris. How quickly the tide turns.

The Head of NHS said staff would start to be tested next week to give workers confidence to go back to work. I long for the testing to start.

I see on Facebook an article about two vans being set on fire in London by vandals. FFS! Although why am I surprised? I wonder how far we are from major looting.

Saturday, 28th March

Today I am excited. We are going out. Just to pick up the video equipment from the office but we have decided to do our daily walk from there around Cams Hill Golf Course. The Government said that we should walk near our houses and not drive to places to walk – however, I feel this is justified as I have to go to work whilst there is no one there. We leave the house at 8.00 a.m. so that there is the minimum of people out.

The motorway is eerily quiet – and I think back to the *Contagion* pandemic film. At the office I cover my hands with my sleeves as I open the doors and go upstairs to pick up the box of work that Dawn has left for me. I look at our bookshelf and pick up 10 business books that I have been meaning to read. I already have a substantial pile at home, but as this is the only time I will be in the office I take them anyway. I go into my office and behind my desk are two trays full of paperwork and proposals; a graveyard of paperwork that has piled up over the years that I never have time to tackle. I grab both trays, pack them into a box and take them too. Might as well aim for a fresh start and a tidy up. As Keith takes the boxes down, I look around the empty office, at my team's desks and am suddenly overcome by grief. I feel as if someone has plunged a knife into my heart and is twisting it. I can't breathe and I sob – will we ever be back here? Will it ever be the same? I can't believe that after twenty-five years it would all end like this. I have been so strong and upbeat with the team this week, but this hits me hard. I vow that if I get another chance, I will be a better leader.

I go down to the car wiping away tears. Keith is now confused – two minutes ago I was fine and now I am a blubbering, emotional wreck. I try to explain and he gives me a hug and tells me it will all be fine – which is pretty empathetic for Keith.

We walk around the golf course and it is beautiful. At first we see hardly a soul but the wildlife is incredible; the swans gliding around the creek and the birds who seem to be braver. Keith comments that maybe this is because there are so few people around – it is good to know at least someone is enjoying the situation. We walk for six miles, moving aside for people as we see them and every single person says, 'good morning'. Despite the sunshine we observe that no one says, 'lovely morning'. Because it isn't, is it? We are still in danger, still in lockdown and still terrified, so whilst we can make the best of things, we all know it will be a long time before it is 'lovely' again.

I read the news – it wasn't so long ago that all we cared about was Brexit and now I couldn't give a toss. I thought it would be Brexit that broke my business, but ironically, from being the most divided we have ever been in the country, in the space of three weeks we are now closer as a nation – the young forgetting their anger at the older generation voting to leave and volunteering to help them. We are all in this together.

We get home and go out to do more gardening. The BBC alert breaks the silence. The number of deaths has risen to over 1,000 – 1,019; another 260 deaths from 75 on Friday. At least 13 were healthy adults. There are now 17,089 cases, the biggest day-on-day increase in the UK since the outbreak began. It is 34% higher than Friday's figure. Alok Sharma, the Business Secretary, takes today's briefing and tells us that if we keep the total deaths below 20,000 we will have done very well – a terrifying statement. He is joined by Professor Stephen Powis, the National Medical Director of NHS England, who again urges us to stay at home, which will result in less deaths.

Testing is starting to filter through – currently about 6,000 people are tested daily but the Government is looking to increase it and there is a goal for 25,000 by mid-April. The tests are antigen tests, which indicate if someone is infected, but what we are really waiting for is the antibody test, which indicates whether someone has recently had the virus. Apparently Public Health England is ordering it in.

The first Royal Family member to die is Princess Maria Teresea of the Bourbon Parma Royal Family, aged 86. Meanwhile, the number of deaths in Spain from Covid-19 is 832, bringing the death toll to 5,690 since the beginning of the outbreak, which means that Spain is the second worst-hit nation. I think of Spain and all our lovely holidays in Majorca, our visit to Barcelona and all of the beautiful places and the friendly people. My heart breaks for them, although at the same time I recognise that this could easily be us in two weeks.

Initially, the lockdown was supposed to last three weeks, but it feels like we are now going to settle in for the long haul. I anticipate it will be at least another four weeks after the initial three and the idea of any normality of life floats further and further away.

I cook dinner and we eat in the dining room to make it feel more special. I have designated tonight as our dinner 'out' with a nice dinner and wine, and once again we are consumed in the normality of being in our home, surrounded by our beautiful belongings and eating lovely food and wine – all feels normal and it is hard to believe what is going on outside. This is the total craziness of this pandemic, if you didn't look at social media or the news you could pretend that you were having a couple of weeks off and just doing things around the house and enjoying relaxing. It feels like we are in a film, and even if we go outside of the house all seems well. Totally bizarre.

Sunday, 29th March

The clocks went forward last night. This is probably the first time in history that the world didn't care that they had lost an hour! As always, I wake up early and as I turn over to try and get my extra hour the cat starts pushing her nose against mine, her paws up on the bed, her big eyes hopeful and her purr extraordinarily loud. I can't resist stroking her, she has been such a wonderful companion in the last two weeks, so I get up and dress and she winds herself round my legs as I struggle not to fall down the stairs and feed her.

I make a pot of tea (a pot, not a mug – small things make me very happy now) and settle down to read. I come across a passage from the field of shamanic healing. The passage was startlingly aligned with how I currently feel, and the methodology I have been using to cope with the changes and reading it gave me strength and insight.

Message from White Eagle, Hopi[1] indigenous on 03/16/2020:

> *"This moment humanity is going through can now be seen as a portal and as a hole. The decision to fall into the hole or go through the portal is up to you. If they repent of the problem and consume the news*

twenty-four-hours-a-day, with little energy, nervous all the time, with pessimism, they will fall into the hole. But if you take this opportunity to look at yourself, rethink life and death, take care of yourself and others, you will cross the portal. Take care of your home, take care of your body. Connect with the middle body of your spiritual House. Connect to the egregor of your spiritual home. Body, house, medium body, spiritual house, all this is synonymous, that is to say the same. When you are taking care of one, you are taking care of everything else. Do not lose the spiritual dimension of this crisis, have the aspect of the eagle, which from above, sees the whole, sees more widely. There is a social demand in this crisis, but there is also a spiritual demand. The two go hand in hand. Without the social dimension, we fall into fanaticism. But without the spiritual dimension, we fall into pessimism and lack of meaning. You were prepared to go through this crisis. Take your toolbox and use all the tools at your disposal. Learn about resistance with indigenous and African peoples: we have always been and continue to be exterminated. But we still haven't; stopped singing, dancing, lighting a fire and having fun. Don't feel guilty about being happy during this difficult time. You don't help at all by being sad and without energy. It helps if good things emanate from the Universe now. It is through joy that one resists. Also, when the storm passes, you will be very important in the reconstruction of this new world. You need to be well and strong. And, for that, there is no other way than to maintain a beautiful, happy and bright vibration. This has nothing to do with alienation. This is a resistance strategy. In shamanism, there is a rite of passage called the quest for vision. You spend a few days alone in the forest, without water, without food, without protection. When you go through this portal, you get a new vision of the world, because you have faced your fears, your difficulties ... This is what is asked of you. Let them take advantage of this time to perform their vision seeking rituals. What world do you want to build for yourself? For now, this is what you can do: serenity in the storm. Calm down and pray. Everyday. Establish a routine to meet the sacred every day. Good things emanate, what you emanate now is the most important thing. And sing, dance, resist through art, joy, faith and love."

Who knows whether there is any portal, but the concept of using this time to test our strength, to recentre and align, and to create a new vision feels very real, today? I print it out and keep it close.

My diary pings to tell me that today we should have been at the O2 for a concert – a present from my daughter that is now not happening. Keith wakes up late and we have breakfast together and then I head out to the garden – it has never looked so beautiful for no reason! There is one border that we haven't ever tackled and I decide to make a start. Two hours later I have filled a massive bag with twigs, leaves and plants and we are ready to bed some new plants in. I get great satisfaction from completing this one.

News comes through that one of the dead today is a 55-year-old doctor, Amged El-Hawrani, at Queen's Hospital, Burton. This makes me terribly sad as I think of his family and the sacrifices he made. Last week an organ transplant consultant died. These people who were putting their lives at risk for us, and leaving behind their families, is heart-breaking. And still idiots won't keep to the guidelines. Facebook reports a big group having a karaoke party at the weekend with pictures – how can they see news like this and still not realise how important it is?

Today the briefing is held by Dr Jenny Harries, England's Deputy Chief Medical Officer, and it brings a depressing thought – it could be six months before life in the UK returns to 'normal'.

She then adds that it did not necessarily mean we would be in complete lockdown for six months, but it did mean that the UK had to be responsible in continuing social distancing. She tells us that the Government will review the lockdown measures in three weeks. That doesn't mean that we will suddenly revert to our normal way of life, and she stresses that if we stop the lockdown then all efforts will be wasted and we could potentially see a second peak. Her estimation is: "Three weeks for review, two or three months to see whether we have really squashed it but about three to six months ideally, and lots of uncertainty in that, but then to see at which point we can actually get back to normal."

She also gives us a stark warning about the total deaths when she adds: "We actually anticipate our numbers will get worse over the next week, possibly two, and then we are looking to see whether we have managed to push that curve down and we start to see a decline."

News from Professor James Naismith, director of the Rosalind Franklin Institute at the University of Oxford, tells us that patients who are dying now were infected around a month ago, which is three weeks before the social distancing rules were put in place. He says he is confident that if we follow the social distancing the increase in deaths will stop but that it can take up to two weeks from infection to onset of symptoms.

After dinner we do a virtual pub quiz with friends. It is

such fun that we wonder why we have never done it before. Miraculously, we win and agree to host it next week. It is funny how quickly a routine can become established. My diary is looking busy this week with a virtual dinner on Tuesday night with a friend, and drinks with two girlfriends on Thursday. Suddenly I wonder what will happen if the Internet doesn't cope.

Once again it has been a really good weekend and I feel refreshed and ready for work.

TOTAL DEATHS – 1,228

Monday, 30th March
Official Lockdown, Week Two

It is my second virtual gym personal training session, and it is actually working really well. I work hard in the gym and as I work out Olivia and I talk about how things are going and her transition to taking personal training online. We muse over the fact that she could earn so much more money if she is not travelling around – it is a big transition and we are all learning.

I switch on the news as I get dressed and Piers Morgan is back. He is calm and sycophantic this morning because he is interviewing a cricketer about him doing Pilates at home with his wife. He then interviews some doctors about PPE – they are speaking out about how they're being forced to reuse masks, gloves, and gowns, and resort to making their own protective medical gear. It is shameful, it really is like lambs to the slaughter.

Another doctor tells us that she is working on a vaccine and this should be ready by the end of the year.

I start work and have a good meeting with the team. They seem on good form today and we agree our priorities for the next couple of days. I have another call with Saudi, who may have another area that needs some webinars. We discuss content and they seem interested, so I leave them to review their needs and pray that they come back to us. I immerse myself back in my work and start analysing a report. As usual my day feels normal and I quickly start to get lost in the data. I don't want to say it too loudly in front of other people, but I am almost enjoying the respite at the moment from travelling, when I manage to not think of the consequences.

On the stroke of midday in Madrid there is a minute's silence for the victims. But then once again there is a glimmer of hope. There are rumours that Italy may be turning the corner, as the number of infections falls to 4,050, its lowest in nearly two weeks. That means the total in the country is 101,739 from the previous 97,689 sadly with the total deaths still climbing by 812 to 11,592. The WHO is hopeful that this is now going to stabilise as it enters its fourth week in lockdown.

And then Elly phones, she is crying and I can't quite make out what she is saying. My heart turns cold, has someone got it and died? Finally, she calms herself and sobs that all her money has been stolen. She has been the victim of a very clever scam, a text, apparently, from her bank, in the same thread as all of her other texts telling her that she needed to phone the Fraud department as someone has bought something on Amazon using her account. She has had this before and she calls them and then they clean out her bank balance of £2,000. Apparently, the new App, Houseparty, might be to blame. The thieving bastards are finding this is a prime time to hack into accounts as everyone is at home consuming digital content/media. I am so angry I could cry for her. She contacts Nat West and they open a case. A different type of victim of the virus; is nowhere safe?

The briefing is early today and Dominic Raab is accompanied by Sir Patrick Vallance, who is bringing the latest data.

In the UK our total deaths dropped for the second day in a row. But that isn't good news. Still 180 new fatalities and cases jump by 2,619 to more than 22,000

He talks about the need to brake and slow the transmission of the virus and how, so far, we have been successful in terms of behaviour changes. He shows slides depicting transport from end of February to now – a dramatic fall-off in tube, rail and all motor vehicles. He tells us that measures are making a difference and decreasing contact is really helping. Finally, we have got the message.

He tells us that 8,000 people have been admitted to hospital, the figures have gone up the same amount each day. About half the cases are in London, but also throughout the UK, and it is expected that this will get worse over the next couple of weeks

In other news, Nicola Sturgeon announces that the Glasgow NEC will join the other major venues in being a temporary hospital.

Prince Charles is released from self-isolation and is said to be doing well. He has spent seven days self-isolating in Scotland after he had tested positive and had displayed mild symptoms. Well at least his mum is safe, God bless her!

TOTAL DEATHS – 1,408

Tuesday, 31st March

I wake up still feeling angry about Elly's money – the injustice of it is just hard to reason. How people can do things like that is just beyond me and I march up the hill to the local shop to try and disperse some of my anger. I hope that today we might get some news from the bank.

I switch on TV to GMB as I get dressed and Piers is discussing whether the police are being too heavy-handed – three days ago they started to hand out £60 fines after being given unprecedented powers to enforce the coronavirus lockdown. They are using roadblocks, helicopters and police drones to catch those members of the public who are not keeping to the rules. People have been 'named and shamed' in drone footage on social media for walking on Snowdon, and bizarrely, beauty spots have had ponds dyed to make them less attractive! Video footage shows police stopping people and telling them they cannot drive to walk their dogs – they must walk close to their homes. I guess it is to stop large crowds gathering in car parks; if we all walk near our houses at different times it is safer. Apparently, it is all Boris's fault – the Government wasn't entirely clear on the guidelines.

National Police Chiefs' Council Chairman, Martin Hewitt, defended the police actions by saying: "This is a national emergency, it's not a national holiday and it's important that people understand that." I feel like some people are truly behaving like toddlers – pushing the boundaries. I want to scream at them to stop. We all must be responsible, what more will it take?

The doors arrive for my study – I am amazed as I didn't think they would get here. I have no idea why this is so important to me, but it is ... I just feel that need for some privacy and also to be able to shut the door on it at night – every time I see my desk, I think I should be sitting at it. But now Keith is doing the builders thing – sucking his breath over his teeth and suggesting he may not be able to fit them as the builder's merchants is shut and he can't get the size wood he needs. I grit my own teeth and try to remain patient and help him find ideas. He tries to phone Wickes to get some timber to put it together – there is a fifteen-minute queue and then his laptop crashes. I lock myself away in my unlockable study and put my headphones on. I have found my noise-cancelling headphones but am beginning to think they are a Trade Descriptions Act contravention.

British Airways are suspending all flights. Yesterday EasyJet grounded all of theirs. I wonder if this is the end of travel as we know it – this year to celebrate my sixtieth I had decided to have six holidays and now it seems unlikely I will get more than one. I now find it hard to believe that I almost flew once a week and Heathrow Terminal 5 was jokingly designated as my second home.

I have a Zoom call and there I am again in widescreen multicolour! I have never liked being photographed, or looking at myself on films, and this is the bit I hate, having to constantly look at myself on these calls. I study my eyes – one is substantially bigger than the other – is that normal? I wonder whether I really should have put some make up on.

Some dreadful news comes through of a mother, father

and two young daughters who are found dead with their dog in west Sussex. The deaths came just days after the family posted pictures of them enjoying a country walk together. Pictures show a beautiful, normal family and they lived in big house in the country, but the report labels it the first lockdown suicide – apparently, he killed them all before taking his own life. I feel sick reading this and worry tremendously about the amount of mental health issues and domestic violence that could occur in this period. I have a horrible feeling that mental health will be a major issue going forward.

I send out the official Furlough letters to my team. I wonder how they feel on receiving them and whether they are nervous? I am missing them already. I get emails back saying that they have been received but nothing more.

The afternoon passes quickly, and I am quite productive, we are still producing material for new products and services. No further actual sales but still lots of projects to work on.

In the news:

- Pregnant prisoners could be granted temporary release from prison 'within days' to protect them and their unborn children from the virus.

- The transaction limit for contactless card payments will increase from £30 to £45 per transaction from Wednesday – that will be helpful in not having to touch keypads.

- British Airways announce it will suspend all traffic at Gatwick – it is quite inconceivable to think of that airport being shut.

- There is a lockdown in the UK mortgage market as lenders pull out of new deals, and I think of my son again and what will happen when it is all over and if he will be able to get a loan.
- Boris is apparently doing well and for the first time ever he conducted the cabinet briefing of senior ministers through video technology.

Cabinet Officer Michael Gove is up today for the briefing joined by Dr Jenny Harries and Professor Powis. The news is even worse – yesterday saw the highest single increase in deaths – 381, making a total of 1,789. Gove is very empathetic as he tells the country: "Every death is the loss of a loved one and our thoughts and prayers are with their families."

He talks about testing and how the UK must go 'further, faster' to ramp up its testing capacity to meet the target of 25,000 tests a day, as it is likely this won't be until the end of April; apparently there is a global shortage of the chemicals required. The comments come against mounting criticism that health workers are being put at risk without testing.

Stephen Powis, National Medical Director of NHS England, describes how he has been to the London Nightingale Hospital this morning – from a standing start to a new hospital ready to take patients this week.

It is an incredibly long and detailed briefing with many questions from the press – capacity, PPE, when will the peak come, could our loved ones come home to die? There is a real range tonight. Michael Gove pleasantly fields them to his colleagues.

Dr Jenny Harries steps in to take questions. Jenny is asked for a comparison with Korea and Germany. Wow this woman knows her stuff – she effortlessly discusses both countries' figures to discuss comparable data. She is one of the most credible, balanced and impressive women I have come across in a long time. I make a note to include her as an example in future Women's Development programmes. A wave of sadness comes across me as I think about the courses and wonder how long it will be until we can start delivering again. But that is just work and this is life or death.

TOTAL DEATHS – 1,789

Wednesday, 1st April

Today is the first day of delivering our virtual learning sessions to Saudi and I wake with a flicker of excitement and nervousness. It is ridiculous that after all these years of delivering training I feel nervous – not about the content, I feel completely qualified to talk about managing to work from home in isolation, but about the technology. And, also, how it will feel building rapport with people when you are not in the room with them. But it must work, this is all we have got at the moment, and potentially all we will have for a long time.

I switch on *GMB* as I dress and Piers Morgan is on an absolute roll in battle with Robert Jenrick, the Secretary of State for Housing, Communicities and Local Government, about why we are doing so little testing and why we are so behind Germany in testing. He doesn't allow Jenrick to get a word in and pushes him again and again to say why this has happened. Once more, I hate to say it but I have to concede, Piers is right and we should be a lot further along with testing, but it is pretty irritating to watch an interview when the other person cannot actually reply. Having said that I am not sure that Jenrick has anything useful to add.

Piers then switches tack to the flights coming from other countries and demands to know what is being done to test people as they arrive on planes. For the third time Jenrick tries to answer and is shot down so many times that he never really gets past his first two words. But actually, this is serious, and it gets me thinking – where are these people going when they come in from hotspots like New York, and why don't the authorities insist they are put in isolation for fourteen days?

Piers then goes on to show pictures of the scenes of people crowding onto trains in North Acton and this time his victim is Sadiq Khan. Khan looks very sombre and tired and he absolutely agrees and urges companies to tell people to work at home if it is non-essential for them to go into work.

On the 8.00 a.m. news, the Dutch cruise ship, Zaandam, has had four coronavirus deaths on the ship, including one Briton, but the US is forbidding them to dock. That must be horrendous for them; stuck in small cabins knowing that the virus has been creeping through the corridors.

And then there is an interview with the family of the youngest victim so far – a child who died yesterday, aged 13, and my heart breaks as they describe Ismail. His relative says that the worst thing was that he died alone. I want to cry; it is a tragedy and I think about the poor mother – no parent should have to bury their child, and even worse, how do you ever get over knowing that your child died alone? We are now in a world where funerals are fast, sparsely attended and no hugs allowed.

This is followed by more tragic news; an interview with Sophia, the daughter of Peter Myles who died yesterday aged seventy-six. He was a vicar, a loving soul who ironically adored caring for people. His daughter explained the sorrow of only being allowed five minutes with him in full protective clothing but considered herself one of the lucky ones that she had any time with him. I think back to my own treasured father's death. My brothers and I spent four days at his side in his hospital room until he eventually passed away, saying everything we wanted to say and holding him tight in his last moments. Every person deserves that final act of love and I feel terrified of the impact it would have on my children if I were to succumb and they wouldn't get the chance. For the first time I seriously wonder if I should make a video or write them a letter to help them in case this happened. By now tears are pouring down my face and when I hear of a couple in America who had to say goodbye to both of their parents by FaceTime due to the virus, I can't take any more. I have a training session to run and I must sound positive, so I shake it off.

The session goes well, technology doesn't let me down and we have a good level of interactivity discussing how to cope with working from home.

The afternoon passes rapidly with Zoom calls, and then the 4.00 p.m. team meeting. I brace myself to be positive. We have had more potential cancellations today and I can see more finances slipping away, but I have to keep the team going; this is not a time to show my weaknesses and vulnerabilities. They all seem OK and we agree on the next priorities. There have been some good sales calls and they are doing all the right things keeping clients warm, but no sales, which is pretty much what I expected.

Unbelievably, it is 5.00 p.m. again and I tune into the briefing. Alok Sharma, the Secretary of State steps up – no word from Boris. The opening statement is grim – another 563 people have died in the UK. He delivers the sombre news that this has taken the total deaths to 2,352; this includes a doctor who came out of retirement to volunteer for the NHS. Such bravery – I find it incredible they will put themselves in such danger to save us. His son pays tribute to him: "My dad was a living legend, worked for the NHS for nearly forty years saving people's lives here and in Africa."

Four medics have now lost their lives. But those are just the ones we have heard of.

Dr Yvonne Doyle, Public Health England Medical Director, picks up the next part of the briefing by saying the UK is not in 'as severe' a position as Spain, the US or Italy, but adds there is 'no reason to be complacent'. Dr Doyle adds that whilst use of public transport had gone down since the Government enforced social distancing measures, an increase in motor vehicle use in the last twenty-four hours was 'slightly concerning'. She urges members of the public to stay home to 'protect the NHS'.

The Edinburgh Festival is cancelled in August. That Is the most concerning cancellation notice announcement to date, as August is so far away. Are people starting to think that we won't be anywhere near over this by then? Wimbledon is cancelled too. It is surreal, all these events are part of the English constitution.

Keith and I watch a Stephen King film and avoid the news – today has been overwhelmingly sad and I can't take any more.

TOTAL DEATHS – 2,352

Thursday, 2nd April

Today is walking exercise and I leave the house at 6.00 a.m. – the best time for me to avoid crowds and do a pacey walk around Southampton Common for an hour. I see three people but still a lot of cars. I get back and put some soup on for lunch. My love affair with my soup maker hasn't waned yet. I get dressed and read some news reports, tidy the house, get my desk ready, feed the cat and have breakfast by 8.00 a.m.

Today is my second Zoom call with my client in Saudi, and we talk about managing effective relationships whilst working from home. It is a good session with lots of contributions. I am feeling more and more confident delivering online.

I am also having a call with one of my clients, a straight-talking Northerner with a wicked sense of humour, and when I see her face on Zoom I feel nostalgic; I miss training with her. There may be a potential of a little work there – every little bit counts at the moment.

The lunchtime news comes on and football unions are having talks about salary sacrifices – it comes after some clubs were criticised for using a government scheme to cut the salaries of non-playing staff, whilst paying players in full. Oh please! Surely the funds that are there are to stop people being made redundant? Footballers will not be made redundant, so if they miss a few weeks wages I am sure that their Lamborghinis won't be repossessed!

It is reported that healthcare workers face mental health challenges during the pandemic due to lack of PPE, what they are exposed to in terms of making life and death decisions. Well of course they would be; imagine being in a situation where it was your job to choose who gets treatment and who doesn't?

The newsreader moves on and there are reports of companies that have told the Government that they could make PPE two weeks ago and not had any response despite daily news that there is not sufficient PPE for NHS workers. Footage shows factories sitting empty with staff laid off who could be making masks and equipment. With the Nightingale Hospital about to open it should be all hands to the deck and every NHS worker should be fully protected.

I get back to work at my desk and before I can blink it is 5.00 p.m. and another briefing. Matt Hancock steps up to announce his 5-pillar testing plan and confirms it is aiming to carry out 100,000 tests a day. Currently it is only about 10,000. The Government has been criticised for not increasing the number of tests more quickly. It was originally thought the target would be for the whole of the UK, but the Government later issued a correction saying the goal will only be for England.

The five-pillar plan includes swab tests to see if we already have it, using commercial partners such as universities and private businesses to do more swab testing, antibody blood tests that can check if we have had it, surveillance to see how the infection is spreading and building a British diagnostics industry.

The number of people with the virus who have died in the UK has risen by 569, taking the total to 2,921.

Hidden in the briefing and the dreadful news is something positive – the government is writing off £13.4 billion of historic NHS debt so that hospital trusts are in a stronger position to deal with the outbreak – I sincerely hope that the Government completely changes their view of funding for the NHS after this.

And then it is 8.00 p.m. and once again we go outside. In the distance we hear a banging – a wooden spoon on a pot, a lone thudding in the still of the night – and then a ripple of clapping that spreads all down the road. I can see lights in the distance and hear people shouting, cheering and whooping. Someone is playing music, but I can't hear the song. I clap until my hands hurt, and that was only two minutes, and then I start clapping again. In some ways it is an analogy – my hands hurt after two minutes and I have the option to stop clapping, but the NHS workers must feel the same way, quickly broken and exhausted but they can't stop. My emotions are rising again as I think about all those people working out there with one mission – to save as many people as they possibly can. I think of Sophie, my son's fiancée who is a midwife in London, putting herself at risk every day. And then I think of all the women and men who go out to work each day to keep our services going and I feel even more humbled. It is all in their hands, out of our control, and we can only pray that they all remain safe and this soon passes.

But terrifyingly, the total deaths has quadrupled this week. The latest victims were aged between 22 and 100, 44 of whom had no underlying conditions. None of us are safe now – although I doubt whether we ever were.

TOTAL DEATHS 2,921

Friday 3rd April

I wake at 5.00 a.m. today with my brain buzzing with all the things that have been going on yesterday both at work and with the coronavirus. I try and push the anxious thoughts away and focus on what I can do today. I attempt to go back to sleep, but it isn't happening, so I get up before 6.00 a.m. and shower.

As always, *Good Morning Britain* accompanies me as I work, and this morning is a lighter show and the presenters are joking with each other about their home décor as some of them shoot their sessions from home. I must admit it has become one of my strange obsessions wondering why people video call from messy rooms; bookshelves in particular interest me. Prince Charles is doing an interview and his book game is absolutely on point – larger books at each end cascading into the smaller ones in the middle. Other people seem to have papers and books stacked in any old piles. I am sure as the weeks go by they will get tidier!

Another lovely highlight of this morning is a YouTube video of a doctor in America that has had over 500,000 hits already. He is singing 'Imagine' and it is absolutely stunning, his beautiful voice brings a lump to my throat as he sings about the world being at one. And his name – Dr

Elvis! Apparently, his mother had a dream the week before he was born that she was at an Elvis concert. But his voice isn't the only beautiful thing about him, his personality shines through as he talks about music helping people to recover and even when pushed as to whether he might now consider signing a music deal he talks about his vocation of helping people.

A Labour MP appears on screen to criticise the Government for changing their promise from 250,000 tests a day to 100,00 a day. I want to shut her up; they really are doing their best and I have actually been impressed with Matt Hancock's 5-pillar strategy for testing. I agree with his philosophy – testing is only valuable if it gives the right result, so if it is a case of ramping up the testing with unreliable kits then I am all for caution.

However, it does get me thinking – where has Jeremy Corbyn been throughout this? I suddenly realise we haven't seen hide nor hair, and I once again feel hugely grateful that Labour did not win the Election before Christmas. Apart from the typically predictable and unhelpful jibes that Labour would have tackled the crisis earlier, we haven't heard anything. The thought of Jeremy Corbyn running this show is just terrifying. They discuss the fact that it is pretty much a done deal that Sir Kier Starmer will most likely take the leadership. Anyone would be better in my eyes than Corbyn, not that I care about politics anymore. For three years I have studied manifestos, read up on policy and prayed that we wouldn't leave the EU. Brexit consumed a lot of my thoughts and concernes about the future of my business, but now I have no interest at all.

And then, of course the inevitable happens – a conspiracy theory emerges and this time it is really left field! 5G masts are being set alight after the most bizarre claim that radiation caused the coronavirus spread. What the actual F@*! Apparently, the theory started last year after a video from a US health conference was release claiming that the reason Africa was not as affected by the disease was because it wasn't a 5G region. It didn't take long for the WHO to quash the myth by confirming there were thousands of cases in Africa, followed quickly by the Governments confirmation that there was no evidence to suggest that 5G has anything to do with it. And who was it who was spreading the myths? Celebs; clearly Z listers, but their posting on social media doing the rounds via a lengthy voice note encouraging people to destroy masts via a 'Stop 5G Facebook Group'. Pictures of the blazing masts were posted on Facebook with people celebrating their demise and one person apparently even keeping a league table for cities setting the masts on fire. Words fail me.

Today passes in a blur of Zoom calls and catch-up with staff members. I do a coaching session and in between I continue to tackle my to-do list, which is getting slimmer by the day. I find myself being so focused that by the end of the day I actually feel that if I wanted to, I wouldn't necessarily need to work over the weekend (apart from one spreadsheet I had promised to update on our final call). I can't remember the last time I didn't need to do anything at the weekend. That sends a shiver of anxiety down me, will we run out of work? In terms of sales we can always find something to do, but I have never in twenty-five years run out of work. Maybe this is what I am learning – to clear the slate, get a new start and do it differently.

I go to the 'pub' call with the team and spirits are higher on Zoom today. After the meeting I think about dinner. We haven't had treats or any takeaways for five weeks and really fancy Chinese, so I phone around. After six attempts of unobtainable tones and messages saying they are closed due to coronavirus, I was just about to give up and suddenly

I get an answer. Yes, they are open, yes, they can deliver. Excitedly I order for 7.00 p.m. and we decide to go in the hot tub first! Sitting in our garden, with the birds singing louder than I have ever heard, on a Friday night, after a busy week, anticipating a Chinese and a film night on the sofa, it is so easy to feel that life is normal and I even feel a bit tipsy. We chat and laugh a lot and again I feel so lucky; lucky to have my husband and my house and my work, for as long as it lasts. Today is our anniversary of nine years since we met so it feels like a mini celebration.

I watch the news and there is more sadness, two nurses have died, Aimee O'Rourke and Areem Nasreem, leaving young families. I just can't process this. I wouldn't blame every nurse in the front line if they downed tools immediately. I silently thank them for sacrificing themselves and pray there won't be any more but in my heart, I know that there will.

Prince Charles opens the new Nightingale Hospital by video link. Sky News shows pictures of Matt Hancock on television in front of the ex-conference centre and the people behind him at the opening ceremony are milling around as if they were at a drinks' reception. Earlier he had shown yellow lines that had been drawn out for social distancing but in the video extract there was no social distancing – even if they were all health workers who had been tested (and they couldn't have been) it is not the example that was needed. Particularly as the Government are sending the strongest message about social distancing.

The hospital looks amazing and I am curious; what did it take to turn an exhibition centre into a hospital in days to equip it and fit 500 beds? I Google it. It took 160 contractors and 200 army engineers who worked 15-hour shifts at a time. The hospital will be equipped with 16,000 staff, 750 St John Ambulance volunteers and thousands of

EasyJet and Virgin air cabin crew who have been urged to help. Just amazing, when everything else seems to take so long to do!

The International Monetary Fund sends a stark warning about the global economy – apparently it is set for its sharpest reversal since the Great Depression and much worse than 2008.

"This is a crisis like no other," said Kristalina Georgieva, Managing Director of the International Monetary Fund (IMF), at a conference organised by the World Health Organization yesterday.

"Never in the history of the IMF have we witnessed the world economy coming to a standstill," she said. "It is way worse than the global financial crisis."

I cannot bear to think of the economy.

Vaccines are still being worked on but the clinical trial process is highly phased and would normally take ten years, however, industry and governments are working hard to speed it up and there is a possibility a preventative option could be available in case COVID-19 tries to recirculate next year. I pray that we never see anything like this again as long as we or any of our children or grandchildren live.

TOTAL DEATHS – 3,605

Saturday, 4th April

After a good sleep, only disturbed by the cat jumping on me at 6.00 a.m. confused that I wasn't up to feed her. After half an hour of my indifference she gives up.

I get up and make tea and go back to bed. No need to rush this morning and lying-in was something I never did. Keith was quite an expert at it, slowly waking up and watching some TV until he was ready to get up, but I was normally up before the alarm at 6.00 a.m. We watch *The News* and look through social media to try and find fun things to show each other. I find the most amazing violin rendition, by two young boys in Italy, of Coldplay's 'Viva La Vida'. I am mesmerised. It just goes to show you what practice can do when you have nothing else to do!

On the television, pictures come through from China of a day of remembrance for the victims. At 10.00 a.m. an air-raid siren echoes out and everyone stops; on bikes, in cars and pedestrians. They all hang their heads and afterwards there is an explosion of car horns and noise. I wonder what we will do when it is all over and we try and remember our dead and hope it is something more than a few minutes' silence.

Another memorable quote pops up on Facebook, which resonates with me.

We will not go back to normal. Normal never was. Our pre-corona existence was not normal other than we normalised greed, inequity, exhaustion, depletion, extraction, disconnections, confusion, rage, hoarding, hate and lack. We should not long to return, my friends. We are being given the opportunity to stitch a new garment. One that fits all of humanity and nature.

Sonya Renee Taylor.

The News continues and another scientific adviser says he hope the restrictions in the UK may be relaxed in a few weeks, followed by sobering news from IMF – the pandemic has stalled the global community causing the worst recession ever, worse than 2008. I try to remain optimistic; we were in business back in 2008 and we weathered the recession. I still don't know if we will weather this.

I get up at 9.00 a.m., which feels deliciously naughty, and I set up exercise circuits in the garden. It is a beautiful day already and for an hour I enjoy working out in the fresh air with just the birds. We start gardening and our resident robins hop hopefully about. Normally when we are in the garden they know that we are weeding, so they generally associate it with feeding time and juicy worms. They come incredibly close to us when we are digging and we have become very fond of the pair. After a few minutes they realise there is no food for them and hop disdainfully off. I sit in the garden and have a long WhatsApp video call with Sarah. Again, something we rarely do on a weekend as we are both normally running around to appointments. As before, I am shocked by the normality of everything within our environment.

But there is something far more exciting going on in the Jones-Williams household – the study doors are going up. Keith is in full workman mode, and I know from experience that once he starts a job it will get finished, and will be done perfectly. I am not in the least irritated by the banging, swearing and drilling that normally drives me crazy, and I offer him regular tea and food.

But the normality and fun doesn't last long; news floods in again and I read a devastating story on Twitter about an NHS nurse who died after contracting the virus. His family claim that he would still be alive today if he had been given proper protective equipment. Thomas Harvey was a healthcare assistant at North East London NHS Foundation Trust and had been unable to eat for several days and struggled to breathe after contracting the virus. The picture of him with his young son makes me want to cry again. Added to that, news comes through of a five-year-old who has died over the past day. No underlying conditions, no good reason. I feel so angry.

In other news, Kier Starmer has been voted the new Labour leader and vows to lead the Labour party into a new era and to work constructively in opposition. It sounds as if it was pretty much a one-horse race with 56.2% of the votes. It probably is the right decision but once again I feel it is a shame a woman hasn't been elected. He apologises for the 'stain of anti-Semitism that has tainted labour' and in his speech pledges to: "Tear the poison out by its roots by measuring whether former Jewish members return." Take that Corbyn!

Michael Gove and Stephen Powis head up today's briefing at lunchtime with more grim news. The latest figures show that 4,313 people have now died in the UK, up by 709 on Friday. Hundreds of ventilators are being manufactured every day and apparently more have been sourced from abroad.

Donald Trump is still being an ass and the press show an interview with him in his normal sycophantic tone telling people: “I just don’t want to be doing – somehow sitting in the Oval Office behind that beautiful Resolute Desk, the great Resolute Desk I think wearing a face mask as I greet presidents, prime ministers, dictators, kings, queens, I don’t know, somehow I don’t see it for myself. Maybe I’ll change my mind, but this will pass, and hopefully it will pass very quickly.”

He follows this by telling people that: “Most people could make something out of a certain material, it’s very simple, but I won’t be doing it”,

What a complete and utter twat!

News pings in that Carrie Symonds, Boris Johnson’s pregnant fiancée, has coronavirus too. So now they are both in isolation.

One of our friends, who is an Elvis impersonator, is doing a garage gig on Facebook and we tune in and put it on the TV screen whilst I write. It reminds me of our holidays in Majorca where we had all enjoyed nights out watching Elvis tribute gigs in the local bar. I suddenly feel melancholy and long to be back there.

The evening news states that the Queen will do a message tomorrow, something that has only happened on a handful of occasions throughout her reign. We are told it is a deeply personal message and will be thanking people and recognising the pain. I look forward to it, I love a bit of Liz!

TOTAL DEATHS – 4,353

Sunday, 5th April

Today I go for a walk as I am still trying to get my miles up in training for the Marathon – I am aiming for eight miles, although I have a very dodgy knee that often starts to sing loudly after about six miles, so I decide to see how it goes. I walk early for a Sunday morning to miss the crowds and at 8.00 a.m. the roads are deserted. I only encounter a couple of people and we give each other a wide berth accompanied by slightly embarrassed smiles. Whilst I walk, I reflect on what I have learnt during the last three weeks prompted by a poem I saw on social media by Monika Misra that resonated with me:

We are billions of caterpillars forced into our cocoons being called on to change, from the inside out, to metamorphosize, to rest, and reflect and sprout wings.

There was no name or anyone to credit it too, but it really struck a chord with me. I remember my yellow butterfly.

I have learnt so much already and my resilience has been tested so much; some days I have been proud, focused, and purposeful and sometimes I have been ashamed of how weak I felt inside.

So here is a list of some of the things I have learnt:

- That I like my life not being so fast (people used to say I would hate it – wrong!)
- That I enjoy being with my husband (and I can speak to him with respect! Well sometimes anyway!)
- That providing I have purpose I can survive.
- With structure and discipline, you can achieve anything.
- I never needed to diet – I just needed to eat healthily and not snack.
- How lucky I am with what I have – my house, family, business, and team.
- That in the end material things are trivial and pointless – all that matters is health.
- That I will never again take my freedom for granted.
- That choosing your behaviour is absolutely critical.
- To stop and appreciate small things – nature, conversations, food, telephone calls.
- To eat slowly and appreciate mealtimes.
- Not to waste food.

Quite a list for only three weeks. I get into my stride and thoughts float through my head. I think of my dad, my wonderful, wise, loving, legend of a father, and wondered what he would make of all this. As always, I ask him for a sign, a sign that things will be all right, a sign that the world will be OK. The next song comes on to Spotify and my heart stands still. It is 'Somewhere Over the Rainbow', my father's favourite song that we played at his funeral. Big fat tears roll down my cheeks as I walk, feeling him near me, within me and soothing me. It will all work out. The walk does me good and I feel positive and strong again.

I sit outside in the warm sun trying to relax and flicking through news and social media. Once again I see Facebook postings of idiots outside in parks and on the beach are filtering through. I feel so angry. Does this mean lockdown will get tighter? Despite videos of nurses sobbing about what they have endured on their shift, they still insist on saying it is no big deal and flaunting the rules. How many more times do people have to say: Just stay inside?

In Scotland, the Chief Medical Officer has resigned after she was caught by police visiting her second home in Fife during lockdown. Dr Catherine Calderwood apologised and resigned, "with a heavy heart." She agreed with Nicola Sturgeon that the example she was setting risked distracting from the pandemic advice.

Figures are coming in as always; worldwide cases pass 1.2 million, at least 65,000 people have died and 252,000 recovered. It's good to hear the recovery figures and there are some rays of hope as Italy sees the lowest death rate in over two weeks and Spain sees another decline with 674 reported on Sunday – a fall of 135 from Saturday – not good news but I am still clinging on to any positives.

On the other side of the coin, the US has more than 312,000 cases, the most of any country, and the US Surgeon General warns this will be the hardest and saddest week of most American's lives.

And then it is 8.00 p.m. and time for the Queen's speech. It is very rare for the Queen to make a speech apart from at Christmas, in fact it has only happened four times in her reign. The beginning of the land war in Iraq in 1991; the death of Diana, Princess of Wales; the death of the Queen's mother and a brief message of thanks after the celebration of the Queen's Diamond Jubilee.

She is sitting at her desk in her beautiful room, dressed impeccably in green, looking amazing for her years. Her body language displays calm determination, just what we need to see. She thanks everyone warmly on the NHS front line, and others carrying out essential roles, for their help and support and asks the nation to join her in thanking everyone. She also thanks all of us who are staying at home and sparing others the pain.

The rest of her speech is rousing, and memorable. One of those speeches that will go down in history and that touches the hearts and souls of her people.

> *"Together we are tackling this disease, and I want to reassure you that if we remain united and resolute, then we will overcome it."*

> *"I hope in the years to come everyone will be able to take pride in how they responded to this challenge."*

> *"And those who come after us will say the Britons of this generation were as strong as any."*

> *"That the attributes of self-discipline, of quiet good-humoured resolve and of fellow-feeling still characterise this country."*

> *"The pride in who we are is not a part of our past, it defines our present and our future."*

> *"The moments when the United Kingdom has come together to applaud its care and essential workers will be remembered as an expression of our national*

spirit; and its symbol will be the rainbows drawn by children."

"Across the Commonwealth and around the world, we have seen heart-warming stories of people coming together to help others, be it through delivering food parcels and medicines, checking on neighbours, or converting businesses to help the relief effort."

"And though self-isolating may at times be hard, many people of all faiths, and of none, are discovering that it presents an opportunity to slow down, pause and reflect, in prayer or meditation."

"It reminds me of the very first broadcast I made, in 1940, helped by my sister."

A picture of her and Princess Margaret as young girls pops up as she talks about her evacuation during the war. She tells us that today, once again, people feel separation, but we know it is the right thing to do. I think of the difference between then and now – sending your children away, never knowing when or whether you will see them again and only being able to write them letters. How did they bear that? We can see our children daily on FaceTime and talk to them whenever we want to as if they are in the room. There is no comparison. This is nothing like the war that our grandparents had to suffer through; sleeping in underground stations, sitting quietly in rooms around candles so that the lights didn't alert the enemy to bomb them. We sit on our sofas being entertained and connecting with our friends. We will get the food we want, even if we might have to queue for a while, but they had to queue for hours for tiny rations. We need to truly remember that.

She continues stoically.

"While we have faced challenges before, this one is different."

"This time we join with all nations across the globe in a common endeavour, using the great advances of science and our instinctive compassion to heal."

"We will succeed – and that success will belong to every one of us."

"We should take comfort that while we may have more still to endure, better days will return we will be with our friends again; we will be with our families again; we will meet again."

"But for now, I send my thanks and warmest good wishes to you all."

It certainly does the job; I feel comforted and grateful to hear from her. I have always been a fan of the Royal Family and I admire her strength. But then my black humour kicks in and I can't help musing that it would be fun if she were to start to sing that golden oldie by Dame Vera Lynn 'We'll Meet Again'!

We log on to the laptop to start our Sunday Pub Quiz, and for an hour or so everything feels normal again.

Concerning news comes in from Downing Street that Boris Johnson has been admitted to hospital for tests, ten days after testing positive for coronavirus. Apparently, he has had persistent symptoms including a temperature, so he was admitted as a precautionary measure and they expect him to stay overnight. I must admit he hasn't been looking very well.

TOTAL DEATHS – 4,934

Monday, 6th April
Official Lockdown, Week Three

My week is looking pretty full on, so I get up early to do my virtual PT session but WiFi is not being helpful today. We finally manage it on FaceTime but are realising we need to be pretty tenacious and patient with virtual sessions.

As I get dressed, I tune in, as always, to *GMB* and there is a strange feel to the programme today. Piers Morgan is being uncharacteristically reserved and is certainly not himself and Susanna Reid's smile is just not touching her eyes. They are discussing the death of Eddie Large, which has clearly hit Piers hard. His widow and son appear on screen with his comedy partner, Sid Little, in another window. Sid looks as if he is barely keeping it together. His son speaks eloquently and with huge passion about his father's career, but his wife, his adorable loving wife, speaks desperately about not being able to be with him at the end. At the end of the interview, they promise, that when they can, they will hold a proper memorial that Eddie would have loved.

After the interview I realise why the sombre mood is hanging over the studio. Susanna then announces that their thoughts are with Kate Garraway, whose husband is seriously ill in hospital. Kate is reportedly 'sick with worry' as her husband battles in Intensive Care. He has been in hospital for the last week.

Kate is a firm favourite with the nation, particularly after appearing on *I'm a Celebrity* last year, and this somehow feels horribly close to home. I remember seeing interviews with her husband and children when Kate was in the jungle and he was the loveliest man – that is the power of TV, you feel that you know people!

My daughter sends me a picture of one of her work colleagues, aged 32, on a respirator, saying they are just deciding whether to put him in a coma. My stomach is really churning today, and anxiety is rising, and I know I have to focus on something else to control it.

Piers then regains control and blasts Nicola Sturgeon for the delayed response to former Chief Medical Officer Catherine Calderwood for breaching the Government's guidelines. Calderwood resigned yesterday but Piers is furious that Nicola Sturgeon would even try to protect her. Fair point Piers.

My working day starts with a one to one with a member of staff who has been furloughed. She is an absolutely valued member who has been with me for twenty years, but the experience has left her feeling concerned that she is going to be made redundant, that she is not being useful at the moment. I am quite shocked that she is feeling this way and I assure her that I would do anything to keep her. I really would and just hope that the economy allows me to do it.

Another day passes in a blur of webinars and meetings and before I know it the clock is showing 2.30 p.m. I have to record a video for a client, something that I hate doing, but I know it is important, on how to motivate team members during the isolation. I ask Keith to help, a situation which would normally cause countless arguments and disagreements, but today it goes well. He sets up the lights and video equipment, is patient and encouraging and we manage to get them almost in one take. Later, as I prepare dinner, I think about this and how our relationship is evolving – we have really worked as a team over the last three weeks, normally we would live pretty separately, me travelling and working whilst he did gardening or other tasks, but now we work on things together, talking about things every day, and I am loving this new aspect to our relationship. I wonder how many other relationships are improving or deteriorating.

Dominic Raab takes the evening briefing and is asked by journalists when the current social distancing measures could be lifted. Professor Chris Witty, out of isolation for the first time, who is supporting him, said the Government must first establish when the peak of the epidemic will come and it was important to feel confident that we are over the peak.

Dominic Raab says it is too early to consider a strategy for exiting the coronavirus lockdown. He tells the briefing that the current measures are beginning to work, but if we shift focus we won't get through the peak as fast as we need to. I feel relieved.

The trio were asked whether the Prime Minister was fit to run the Government from hospital and Dominic neatly sidesteps saying that Boris will follow medical advice. Apparently, Donald Trump has sent his wishes to his 'great friend' Mr Johnson (cue sick bucket!)

No. 10 announces that 27,000 former healthcare professionals have registered to return to the NHS – there has been a great ad campaign to ask for retired personnel to return.

As I feared, news from the charity Refuge, the National Domestic Abuse Helpline, has experienced a dramatic rise in calls and online requests for help since the lockdown. There will, no doubt, not be any additional support for these victims and I fear for the rising death rate here.

After dinner I watch a short video of Bill Gates doing a TED Talk in 2015 on what we need to do to prevent a pandemic such as coronavirus. It feels chillingly accurate. During the video he describes what happened with the Spanish flu in 1918 and states clearly that the world needed to invest in better health systems, increase international collaboration, start a reserve of medical staff in co-operation with the army and invest in vaccine research. He describes how failing to do that in the face of a pandemic could cost millions of lives and trillions of dollars. He declared that the world was not prepared for an epidemic and urged us to get going because time was not on our side. Since then, apparently, the US has cut some of its virus programmes.

And then a shocking newsflash – Boris Johnson has been moved to the intensive care unit of a London hospital, after being hospitalised on Sunday for persistent coronavirus symptoms.

"Over the course of this afternoon, the condition of the Prime Minister has worsened, and, on the advice of his medical team, he has been moved to the Intensive Care Unit at the hospital," said a spokesman.

"The Prime Minister has asked Foreign Secretary, Dominic Raab, who is the First Secretary of State, to deputise for him where necessary," he added.

I never thought I would say these words, but I pray he recovers quickly.

TOTAL DEATHS – 5,373

Tuesday, 7th April

It all has got horribly real now that Boris is in Intensive Care. He is in St Thomas's Hospital. There couldn't be a stronger message to the world about how dangerous this is than for our Prime Minister to be facing this. Messages are flooding in from the whole world for him and his family – Trump, of course, offering to throw money at it for medical care – has he really not got the point yet that there is NO medical care that can help other than oxygen? The Queen is being regularly updated. I feel deeply sorry for his fiancée who has only recently announced that she is pregnant. It is really hard to process this and the news is full of medical experts, friends, and politicians discussing the situation both medically and debating who will now be making decisions. Each day I see Piers and Susanna becoming more and more worn down with the terrible situations they have to report and whilst they try and remain cheery and positive wherever possible, you can sense the fear in their voices as they present more and more tragic news. They show some videos of people who have survived coronavirus and the NHS workers all applauding a senior citizen as he leaves the hospital. Every single survivor is a victory for the NHS and must provide them with a massive lift during their relentlessly hard and emotionally draining days.

An interview is held with a man who was in ICU and recovered and this particular interview again terrifies me. He tells the story of how he went in after two weeks and all that the medical experts can do is to give you oxygen as your lungs are incapable of providing any. If the respirators don't help and your lungs worsen, that is when the invasive treatment begins and you are put into a coma on a ventilator so that your body can fight the virus whilst your lungs get help. When you get to that point, he tells us, it is 50/50, chilling odds. He talks about his dark moments realising there was no antibiotic or injection they could give but just this support to fight.

Michael Gove appears and is asked who is in charge of the country? He answers that Dominic Raab will be chairing all the important meetings today. He will be asking the tough questions and marshalling the team. Piers asks who the person is, who, in a case of nuclear war would 'press the button' and Gove refuses to answer by saying that they don't talk about matters of national security. Susanna changes tack and asks about lockdown and who will make the decision about when it is lifted – will it be delayed because Boris is in hospital? Gove responds rapidly that it won't be delayed, and they will make the decision as a cabinet. He reiterates that the Prime Minister's condition is a stark reminder of the dreadful power of the virus and the importance of lockdown. Piers thanks him sincerely at the end, to the extent that Gove tells Piers to keep challenging and just be himself!

My day is busy again, I do three coaching sessions with women, which is my passion, and it is really nice to get back into proper coaching. I move into the dining room temporarily as Keith sets to work on the doors of the study. I don't even care that my calls are peppered with the sound of drills screaming; I am getting doors on the study! The team are emailing with some positive news of clients interested in products, again not huge amounts for now, but if we get through this some very positive business that could be done. It is good to know that clients are responding and interacting.

By lunchtime Michael Gove is in isolation due to a family member displaying symptoms and by 2.00 p.m. news comes through that Boris is stable and in good spirits. A spokesman said he is receiving standard oxygen and breathing without any other assistance and definitely does not have pneumonia. Fingers crossed he continues to improve.

Feeling slightly relieved, I start to giggle at the next part of the newsflash: "The Prime Minister's weekly audience with the Queen will not go ahead." No shit, Sherlock! Of course, he wasn't going to Buckingham Palace today and the thought of dear Liz conducting a FaceTime whilst he was in his PJs in Intensive Care was just, well unthinkable!

On a lighter note, people around the world have been trying to brighten things up with humour. Dressing up to take up out the rubbish has become a thing and there are wonderful videos of burly men in princess costumes and tutus, people in animal costumes and superhero fancy dress, not just walking to the bins but acting and dancing on their way. In England, a postman is dressing up in a different costume each day and the community are logging on in the morning to see what he is wearing. Other people are setting up giant teddy bears on their lawns doing daily chores to amuse people on their walks. That's the spirit, that will get us through!

Rob sends me through the finished video for the Middle East that I had recorded on *Keeping Your Team Motivated*

– I am pleasantly surprised. It is the first time we have tried video in an interactive format and it looks very good – I also like the fact that I am in a small window to the side rather than in full HD on wide screen!

More news comes through and by 3.00 p.m. it is cited as the deadliest day for the virus today with 758 deaths recorded in England alone and the total death toll passing 6,000. The ages of the deceased are between 23 and 102 with the 23-year-old having no underlying health conditions. It is totally unimaginable and again I think about my 2 children and how indiscriminate the virus is.

I check the Dow Jones and today it jumped 857 points as countries report coronavirus infections are slowing. Airline and hospitality shares are swinging wildly which is not surprising, and once again I wonder if we will get to Mauritius in July. Selfish I know when I read that New York is recording 731 deaths – the largest single rise in a day. And for some reason, US gun sales reach an all-time high – both dreadful pieces of news. I ponder on whether there is a link.

One of my friends phones me to talk about a volunteering scheme to coach and counsel NHS members and I sign up immediately – it is the only thing I can do as I can't leave home, but these amazing people need help and if I can help I will.

TOTAL DEATHS – 6,169

Wednesday, 8th April

When I wake today, I grab my phone to check on news of Boris – thankfully, he is still in good spirits and not deteriorating. I also read that Wuhan has finally been released from lockdown. Travel is now allowed and limits on economic activity and individual movement have been eased. China has reported no new deaths for the first time since the beginning of the outbreak but there are still some concerns over whether this reporting can be trusted. Last week Michael Gove had said that some of the reporting was: "Not clear about the scale, the nature, the infectiousness of the virus," and Trump added that: "It was a little bit on the light side." I wonder about the future of economic relationships with China.

This morning I have a very mindful walk, taking in the beautiful sights of spring, the budding flowers, the early blooms of the camelias and the beautiful cherry blossom trees that flank the road. It is like walking through a tunnel of nature's most magnificent attempts. It is 6.00 a.m. and the sun looks beautiful as it rises, and I catch a waft of honeysuckle as I walk. I like these early walks; I feel safe and calm and it helps me to ground myself. We have made inroads to some future business and we have developed some really innovative products that we have been trying to get the time to create for a long time. We have had some good conversations with key clients and have kept our profile high. But we aren't really making money, so I can only pray this will be enough for whatever the world looks like when we come out of this. And that is one of the most difficult things, just not knowing what business will look like on the other side. Will people have money to spend on training anymore? Of course, budgets are going to be tight and companies will have to change but we just don't know what the business landscape will be.

Back home I tune into *GMB* and Piers is back on form tearing apart Sadiq Khan. Fourteen London Transport workers have died including nine bus drivers, and an argument ensues over whether they should have worn PPE. Khan tries to argue that they are following WHO guidelines but Piers will not let this go and then the discussion becomes fraught. Sadiq Khan is sincere in his sorrow at the deaths, even mentioning that he has many friends who work for London Transport but still Piers insists that they should have PPE. Ten minutes later GMB have on screen the mother of one of the bus drivers who died aged thirty-six. The screen is shaky as she holds the phone, and she is composed and eloquent as she describes how he had told her the buses were dirty and his fear of the virus. At the end of the interview her voice breaks as she tries to describe her son and how much she will miss him. It turns me cold when I hear these stories; ordinary people doing their jobs and families left in tatters because we were not sufficiently prepared. Why? As Bill Gates had said, why were we not preparing for this? No doubt once this is all over there will be many questions to answer.

On a more cheerful note they interview Katherine Jenkins who announces that the duet she recorded with

Vera Lynne on the 70th anniversary of D-Day, 'We'll Meet Again', has been re-released and all the proceeds will be going to the NHS. I watch it on YouTube with tears rolling down my face. My emotions really are all over the place today.

At today's briefing, The Chancellor, Rishi Sunak, is back joined by Stephen Powis – and, as has become normal, he is doing a recap of what the Government have done so far to help us. As always, he is pristine, articulate, and empathetic, particularly when he delivers the bad news from today – daily figures of the total deaths is up by 938 in the last twenty-four hours. I can't even compute those figures.

Rishi gives an update on Boris – he is receiving excellent care and he remains in Intensive Care where his condition is improving. He has also been sitting up and engaging with the team, so fingers crossed he is over the worst. He talks about the virus being indiscriminate in terms of who it will attack, and it is so true.

Rishi also goes on to talk about how the Government is supporting businesses and tonight his focus is on charities and particularly those that are on the front line in supporting the public. £750 million for the charity sector, £370 million for those who look after the vulnerable. The £370 million of the support will come from the National Lottery Fund (I was just wondering where that would come from), Rishi really does seem to have endless pockets but I know who will pay for this eventually.

I feel strangely reassured as he consistently talks about doing whatever is needed to support us and his comments about trying to put us in a position to bounce back quickly. If only that could be true – I want to stay positive but not be overly optimistic. Exactly the subject of my webinar today – Managing Resilience.

Rishi Sunak is asked about when we will come out of lockdown and he answers earnestly that there will be a COBRA meeting chaired by Dominic Raab, which will make the decision based on data. Pushed on whether different groups of people will emerge at different times, he refuses to speculate on the future.

Deaths in Spain rise to 13,455. That seems unbelievably high but at our current rate of multiplication we could reach that in less than a week.

TOTAL DEATHS – 7,098

Thursday, 9th April

Today I wake feeling surprisingly positive about the Easter holiday. I have already decided to split the days between enjoying reading books in the sun, gardening and doing some chores indoors. Along with spring cleaning and ironing, I also want to have a concerted effort sorting out my wardrobes.

Today's news is dominated by football and whether the rest of the season will be played. There is no conclusion. However, there is an announcement that the Premier League teams have all come together to raise money under the heading of Players Together. They will be targeting NHS charities with £4 million already paid and hope that they will raise more. They are quick to announce that the plan was already underway before criticism regarding the furloughing of non-playing staff. Donations will be anonymous, but the hope is to raise millions.

Today I feel at peace with myself and the world. I am looking forward to my webinar this morning and then a day of design and creative work. We are working on a Children's playbook with a thirty-day challenge to keep children occupied after Easter. I want to send something free to my clients to support their people, but also to keep us in the client's minds for when business restarts. There is not much we can do at the moment, so things like this keep me motivated and purposeful. My rollercoaster is on the upward trajectory today, the webinar seems to go well, and I feel I really have the hang of virtual learning.

I flick on to social media and I read this post. As it has been asked to be shared, I want to include it in the book. This post touched me on so many levels and really bought to life for me the daily terror that people in the front line are feeling, the connection that they have with their patients and the compassion and joy they experience when the treatment is successful. The post is from a doctor named Halen Albania.

> *"I have been an Emergency Medicine Physician for almost 20 years. I have worked through numerous disasters, and I'm used to the daily grind of heart attacks, gunshots, strokes, flu, traumas, and more. It's par for the course in my field. Yet nothing has made me feel the way I do about my "job" as this pandemic has—that knot-in-the-pit-of-your-stomach sensation while heading into work, comforted only by the empathetic faces of my colleagues who are going through the same. I am grateful for their presence, knowing they are both literally and figuratively with me, that they understand and accept so profoundly the risks we take each day. I also hope that my friends and family forgive me for my lack of presence during this time—precisely when we need each other most—and that they realize that their words, their encouragement, and their small gestures that come my way daily are the fuel that gets me through each day. This is a story for all of us.*

I met my patient, Mr. C., on my first real "pandemic" shift, when what we were seeing that day was what we had been preparing for. He was classic in his presentation, his X-ray findings, his low oxygen levels... we just knew. And he was the nicest man I had met in a long time. Gasping for breath, he kept asking if we needed anything, and that it would all be okay. He told us he was a teacher but that he was learning so much from us, and how much he respected what we were doing. The opposite could not be truer.

We had to decide how long we would try to let him work through this low oxygen state before needing to intubate him. His levels kept falling and despite all our best efforts it was time to put him on the ventilator. He told us he didn't feel great about this, "but Doc, I trust you and am putting myself in your hands." That uneasy feeling in my stomach grew even more in that moment. But he, with his teacher's steady voice, kept me grounded, where I was supposed to be. I saw his eyes looking at me, seeing the kindness in them, even as we pushed the medications to put him to sleep. To say this was an "easy" intubation is an understatement. It was not. He nearly left us a few times during those first minutes, but he kept coming back. We fought hard to keep him with us. The patience and strength of my team that day, truly remarkable.

I handed him over to my friend and colleague, Beth Ginsburg, and her team in the ICU, and her calming voice reassured me that they had it from here. And then for the next twelve days, I waited and watched his progress, knowing the statistics, and how sick he was when he got to us. They did their magic, and just yesterday my new friend Mr. C was extubated. I decided to go "meet" him again.

Mr C. was in the COVID stepdown unit, recovering, without family. Nobody was allowed to visit him; even worse, his wife had been home alone in isolation for the past fourteen days, too. My heart broke thinking of how that must have been for her. I cautiously went into his room, donned in my PPE, and when he saw me, he stopped for a second. A moment of recognition.

I introduced myself. "I'm Dr. Albania, Mr. C. I was the last person you saw in the ER. You told me you trusted us to get you to this side. Looks like you did just fine." He started to cry. He said, "I remember your eyes." And I started to cry. What he didn't know is that, at that moment, I realized that we do what we do exactly for people like him, for moments like these. His strength, his kindness, his calming words to me meant everything. At that moment, my heart (which had been beating over 100 bpm since this pandemic began) finally slowed down.

I sat down and we talked. I told him that while he is here, we are his family. He will always have a place in my heart. And whether he knows it or not, he will be my silent warrior and guide as I take care of every patient, COVID or not. He will fuel me until the day I hang up my stethoscope."

(Facebook notes: *Story posted with full permission from patient.*)

A stark dose of reality in a newsflash comes from the Head of the IMF, Kristalina Georgieva, who said that the coronavirus pandemic is likely to cause the worst recession in almost a century. Apparently, growth across the world would turn 'sharply negative' in 2020 and that most countries – regardless of their income – would face a fall in incomes. Not unexpected, but when she states that they anticipate the worst economic fallout since the depression it feels very dark. She does follow this by saying a partial recovery next year is possible, however, this can only happen if the virus began to fade later this year.

We have our end-of-week pub meeting on Zoom and the mood is still uplifted. I wish them all a Happy Easter. In previous years I would have given them all Easter eggs but this year they will have to make do with a greeting.

Dominic Raab takes the briefing and tells people that things will not change for the next few weeks; the death rate needs to go down and there were concerns that the warm weather could tempt people outside this Easter Bank Holiday. The thought is that the lockdown is likely to be extended; Nicola Sturgeon had already been fairly explicit about this in Scotland. Raab states that there will not be a firm announcement until the end of next week as they need to examine all the key data.

By law, a review of the lockdown has to happen by next Thursday, however, I am pretty convinced that it will be an extension at least until the beginning of May. In theory, I am in until at least mid-May.

The Foreign Secretary also revealed that he hadn't had any contact with Boris Johnson since stepping in as his deputy – making the point that the Prime Minister must focus on his recovery.

Later that evening news comes through that the PM has been moved from Intensive Care back to the ward where he will receive close monitoring – they add that he is in extremely good spirits.

And then we all go out to clap. Tonight, I take a pan and a wooden spoon so I can make more noise for longer, and even find a whistle. Again, the clapping starts with a firework and then an amazing noise – it is weird as I can't see anybody from my front garden, just hear them and I blow loudly on my whistle. Each blow is followed by hoots and whooping. I hope it means something to the staff to hear our thanks. The television shows different streets around the country and even a whole car park full of police cars who all turned on their blue lights for the five minutes. Highly moving. My emotional rollercoaster hits again as I battle with tears – it doesn't take much these days.

TOTAL DEATHS – 7,978

Friday, 10th April – Good Friday

It's Good Friday and a beautiful sunny day, and once again I allow myself a little lie-in to watch *The News*.

A few snippets of good news come through; a 101-year-old man pulls through the virus. It is wonderful when you see stories like that and I hope today, as I do every day, that there will be more positive news. However, as always some news catches my eye to change the mood and this is truly hideous – the New York total for deaths is now 7,844 – the highest of any single city – but drone images emerge of coffins being buried in a mass grave with workers in hazmat gear seen stacking the coffins in deep trenches in Hart Island off the Bronx on Long Island. It has long been used for people with no next of kin and would potentially intern 25 bodies a week, but now they are burying 24 per day. Apparently, it is unclear how many of them have no next of kin or cannot afford burials, and New York City Mayor, Bill de Blasio, indicated that temporary burials may be needed until the crisis has passed. I cannot bear the thought of all of these people unable to grieve properly, with no headstone for their loved ones. The US has had, in total, about 16,700 deaths but our 8,000 doesn't feel that far behind.

I try to shake it off with a circuit's workout in the garden, and then some weeding in the front garden, but actually start to feel quite unwell. Headachy and nauseous; the first time I have felt under the weather for weeks. By 2.00 p.m. I decide to go and sit in the garden and read. I stay there all afternoon reading and dozing.

The briefing comes on led by Matt Hancock and joined by Chief Nursing Officer, Ruth May and Chief Medical Officer, Jonathan Van-Tam. Ruth May pays an emotional tribute to front-line staff who had died after contracting coronavirus and says: "The NHS is a family and we feel their loss deeply." Jonathan runs us through the slides of the figures, and we can see the trends – in one of the graphs we are bang on the same trajectory as Italy was days ago. He is asked by a journalist what signs will we be able to look for that will tell us that lockdown might be ending and he says it is impossible to tell.

Fielding questions, Matt Hancock once more reiterates that they are following scientific advice, i.e. that masks are not protective for individuals and no other countries advise. More PPE is now being delivered following criticism that the Government was not doing enough to protect staff and Hancock confirms that 15 drive-through testing centres have also been opened. He also mentions that other labs have now been discovered to work on tests and this is their hope for increasing the amount of testing.

The figures are still grim with another 980 hospital deaths and we are told that whilst the lockdown was beginning to pay off it was still a dangerous situation. More urging from all three of them to stay inside.

On the plus side, Boris is now out of Intensive Care and on to a hospital ward (I wonder who with?) and has now been able to do short walks. I am glad for his fiancée as she must have been worried sick, and to be pregnant and have coronavirus and have to cope with him being in Intensive Care must have been a very anxious time.

I do a Zoom call with one of my best friends Lauren, and her husband in California. We haven't spoken since this started and it is good to catch-up. They are fairly well protected there as they live in a quiet area. I decide not to watch *The News* tonight; we have started to watch *Gavin and Stacey* from the beginning again and we settle in for a comedy binge – sometimes not knowing is the best.

TOTAL DEATHS – 8,958

Saturday, 11th April

I awake thinking it is Sunday and then remember it is Saturday and can't get back to sleep. So, I decide to go and walk early.

The streets are deserted until I reach the Common and then it gets busy, so we play the game of 'who will social distance first?' When a person approaches one of you has to move (although not everyone has read the game rules) and then we give each other an embarrassed smile, which is supposed to mean, "I know you are a really nice person but get away from me!" Most people are adhering to guidelines although a few people had set up circuits or were boxing with pads on the grassy area of the Common. My knee is sore today after gardening yesterday, so I only do six miles before I go home. We have breakfast in the garden and spend half an hour discussing which plants were blooming – when did we become such avid gardeners? The peace and quiet is lovely and the birds are loud and distinct, and it is easy to go into our bubble of contentment. I vow to avoid all news until the end of the day and try and enjoy a day off. Keith tells me that he thinks we have just about finished the garden and I manage to find at least another five jobs –

well, it is going to be a while before we get out and I don't want him to feel that he has nothing to do!

It's twenty-one degrees, hotter than I can ever remember at Easter. For an hour I tackle the front garden borders whilst Keith finishes painting the fence, and then decide to hit the helicopter chair for some reading. I choose a book on purpose for leaders – it is slim and a bit repetitive, but it does remind me that I probably need to revisit this. I can't sit still for long and finish the book in two hours (I learnt many years ago that if in a business book someone puts a summary at the end of each chapter that is probably all you need to read) so I start sorting out the big box of papers I brought home from the office.

Our friend Tony, the Elvis impersonator, is doing another garage concert at 5.00 p.m. so we put it on television and have a drink. Again, another nice day – probably the type of weekends that normal people have and I vow that when we get back to normal (I must find another name for that as it won't be normal and I don't even know if I want it to be) I will make more of my weekends.

But when I turn on the news my mood soon changes.

The headline states that as Boris recovers, his government faces mounting problems on political, health and economic fronts as it battles the pandemic in his absence.

Whilst the senior ministers are urging him not to rush back, they do believe he should act as a chairman of the board whilst he recuperates. One minister said that the current lockdown was likely to continue until early to mid-May at the earliest to allow Johnson some time to make a phased return to work. Apparently trust between the Downing Street political team and civil service officials is at an all-time low. Bloody typical, the minute the headmaster is away the kids start fighting; clearly Boris Johnson's incarceration in hospital has thrown them all in turmoil as his absence has led to a political vacuum with uncertainty and confusion around who is actually in charge. I stop watching as it is making me so irritable – this is the last thing we need.

And once again the UK is told to stay at home as the news comes through, that 917 new deaths are reported, which could even be an underestimate as there is often a lag in reporting at the weekend. This was the second day in a row that the daily total deaths exceeded 900. Having said that, the growth in deaths has stalled in the last four days.

The police have handed out over 1,000 fines to people who are still flouting the rules and playing games of football, sunbathing, and having gatherings in parks in London. I really can understand how hard it is for people who don't have a garden when the weather is like it is. But we must comply.

The Home Secretary, Priti Patel, hosted today's daily press conference, joined by Martin Hewitt, Chair of the National Police Chiefs' Council and Professor Stephen Powis, National Medical Director of NHS England. Professor Stephen Powis revealed that drug treatment could come BEFORE a vaccination.

Priti Patel announced £2 million to support domestic abuse survivors – nowhere near enough but at least it is something. She also announces that whilst total crime has fallen during the lockdown there was more activity from fraudsters who had already exploited the virus with £1.8 million through a variety of frauds on cures, COVID-19 Tax refunds, WHO announcements, fear mongering and donations.

An article in my feed comes up about NHS workers who have died, and the roll call is heart breaking. Some of them are people who were retired and volunteered to come back.

The pictures and the stories of each of them, with ages ranging from 29 to 76, all who had fearlessly approached the front line to do their job and left behind families and loved ones. I read every story – these are the people who deserve to be remembered and it is their families I want to help. It makes me even more angry when I hear of people flouting the lockdown rules and these families losing their loved ones.

I read an article about the Spanish flu in 1918. It alludes to the fact that in 1918 Philadelphia prematurely ended its quarantine from the Spanish flu to throw a parade in order to boost morale for the war effort. Some 200,000 people lined the streets. Within seventy-two hours every bed in Philadelphia's 31 hospitals was filled and 4,500 people ended up dying within days. Whether that is true or not, I wonder if the Government have looked at any of the lessons from the Spanish flu?

And we are surprised with another message from the Queen – her first ever Easter message. It is pre-recorded, and she urges the UK to maintain coronavirus lockdown over the Easter weekend. She tells the country that by keeping apart we keep others safe. She talks about religious festivals and candles and how they would normally, at Easter, pass one light to another to show the good news of Christ's resurrection. She mentions that this year Easter will be different but that it isn't cancelled. She says that just as the discovery of the risen Christ on the first Easter Day gave his followers new hope and fresh purpose that we can all take heart from it. She finishes by saying that we know that coronavirus will not overcome us. She wishes us a heartfelt Happy Easter. You too Liz!

TOTAL DEATHS – 9,875

Sunday, 12th April

Easter Sunday. No chocolate eggs here; we are pretty much off sugar since this all started and I have to say my sweet tooth has definitely started to abate.

The weather is starting to change, a little cloudier today but I marvel about how lucky we have been in the last three weeks with the weather. It has been simply astonishing how sunny for March and April it has been (not helpful if you live in a flat but at least going for walks if it is dry) and I reflect on how different this might be if it had been windy and rainy.

I head for the gym – with my knee still being temperamental I am just going to do a long ride on the exercise bike to try and loosen it up, and Sarah phones me – perfect timing. She keeps me company as I cycle and we talk about everything. Her mother is still up and down in the care home and whilst she is speaking to her regularly it is still incredibly hard. I pray that she is able to see her before it is too late – the Alzheimer's is rapidly taking away all semblance of her mother and some days the calls are heart-breaking. We talk for forty-five minutes and as always I feel uplifted – Sarah s the only person in my life who can always cheer me up however dire the situation is. I cannot wait to see her – she is off her cancer drugs to boost her immune system and it worries me tremendously. We touch on it briefly and make light of it – I tell her she is going nowhere, we have far too much mischief to make in the world yet, and we laugh. She mentions that she has heard that Sweden has not locked down and I make a mental note to take a look later and see how that is working for them.

Bill Gates is on morning TV being interviewed about the fact he had said this was the greatest potential threat back in 2015, and says that we definitely will look back and wish that we invested more so that we quickly could have the diagnostics, vaccines and equipment. He says there will be time later for those post-mortems and very few countries 'will get an A grade', we didn't simulate or practise and therefore found ourselves in unchartered territory. Interesting statement – 'no countries will get an A grade'. Too right, we have all flunked this one big-time, publicly and with tragic consequences. Oh, I wish this man was the president.

I decide to check in on Sweden and find an article on CNN stating that Sweden challenges Trump, and the scientific mainstream, by refusing to lock down. Apparently, restaurants and bars are still open in the Nordic country and schools and playgrounds haven't closed either.

Compared to the rest of the world this is certainly a controversial move, and of course Trump didn't let it pass without commenting in his own inimitable way: "Sweden did that, the herd, they call it the herd. Sweden's suffering very, very badly," he dribbled out in his fake sympathetic tone on Tuesday.

However, the Swedish government is confident that their approach can work, and the Foreign Minister even went as far to suggest that Trump was factually wrong to suggest that they were following the herd immunity theory.

This theory suggests that letting enough people catch the virus whilst protecting the vulnerable means a country's population builds up immunity. Ann Linde, Sweden's Minister for Foreign Affairs, stated that Sweden's strategy was to rely very much on people taking responsibility for themselves. According to John Hopkins University's figures Sweden has 9,141 cases and 793 deaths. They very much are allowing Swedes to make their own decisions and take personal responsibility, so Easter for Sweden is still about Easter parties. In some ways they have an advantage as about 40% of the population work from home anyway. I guess we will see in the next month whether the Swedes were right.

I settle down to read. Today's book is *Atomic Habits* by James Clear and this one is brilliant. It really helps me to think about what I am trying to achieve in this twelve-week period and focus on not just my goals, but the systems and processes that are taking me towards the goals. I gain some good information for a virtual learning session I am doing this week on 'Reprogramming Your Mind'.

Matt Hancock takes the briefing and tells us it is a sombre day. He says the future of the virus is unknowable – a strange word but to me it means there is really no idea of when and how it might abate. So, more uncertainty ahead. Apparently, ministers are split over whether to lift restrictions in either three, or six weeks' time.

A further 737 people have died, not as many as the last two days but still far too many. However, it could be more as weekend reporting often has a lag. The John Hopkins University confirms that 1.8 million cases have been confirmed globally, although I wonder how accurate that is considering many people have not been tested. Worldwide more than 112,000 people have died whilst 415,000 have recovered.

Pope Francis broadcasts Easter Sunday Mass from St Peter's Basilica – the first time he has ever broadcast to an empty cathedral.

And finally, Boris Johnson has been discharged from hospital – he still has been advised not to go back to work, although Dominic Raab says that the Government is operating perfectly efficiently within the strategy he set out. He profusely thanked healthcare workers for saving his life and said: "It could have gone either way." He said that he had witnessed the personal courage of hospital staff.

As it is Sunday it is Pub Quiz time – our third one. I think we will count down the lockdown with our pub quiz nights and I predict at least another six!

TOTAL DEATHS – 10,612

Monday, 13th April
Official Lockdown, Week Four

Easter Monday, but today is going to be a working day for me as I have a webinar at lunchtime and another one to prepare for tomorrow. I still take a walk first and the streets are completely deserted this morning. It is 8.00 a.m. and the weather has turned, so I suspect people are just having a good lie-in.

As I walk today, I start to think about the economic impact that this is going to have on the UK and the world. There is no question that this is the biggest global crisis since the Second World War. Now I am no economist, and I don't pretend to understand the stock market, but what I do understand is that the fabric of our economy is being ripped apart and I am not sure what pattern it will make when we start to sew it all together. When we run change workshops we talk about the knock-on effect and get people to draw diagrams about how far the ripples will be felt, and as I walk, my brain winds itself around in circles with a huge amount of questions. Will the homeworking mean that many big organisations give up their offices? Will we now be so used to shopping online that we no longer go into towns? Will more kids return home now as they can't afford to buy houses or will the housing market slump so deeply that they can afford them again? This would be more dreadful news for us as we have a portfolio of houses that we rent out and we have built up a large amount of equity in them – hopefully, we still would be able to rent them out but we could lose a huge amount of money. What will be the impact on our relationship with Chinese commerce? Will we now realise that we can manufacture quickly and cheaply at home and create more jobs? Trump has caused a good deal of damage with his Chinese flu branding, and many people I know talk about the fact that they are angry about the Chinese markets as they feel this started it. Certainly, many organisations have proved during this time how quickly they can manufacture urgent equipment and provisions. Will there be greater family care with more people now deciding to move their elderly parents in to live with them? Will we move to a far more virtual-reality world? We are already realising that Zoom (oh I wish I had shares in that company!) can be as effective as group meetings, so will we stop travelling so much? What will be the impact on airlines? And will the Far East stop visiting us as tourists? We all know the impact on the economy when the hospitality business drops.

There is so much to think about, and my brain intertwines these economic thoughts with personal concerns. I don't think that there will be a return to business as usual – but then actually that it could be a good thing, as business was pretty much a disaster. I remember in 2008, Rahm Emanuel, the former Mayor of Chicago, discussing the recession and saying: "You never want a serious crisis to go to waste." And that is true, if we don't learn and evolve then this pain has all been worthless. On the positive side, I hope that we have more patriotism, care for others, relaxing on pointless regulatory barriers, and most importantly, a realisation that we can do something about the environment and climate change.

But what does this all mean for me, Keith, my family, my team, and my business? We really can't predict this, but as I walk I think again about whether my business will survive, and if it does, in what shape? I take a different route today; we live in a pretty leafy area but within fifteen minutes' walk there is a housing estate. As I walk around looking at the houses and appreciating how lucky I have been with our house and garden, I think about these people who live perfectly happy lives in smaller accommodation, and if the worst comes to the worst, we could downsize. It would be such a shame after finally getting to the point where our house was exactly as we wanted it to be and thinking we had a house we were happy to live in for the rest of our lives, but if we had to sell and buy something smaller we would be OK. Others, if they lost their jobs, might not be and could end up homeless. If we lose all the equity in our houses then hopefully we could still rent them and have an income, so again, worst-case scenario – not everything will be lost. And whilst I didn't really want to have to work at this pace for another ten years, I certainly could, and rather than this being the year I started to slow down then, if I have to ramp up at age sixty, I can do it. Yes, after working crazy hours for twenty-five years doing everything I can to build up the business and just preparing to ease into retirement, it is a shock to have to think about losing everything and starting again, but I have to get my mind set and ready to consider all eventualities.

I work for a few hours to prepare a webinar for tomorrow and then deliver a webinar to Saudi on resilience. As I teach the subject I try and think of my level of resilience and how I am doing – generally, not bad, but it can really vary. It goes well and I finish at 2.30 p.m. A Facebook notification pops up – someone is going live. It is a lovely lady that I met at the Body Camp in Majorca last year; my daughter and I really enjoyed her company. I tune in to find that she is going live with her father's funeral. Because the family aren't able to go, they are giving them the chance to be with them as they take the coffin to the grave. As I watch the party walk to the grave I notice that already another eight graves are dug beside it. It feels so strange to see this – just the five of them walking to the grave to say goodbye. I don't know whether it was coronavirus or not, but I feel desperately sad for her.

I decide to go and clean out some cupboards to distract my thinking; I still have many jobs to do and keep myself occupied for the next month at least. I have the news on in the background, and as I sort through clothes, I hear an interesting comment about how many people die of seasonal flu every year.

Apparently, on average the flu is estimated to kill between 290,000 and 650,000 worldwide including about 17,000 in Britain. Seasonal influenza has almost certainly claimed more lives this year. Now I am a bit confused – if we are trying to stop the death rate passing 20,000, which is not far off what it normally is, the question to me is, how dangerous is coronavirus? Or is seasonal flu separate to COVID-19 reporting? It can't be, surely? The number of figures being thrown at us is now getting quite confusing.

At 5.00 p.m. the briefing comes on led by Dominic Raab and accompanied by Sir Patrick Vallance. He still looks uncomfortable as he reads his speech; his words are sincere but his fluency in being able to read and connect with the camera a bit disjointed. Again, massive thanks to the NHS and to us for, on the whole, keeping to the social distancing rules over the weekend (even though there had been some pictures of police breaking up parties).

He tells us that the UK's plan is working but we are still not past the peak of the virus and reminds us to keep it up. He says: "We have come too far, lost too many loved ones and sacrificed too much to ease up."

Charts come up and we look as if we are still on the same trajectory as Italy.

No change to lockdown yet, we will have to wait for the scientific advisers to review the evidence, although it appears that China could be looking at a second wave as cases rocketed by 108, the highest increase in five weeks.

In France, Macron has extended the lockdown until the 11th of May but will be progressively opening schools and creches from mid-May – bold move Emmanuel, is it not too early to tell? He also said that France was not sufficiently ready for the outbreak of the new coronavirus; they lacked protective clothing, gels, masks, like other countries they have made difficult decisions. Slightly different from Priti Patel's 'sorry, not sorry' statement on Sunday when she said, after reports of the highest daily hospital death rate in Europe: "I am sorry if people feel there have been failings." Err, don't you mean that there have been failings? The press had a field day with that today, some going as far to call it a statement of 'microaggression'.

Once again, I feel depressed as I cook dinner but this evening has a small treat in store for us – *Killing Eve*, Season 3, has started. We finished *Gavin and Stacey* last night so this will keep us going for a few nights.

TOTAL DEATHS – 11,329

Tuesday, 14th April

Wide awake this morning and up early for my virtual gym session. I feel motivated and positive to start the week. We are gradually working through tasks and the more organised I get, the more organised I want to be, so before I even go for a shower I tackle all the ironing.

I switch on *GMB* as I get ready and Piers is in light-hearted mode today as he talks to Captain Tom Moore. Captain Tom is a darling of a gentleman, a 99-year-old, who fought in World War 2. He wanted to raise money for the NHS and so he set himself a goal of completing 100 laps of walking around his garden before his 100th birthday. When he was featured on GMB he had already raised £350,000 and Piers had urged the public to donate and get him to £1 million, and he was getting close. As the day goes on, he raises more and more finally hitting over £3 million – what a man!

I start work and have a productive morning so by the time I look up it is almost 12.30 p.m. and time to get ready to do my webinar to Saudi. I get set up and just before I should log on the Wi-Fi crashes. Bloody brilliant! I shout for Keith who is working in the garden and we manage to get back on with five minutes to spare; nothing like a bit of a panic to get your adrenalin up. Today's subject is about 'Positivity and Reprogramming Your Mind'. The audience is chatty, and it is a subject I love, so I really enjoy it.

After the webinar I grab some lunch. Whilst I eat, I flick through the news and an interesting item catches my eye. Apparently, the Medical Protection Society has called on the Government to safeguard doctors from claims against some of the decisions they are making during the coronavirus – emergency laws would be required. They are already adopted in New York State to ensure that medical staff are not exposed to criminal investigations following decisions that they may need to make in terms of whether, and when, emergency treatment can be withheld or withdrawn. This has bothered me for a long time – doctors are under huge amounts of pressure and whilst decisions would normally be made on what is in the best interest of the patient, in these conditions, where respirators may not be available, there is a lack of clarity as to whether it is lawful. Now that the Government have shown how quickly they can introduce laws, it seems critical that they are introduced rapidly to protect healthcare professionals.

There is also continuing speculation and differing opinions coming through around when schools will reopen. Last Wednesday, Number 10 clarified that schools would not be opening after Easter, which was closely followed by two other unions representing headteachers suggesting that schools should open before the summer holiday rather than staying closed until September. However, this could only happen if it was safe to do so. I am really unsure how this would work – you can't socially distance children and the minute that they open schools I fear everything we have achieved so far would be undermined.

We are now starting to get some clarity on the accuracy of reporting. Apparently, actual coronavirus-related deaths could be 15% higher than the daily briefings are suggesting. Nick Stripe, who is Head of Health Analysis and Life Events at the ONS, (Office for National Statistics) showed that on the 3rd of April the latest comparable data for deaths involving COVID-19 showed that there were 6,235 deaths in England and Wales. Apparently, when looking at data for England, this is 15% higher than the NHS numbers. There is also a huge amount of controversy about the amount of deaths in care homes and whether these have been counted. Apparently, two of the UK's largest care home providers recorded deaths of 521 residents in recent weeks, which fuelled claims that there might be a cover-up in the official figures.

And then it is time for the briefing, and this time Rishi Sunak is not the good-news fairy. He is flanked by Steve Powis and Yvonne Doyle.

He gets straight into it telling us that the OBR (Office for Budget Responsibility) have warned of a 35% shrink in the economy in the second quarter of the year – he shows a chart that shows the impact on the economy of all the major events since the Spanish flu and when it gets to the coronavirus the dip is extreme, surpassing any other event, but then the Chancellor shows us a fast upward spike and says that it might be a fast comeback. It is clearly not a forecast but just a prediction apparently based on the OBR's consideration of a scenario illustrating the possible effects on the economy and public finances of a three-month shutdown, however, it is a very sobering thought. Potentially, unemployment could rise by 2 million – 1 in 10 people out of work. I can still remember the days of 3 million unemployed back in Maggie Thatcher's reign.

But Rishi is strong and tells us earnestly that it is important we are honest with people about what might be happening to our economy and warns us that these are tough times and there will be more to come. However, he does remind us that we came into the crisis with a fundamentally sound economy. Did we? I need to think about that one. He goes on to guarantee that 'we' are not just going to stand by and watch this happen; I presume he means the Government.

He goes on to talk about testing and confirmed that over 300,000 people in the UK have been tested with over 93,000 people testing positive.

He hands over to Steve to take us through the figures. There have been 778 fatalities since yesterday. A tiny dip today but not a lot.

I feel very troubled – as usual I have spent my day focusing on work but when I get my head up and hear news about the economy, panic starts to rise and I have to consider the long-term – I realise my strategy of coping with each day and just working on what I can do is all very well but I still have to make decisions about the future.

TOTAL DEATHS – 12,107

Wednesday, 15th April

We have lost the cat. When I wake up at 6.00 a.m. she is nowhere to be seen and as I get dressed to go in the gym, she is not winding herself around my legs and crying for food. I look around the house; she isn't in any of her normal places and I feel a bit concerned. After half an hour in the gym I give up and walk around the garden calling her. I suddenly realise how devastated I am going to be if something has happened to her, but then I realise that there are hardly any cars on the road and she barely ventures that far; she is a very nervy cat. I come back in and tell Keith I can't find her. He shoots out of bed. I have never seen him get up so fast but inside that hard exterior is an immense soft spot for Maisie. He agrees it is totally out of character for her and he rushes downstairs in his dressing gown calling her. She suddenly strolls into the kitchen totally oblivious to our panic. I feel immensely relieved; on top of everything else losing Maisie would just finish us off. I go downstairs and tell her off for worrying me – she disdainfully raises one eyebrow at me and goes back to sleep on the sofa.

GMB is in full swing as I start work and I have Piers and Susanna in the background whilst I prepare for my first webinar. As my friend Lauren says: "Who will he be spewing his vitriol about today?"

Well today he is interrogating Sir Kier Starmer, who is coming across as pretty weak, even though Piers is relatively gently with him. Starmer is calling on the Government to make public their strategy for releasing the country from lockdown. Whilst he insists that NHS staff should be given the priority for testing, he refuses to be drawn on Gove's behaviour. Pretty underwhelming start, Starmer.

Meanwhile in the US, President Donald Trump has halted funding for the WHO amid heavy criticism. Bill Gates said: "It was as dangerous as it sounds," but Trump feels that the organisation had failed in its response to the pandemic. It will be a massive cut in funds to the WHO and I wonder what impact that will have on its ability to deliver what we need.

Piers is calling for Captain Tom Moore to be knighted. Fair point, Piers! His total this morning is £4,462,000, what an absolute legend.

Now he is launching into the care minister, Helen Whately, about the amount of people who have died in care homes. This turns into a complete car crash of an interview – she laughs nervously when he tries to hold up a newspaper that she can't see and he is like a headmaster asking her why she keeps laughing and keeps telling her that it is not funny. It is an excruciating interview and he absolutely crucifies her. She tries to explain how they collect data but there is nothing that she can do to get the interview back on track.

I switch off and start my first webinar. I am delivering 2 today: 'Resilience and Reprogramming Your Mind' and 'Emotional Intelligence'. I mentally calculate that with the 4 webinars and 4 coaching sessions I have done I have earned over £3,000 for the business this week. If I was working on my own that would have accounted for approximately twelve hours' work – if I didn't have the big machine I have to feed with work, I could be working a lot less hours. But I want to keep my business. I am still finding the webinars quite hard work – there is a lot to concentrate on whilst you are delivering.

Today is particularly intense as I have a full two-hour coaching session, followed by another virtual webinar, followed by another meeting. People have started to ask me if I am bored at home – I wish! Keith, on the other hand, is in the garage sorting his big tin of screws into Tupperware containers. I think he may be getting to the end of his tasks! Note to self to create new list.

Some news comes through that government ministers are pushing for schools to reopen by the 11th of May so that parents can go back to work. This is in light of the predictions of up to 2 million unemployed if the lockdown continues. This feels far too soon.

In other news, Captain Tom is up to nearly £7 million, wow! And then, conflicting emotions as we hear that a 106-year-old has fought off the virus, but a heavily pregnant NHS nurse, aged 28, dies from it. Medics have apparently saved the baby but how dreadful for her partner and family.

There is news that the first wave of financial support will start being paid on the 22nd of April to people who applied for Universal Credit (apparently a record 1.4 million people claimed).

We have our Wednesday afternoon team call and it is good to see everyone. They summarise what they have been working on, and again, some good conversations about business for the future, but we all agree we have to try and sell more now.

It's time for the briefing, so I tune in to see what Matt Hancock has to say today. Once again, he starts with heartfelt thanks to all and a plea for us all to continue to stay at home.

He announces that one thing he is changing is giving people the right to say goodbye by changing the guidelines. He recognises that it is a deep human instinct to be there at the end and sounds very moved and upset as he describes the stories that he heard of people dying without loved ones there. With a flourish he says: “I am pleased to say,” (very strange words for the subject) “we are introducing new measures and making it clear that DNRs (Do Not Resuscitate orders) cannot be applied in a blanket fashion.” I feel so sad for all the people who have missed the opportunity to be with their loved ones and to have a proper funeral, but relieved for Sarah that if anything happens she can now be with her mother.

Hancock is joined by Angela McLean, Deputy Chief Scientific Adviser, and Professor Chris Whitty who says he thinks the death rate is probably reaching its peak. However, he is expecting the death figures to go up tomorrow; apparently, after a weekend the death numbers tend to go down for two days before going up again.

Angela is here to share the slides – evidence about how people are staying home and shows us the graph of different types of travel, now down to less than a third. Tube and National Rail particularly low. Gold star for us!

She then demonstrates that this is further reflected by people in hospital beds and she can also see evidence of a slight drop. It is having the impact we wanted it to have but we need to continue to stay at home. The final slide is comparing deaths in our country to other countries. We can see the UK’s trajectory is still climbing as the data is lagged due to the time it takes to succumb to the disease and the time it takes to get the data. She says she is hoping that they will soon start to show a flatter trajectory.

Questions from the journalists come through – are we past the peak? In other countries, apparently, they are starting to discuss easing restrictions. Are we not trusted to do this? Again, this is batted back, Whitty says that at this point they do not know what the transmission rate is and that they need to know more before they can determine when it is safe to relax the social-distancing measures.

I switch off my laptop and decide to have a night off – we have decided to binge watch *Killing Eve* from the beginning before we start the new episodes. We have never really been TV binge watchers but sometimes escapism is the only way.

TOTAL DEATHS – 12,958

Thursday, 16th April

Today I have a bit of a lie-in until 6.45 a.m. and then walk for an hour. Another beautiful day and the sunrise feels hugely uplifting. I like these walks as they allow me to think, and today I start to think about the future and what I want, and what may happen. I reflect on my life and it has been pretty amazing. I have been incredibly lucky – I decide it is time for me to remember and celebrate what I have to be grateful for first – and there is a lot. I have had a career for twenty-five years that I have absolutely loved and that has taken me all around the world to the Middle East, the Far East, Australia, America, and most of Europe. I have stayed in the most beautiful hotels and eaten at the most stunning restaurants. I have worked with incredible companies, coached executives and CEOs and even a Dame, and delivered my 'Women's Development' programme to delegates all around the UK and the Middle East. I have had the most loyal, dedicated and fun team, some of whom have been with me almost since the business was founded. And we have a property company, which, if the bottom doesn't fall out of the housing market, can help us to keep afloat.

But even more importantly, I have two of the most beautiful children imaginable, who have grown up to be driven, kind, creative and emotionally intelligent adults, and who are both in their perfect careers and with partners that parents can only dream their children will find. I have helped Elly to buy a house and we are just about to help LJ to buy a house and, he hopes, to get married in 2022. I have a wonderful house, a loving and caring husband and a loyal, fun group of friends. I work incredibly hard – often seven days a week up to fourteen hours a day, but I also party incredibly hard; brunches in Dubai, boats, holidays around the world, throwing big BBQs and parties. When you write it like that, I then feel I deserve some hardship, but anybody who knows me will say that they have never known anyone who works as hard as I do, and my success wasn't through luck. And then, a strange and morbid thought went through my head – if I did get the virus and this was the end of my life, I would feel it had been really worthwhile and I would hope that I had left a legacy. Where did that come from? But inside me I have so much more to give, I want to help so many more women, I want to contribute to charity and I really want to meet my grandchildren (no pressure there, both children have made no secret of wanting to have a family, so their choice and not mine). My emotions are torn between gratitude and guilt and for the first time in a long time I am struggling to really know what I want in the future. For some reason, my brain is clouded. Well, that's OK, as I am assuming that the Government will tonight be announcing at least another three weeks of lockdown, so plenty of thinking space left.

As always, I turn on *GMB*; it's becoming compulsive now and whilst my feelings about Piers Morgan haven't changed, I occasionally respect his challenges to the Government and his support for the underdog. I don't think I will ever like the man, however, I am trying to be objective. But today is beyond ridiculous; he is interviewing Matt Hancock and it turns into such a childish exchange with Matt Hancock telling Piers not to interrupt him and them arguing like 10-year olds about who was interrupting who and who was doing their job. Picking the interview apart there were some useful challenges around, i.e. whether we were prepared for the pandemic and the testing promises that Raab made, but it was impossible to stay focused on it due to all the pathetic bickering and point-scoring. Piers wins in the end when he asks if the Government, and indeed Raab, will be taking a 20% pay cut as the New Zealand ministers are doing, and indeed, as Raab had taken the footballers to task over? Hancock tries to sidestep the question but, in the end, has to say that he doesn't intend to do that, but he does intend to work 24/7 to fight the pandemic. Piers quips that the world would expect that anyway.

Captain Tom Moore, the legend that he is, has completed his 100 laps around his garden two weeks before his 100th birthday. And he has now raised the most incredible amount of money – £12.4 million. He looks as bemused, as we all are, about how this has happened – when Queen performed at Live Aid, they raised about £1.2 million, so he is right up there with the legends of fund raising.

But the bad news is still all around us – a pregnant young nurse, Mary Agyapong, aged 28, died on Sunday. Lorraine Kelly tells us that her baby had been delivered by Caesarean and is doing well but that is not good news; a poor child growing up with no mother, a family torn apart, all because she went to do her duty. There are calls for her and others to be given the George Cross medal, posthumously. The George Cross is the second highest award of the United Kingdom honours system awarded 'for acts of the greatest heroism or for most conspicuous courage in circumstance of extreme danger', and that seems pretty apt to me.

Today ITV are celebrating the NHS all day – I keep it on whilst I work and there are many lovely videos and pictures of children dressing up as NHS staff and thanking them, and a fab video of the bin men who dressed up as the characters of YMCA and did the dance for the street. Little things like that really raise spirits. And my spirits need raising today; we have just had another programme cancelled at the end of June – another £9,000 gone. In my head I had really hoped that by then we might be able to be back on our feet but that sent me spiralling a bit.

Before I know it, the briefing is on and as expected Dominic Raab announced that the lockdown is to be extended for at least the next three weeks until five key targets are hit. These are:

1. The NHS must still be able to cope and that there is sufficient critical care.
2. The death rate falls consistently.
3. There is reliable Sage data showing that the rate of infection is decreasing.
4. Confidence that providing PPE and testing is under control.
5. Confidence that making a change will not risk a second peak.

Although it is still dreadful for business, I feel relieved as I would far prefer to be able to see it off completely than to have a second spike. Deaths have risen by 861 today, so they are levelling out a bit, but it is still far too early to predict the outcome.

An interesting question comes from Sky – their analysis is showing that of the NHS staff and health care staff who have died from coronavirus, 70% were from a BAME background. Raab says that needs to be investigated. I wonder what the stats are on the people who have died and if there is also any correlation?

Well, that's it, we prepare to continue to lockdown; looks as if we will be finishing the full three series of *Killing Eve*.

But before we settle down, we remember it is Thursday and it is NHS clapping day. I grab my whistle, wooden spoon and pan and wait in the garden for it to start. It makes me feel connected as I hear everyone else wildly making a noise.

TOTAL DEATHS – 13,729

Friday, 17th April

I am procrastinating this morning. I feel a bit antsy, and whilst I should go for a walk, am worried about my knee. My procrastination techniques include cleaning out the fridge – but I rationalise that this is needed as today we get our Click-and-Collect order from Sainsbury's. I almost feel excited at the thought of some different foods; the local Co-op doesn't stock a lot of vegetarian or vegan. It is amazing how we habitualise and normalise things after a period of time. Who would have thought that receiving a delivery of food would be the thing that really got me excited?

GMB is light-hearted this morning; no Piers or Susanna and there is a lovely interview with the husband of a woman who was told there was no hope for her. Stacey Fresco had been in Intensive Care a few weeks ago and the doctors had told her husband to bring in their children to say goodbye. They came in with their Mother's Day cards and read them to her and prepared themselves for the worst. The doctors then said they would try one more technique called 'proning', which was turning her over onto her stomach to release the pressure on the lungs (but a very dangerous one as it could potentially cause a heart attack). But it worked and she survived and days later made a miraculous recovery to return to the family home and begin the journey back to full health. Amazing.

I wonder about Kate Garraway and how her husband is – there has been no news for days and I pray he will survive.

Captain Tom has become the biggest hero ever – it is all anyone is talking about. The sum he has raised is jumping each day and is now over £16 million. Yesterday there was a socially-distanced guard of honour for him as he finished his last lap. I am invited to join a Facebook group to organise a Spitfire flypast for him and within hours it has been arranged. Bloody marvellous – he will go down in history.

Sadiq Khan sticks his head above the parapet and says he would like to see it made compulsory that people wear face masks on public transport. Whether it works or not I think I would feel more comfortable if that were the case; I am still feeling extraordinarily nervous about getting on a train again.

There is much debate about testing – Downing Street has said that we have the capacity to conduct 35,000 coronavirus tests a day, however, in the twenty-four hours up to 9.00 a.m. on Wednesday only 15,994 tests were carried out. It is really hard for us to get to grips with why testing is not accelerating. I know that this is massively key to our ability to get out of lockdown safely but there is no clarity on why the testing is not up to the promised figures.

It is another packed day of Zoom coaching sessions and calls. At 3.30 p.m. I have a quick call with Barry about the accounts. Gemma is working on the projections to present to me and he is preparing me for the meeting on Monday. We discuss my gamble on the business and the realisation that it is now too late to stop the 'train' – I need to follow through on my decision and have faith. He talks of potential bank loans for six months. I feel sick; so not only will I lose all of the money I had invested in the business I also might have to borrow some to keep going, depending on how long this goes on?

News comes through that the football legend, Norman Hunter, has died, and on LinkedIn I see a memorial for one of Elly's tutors from Lincoln University. I wish I could say I was becoming used to the deaths, but I am not.

In world news there have been more than 2.15 million confirmed cases and 145,000 deaths, and as of today's figures in the UK we account for 10% of those deaths. Germany is saying that its outbreak is now under control – the infamous 'R' value coming in below 1. China has revised the total deaths but still denies covering up the scale of the outbreak, although Emmanuel Macron has joined the growing group who are questioning China's handling of the outbreak. The Chinese economy is taking quite a battering and shrinks for the first time in decades.

The briefing tonight is led by Alok Sharma, Secretary of State for Business, and joined by the Medical Director of Public Health England, Professor Yvonne Doyle and Chief Scientific Adviser to the Government, Sir Patrick Vallance. Alok is asked about his definition of the 'new normal'. A journalist pushes as to whether that means people will need to work from home until there is a vaccine. Alok sticks to the next three weeks and reiterates the PHE guidelines, so nothing concrete for us there.

The Secretary of State announces that a vaccine task force has been set up but there is a heavy dose of caution – no guarantees that a vaccine might be produced, whether it will work or when it might be ready. Does this mean that the Government is going to get ahead on vaccines, as we seemed to be behind the curve on testing?

The Duke and Duchess of Cambridge appear in an interview discussing the impact on mental health. It is a delightful interview with them talking about their daily routine, their struggles with home schooling (Kate announcing that she felt a bit guilty they had continued home schooling through the holidays but 'don't tell the children') and William talking about their keep-fit routine – they haven't tried Joe Wicks yet but might do soon!

After dinner we head for the sofa. We have become binge watchers; I don't know how it happened, we had barely watched television and now I am staying up late begging for another episode of *Killing Eve* – is there support group I can join?

TOTAL DEATHS – 14,576

Saturday, 18th April

I can't believe it is Saturday again and we stay in bed until 8.45 a.m. watching news and scrolling through social media. I really have enjoyed these lie-ins; normally I am rushing around on Saturdays to my gym class, to get my hair done or other beauty appointments, to shop and do other chores. It is really quite nice to be low-maintenance; I don't do my hair or wear makeup at weekends – it is actually quite liberating. The news, as always, is dedicated to coronavirus, and in particular, the lack of PPE.

We are running dangerously short of PPE and there is a debate about reusing it – there are fears that we may run out of protective gowns this weekend – this would leave the staff totally exposed. Apparently, at the Commons' Health and Social Care Committee on Friday morning, Matt Hancock couldn't say whether there would be enough. It seems there are another 55,000 gowns arriving, but it is likely that these won't be sufficient. As the newsreader discusses it, we watch pictures of NHS staff around a bed wearing PPE. There are about 6 staff around the bed, reinforcing the level of care people describe they are getting but it is a terrifying scene. I think about what it must be like to be lying there, fighting for your life, with this amount of staff in their gowns and masks around you – it must feel like a scene out of a sci-fi horror. I have been in hospital many times and know how soothing it is when the nurses or the surgeons come and sit with you and hold your hand or pat your arm and show the kindness in their faces and words. But this must be so different, to barely be able to see their eyes and to realise the danger that you are in due to their gowns and aprons. This is the reality of what is happening

Captain Tom has now raised over £20 million and people are not just calling for a Spitfire flypast and a knighthood but for hospital wards to be named after him. He has captured the heart of not just the UK but the world. It must be completely bewildering for him to suddenly have become the symbol of the coronavirus, the hope that we all cling to and that at 99 he has become a massive celebrity. Not only has he raised the money by walking, but he has now recorded a song with Michael Ball – 'You'll Never Walk Alone'. I listen to it on YouTube; the stunningly powerful voice of Michael, the beauty of the choir and then the wonderful inputs from Tom, who is one of the few men in the country who knows what it feels like to not walk alone. Tears roll down my cheeks (I am never far from a sobbing wreck these days), it is so emotional to hear and there is talk of trying to get this to number one in time for his birthday. How amazing would that be? And I can't think of a more fitting tribute. In years to come, when we talk about the days of coronavirus, we will all remember Tom and thank him for his amazing contribution.

I go in the gym and do a really hard session, and as today is cloudy, I decide I will finally sort out the rest of my wardrobes. I tackle them with relish and before I know it have cleared out all wardrobes, drawers, bathroom cabinets and cupboard shelves! I am quite shocked by how much I have hoarded over the years, and four exhausting hours later, I have five bags ready to go to charity. It feels great and being busy really helps, although I feel ridiculously nostalgic as I take all my beautiful dresses out and wonder when I will next wear them. I really miss wearing them and I vow that when I go back to work I will dress up every day regardless of whether I have client meetings to go to. That's if I have work to go back to – a quick reality check hits me.

The Queen has made another statement to say that there should be no gun salute to mark her birthday on Tuesday – apparently this is the first time the Palace have made such a request in the British Monarch's 68-year reign. I am sure the Palace will find another way to mark the event for her Majesty.

The Government Secretary of State for Housing, Robert Jenrick, is in charge of today's briefing. Councils in England are to get an extra £1.6 billion in funding to help them to cope with the pandemic – no doubt that will be put on our taxes next year. Jenrick addresses the issue of PPE and did admit that aprons and gowns were still in short supply and that the Government must do more to get supplies to those on the front line. However, apparently, we do now have sufficient ventilators across the country with a total of 10,606 – I fervently wish that they wouldn't be needed.

Our friend Tony Fletcher is doing his Saturday night concert from his garage, and we listen for the whole two hours – all our other friends are watching and commenting and once again we feel strangely connected with each other for this period. I feel a bit melancholy and I can't wait to be able to see them all again.

I have produced a massive pile of mending from my wardrobe sorting, so we settle down to our evening binge and a lot of sewing. What am I going to do when I start to run out of all these jobs? And when we run out of episodes of *Killing Eve*?

TOTAL DEATHS – 15,464

Sunday, 19th April

Last night I had a bad dream – we were skiing and people were falling over and dying on the slopes all around. It was pretty horrible and I awake sweaty and disorientated, but my thinking keeps going back to that skiing holiday, when we tried to avoid what was going on and didn't want to know about it. I draw a parallel with the Government. On the 11th of March the WHO declared a pandemic, so I start to think about those eleven days and whether, in that critical time between the 12th and the 23rd of March, if the Government had done something rather than deciding to practically give up tracing, how many lives would have been saved.

I go for my Sunday morning six-mile walk, but it is all I can thing about. I think back to those days and remember the mass gatherings that were still happening, and there were still concerts and even Champions League football. The Cheltenham Festival went ahead with massive crowds of 60,000 racegoers – how many of those didn't make it? I wonder how the Jockey Club feels now about insisting it continued to go ahead?

Like us, who were going out every night in La Tania, people were all going to pubs and restaurants, and how many people were they infecting? I remember then, people in Italy, saying that we will be in trouble in three weeks, but I didn't believe it would ever get to that point. I consoled myself with the fact that Italy had a very high elderly population, which was why they suffered such a high total death rate. Alex, our ski guide had been right and whilst people were all stockpiling and were asymptomatic with COVID-19 they were spreading it around the supermarkets. Whilst I have been supportive of the Government, I can't help reflecting on how much those eleven days cost us and how many lives could have been saved if we had locked down earlier. We put our faith in our government, but should we be so trusting? I feel confused and scared today. What about when they start to release us from lockdown – will it truly be safe? They are saying they don't agree with Sadiq Khan about wearing face masks on public transport but how do they know? At this rate I will stay locked in my house until September or until a vaccine is found.

This run of thinking continues as I watch Andrew Marr's show on BBC as he interviews Michael Gove. There had been a damming article in *The Sunday Times*, which accused the Prime Minister of missing five COBRA meetings in the build-up to the crisis. Further criticism was that the UK had shipped protective equipment to China in February. Gove initially insisted that *The Sunday Times* article was inaccurate and indeed it is quite normal for a PM to miss COBRA meetings but these particular meetings would have been critical. Apparently, Boris had spent an entire parliamentary recess out of sight at Chequers and quoted an unnamed adviser as saying that Boris didn't do urgent crisis planning. Gove defended the PM vehemently but did admit that PPE had been shipped to help Wuhan. Gove sort of accepted that this had been a mistake by saying all governments make mistakes including our own. "We seek to learn, and to improve every day ..." followed by stating that: "There would be some profound lessons to be learnt in the future." You bet there will be. I wondered if any of the families of people who died through coronavirus would sue the Government for their lack of early activity? You can pretty much fathom that people who died in the period from the 20th of March onwards could have been infected in the period from the 11th of March during this so called period of inactivity. If we look at the figures from the two weeks from the 20th of March, almost doubling every day, you can see that even if only 10% of those figures were contaminated during the eleven-day period that still would amount to hundreds. I am really trying not to be judgemental and to have faith in the Government, but I now wondered whether my changing faith in Johnson was caused by desperation of needing a leader and feeling sorry for him in Intensive Care. All I can hope now is that decisions are being made in the right way at the right time.

I go to spend some time in the garden reading and the sun is beautiful, providing a few minutes of respite from the news.

During today's briefing, taken by Gove, the death rate figures report a rise of 596, which is heart-breaking but less than the past few days, although sometimes the figures lag at the weekend.

But the big news is that trials on a vaccine might be started in the next week with researchers at Southampton General Hospital (just half a mile from where we live) beginning trials on up to 510 healthy volunteers aged between 18 and 55. Wow, what does it take to be a volunteer for a trial like that? I would be terrified.

Experts are warning that up to 6.5 million jobs might be lost – that is a chilling figure for the economy and not good news for our business. Which reminds me that tomorrow I need to have a discussion with Gemma and Barry, and I start to feel anxious again. When you are enjoying a weekend in your own home, basking in the sun and reading, it is so easy to forget what is really happening out there. I decide to have a glass of wine and go in the hot tub – I am trying to avoid using alcohol to self-medicate, often not particularly successfully.

Keith cooks a fabulous roast dinner whilst I shower and wash my hair – and stupidly try and cut my fringe. It has got to the point where I can't see properly so I attack it with the hairdressing scissors. Three attempts later I stop, before I get to the point where I will need to wear a hat on Zoom calls. It's quiz night tonight; it's raucous and fun and now the new normal on Sundays. We start it later tonight so we can watch the wonderful One World concert. They raised £128 million. Only just over £100 million more than Captain Tom raised! Lady Gaga put it together, with Paul McCartney, The Stones, John Legend, Sam Smith and Elton John performing.

Another lovely weekend in this weird, lonely, twilight zone that we now inhabit.

TOTAL DEATHS – 16,060

Monday, 20th April
Official Lockdown, Week Five

Although officially only five weeks, this is the start of our sixth week in isolation. If I am honest, it hasn't been that hard, but again I reflect that is because we have the luxury of a beautiful house and garden and that I have work to focus on, and if I am even more honest, because I probably needed a real break after ten years of hard slog, stress and ridiculous hours. And I don't have children to home school and juggle with my work. I think about others who are in flats looking after children and feel for them. But for me, it probably has been what my body and mind needed, a complete rest from the travel and craziness, an opportunity to organise my house and do some life laundry – but I am ready now to go back to work, and if the world was continuing to turn and the economy was the same, then apart from missing my family and friends, this would have been a wonderful experience. But it isn't and it won't, and in some ways we are locked in a bubble and the real trauma will happen in the next three months. I turned sixty this year and felt I had at least another five years in me of working full-time and building the business, but that was when work looked promising and the business felt solid. Should I just bow out gracefully, go freelance and work for myself? I seem to be riding this crazy seesaw and for the first time in my life I have no idea of how it might end.

I do a great virtual workout with Olivia; we have really cracked the Zoom sessions and I work hard, which feels good and helps my mental state a lot. My need for structure has become really apparent in this crisis. I go to do battle with my fringe, and with a bit of jiggery pokery with the hair straighteners, if I keep my head to one side, I might just get away with it. Sadly, I need to do a lot more videos this week, so I am going to have to conceal my hacked hair somehow!

On *GMB* this morning there is a lovely interview with the phenomenon that is Captain Tom – he really is so adorable. Over the weekend his song went to number one in the chart, 850,000 people have campaigned to get him a knighthood, people have been re-recording David Bowie's song 'Major Tom' and changing the words, and his fundraising has achieved over £22 million. Piers tells him that he hears Vera Lynn has sent him a note and Tom is clearly completed chuffed with this. Piers asks what she said and Tom cheekily tells him that he won't reveal it, it is between him and Vera! His fast wit and cheeky humour is so reminiscent of my dad and it makes me so happy to hear him. Piers talks about the knighthood and he says he couldn't believe that would ever happen, but I so hope it will. But he was also over the moon that Joe Root, the England cricket captain, had invited him to a cricket game. Just a wonderful moment – ten days ago the only people that knew Captain Tom were his friends and family and now the whole world knows him. The number of portraits that are being painted of him and posted on Facebook is incredible.

However, that is the only good news; in Canada a gunman kills at least 16 people in a rampage in Nova Scotia. He apparently was wearing a military police uniform. The premier of Nova Scotia called the shooting spree: "One of the most senseless acts of violence in our province's history." With all the deaths from coronavirus I had almost forgotten about the other tragedies in the world and this is a massive tragedy for this little province.

In America lockdown is now being released and people have flocked to the beach – for the sake of the people I sincerely hope this doesn't come back to bite them but my gut feel is that it will. The riots have got stronger in the US with people in San Clements marching together holding up boards saying: "My body, my risk, my choice." No, it is not your body, it is everyone around you having no choice, you stupid people! There are even people holding up boards saying COVID-19 is a lie, and bizarre conspiracy theories have started to emerge that Bill Gates is at the centre of the coronavirus crisis claiming he had prior knowledge.

I start work and feel very focused this morning. I make a call to a big client who has suggested partnering with them on a coaching bid and it is positive. We have our Monday 10.00 a.m. meeting and everyone seems quite upbeat – they all seem focused too and are working on some really positive projects to help us to get some income in and to maximise our client base. They inspire me and when we are all together I really can believe we can do it. I try to come across as strong and decisive; I don't want any of them to know how scared and emotional I really am.

Finally, it is 3.30 p.m. and I take a deep breath and have the meeting with Gemma and Barry. Gemma has been very thorough with the projections and I can now see the full picture. This month we haven't even made half of our break-even figure and next month it is unlikely we will either. But I can now see how long it will take before the money runs out. I have committed to this now and I remind myself that I have never run anyway from anything yet and this is not going to be the first time, I am going to fight with every inch of my being to get through this and to come out the other side stronger than before. Gemma talks about tomorrow when she is going into the office as she needs her hard drive to do the Furlough application and run payroll. I feel nervous about her going into the office and she promises to be careful.

Before I know it, it is 5.00 p.m. and Rishi Sunak is leading the briefing tonight with Dame Angela McLean and Yvonne Doyle and starts by talking about the promise he made about saving jobs by government funding through the furlough scheme and how over 140,000 people have now applied for the furlough job-retention scheme meaning that many people's jobs have been saved. In a Tweet, the Chancellor said today: "We promised support would be available by the end of April – today, we deliver our promise."

Professor Dame Angela McLean takes us through the dreaded slides of today's figures. For the second day in a row the amount of people going into hospital has dropped and people going home has risen. She says figures were pretty much stable and flat. Deaths have sadly risen by 449 today.

A good question from a journalist comes through regarding the news that the Government has downgraded recommendations on the wearing of PPE due to the shortage. Doyle answers and says guidance remains exactly the same but over the weekend, to cover people in exceptional services, advice has been given as to how to stay safe in times when there isn't enough. She says this is quite the opposite to guidance being downgraded. Medics have told them they feel that the guidelines are based on availability of equipment as opposed to WHO guidelines. Rishi confirms that 12 million pieces were delivered yesterday and they are improving their sources in a very challenging international context. However, 90 NHS staff have already died in service, how many more will it take?

We have dinner outside tonight for the first time, which is nice after a briefing like that.

TOTAL DEATHS – 16,509

Tuesday, 21st April

Pivot. That's where I was getting it wrong. I need to 'pivot'. Those are my waking thoughts when my eyes ping open at 5.45 a.m. I get up quickly, dress and go for a long walk. When my mind becomes active like this, doing a six-mile walk is generally the best way to work things through. I had gone to sleep thinking about the figures and the future of the business, so clearly my unconscious mind had been busy overnight.

The sun is just rising and it is a beautiful morning, the air feels clear and I notice that as I tackle the big hill at the beginning of the walk my lungs are better. I can do it in one now, whereas before I would have had to stop halfway up, gasping for breath. I don't know whether it is my increased level of fitness, a few pounds lost or that the air is clearer, but it feels good and I walk fast.

I think about pivoting; it is being talked about a lot as businesses start to rethink their strategy, but I suddenly realise that the big problem is I had been thinking about what we were doing as a short-term strategy to help us get through but I need to realise that we actually do need to pivot our business permanently. The world is never going to do the amount of face-to-face training that it did previously; travel restrictions, fear, more working from home, a whole variety of reasons are going to change the way we do business and we need to embrace this fully. We have always steered away from webinars and online training as we felt that there were other big players who did it better and that we couldn't connect in the same way with people if we weren't in the room with them, but now we need to recognise that if that is the new landscape we have to be ahead of the curve. We have to learn how to be the best and be creative with, i.e. push harder than we ever have; we need to see what our competitors are doing and we need to do it better. I send a long email to the team. I give them some transparency over the figures but remind them that I am continuing to fight for the business and want to keep them all, so they do not need to worry about their jobs. I tell them about my plan to produce a video on supporting staff through furlough and then a series of videos for furloughed staff to support our clients.

Within minutes every one of them has replied to me, thanking me, supporting me and assuring me they are on it. And then without any warning, I break down and sob and when Keith walks in I am uncontrollably crying. He is concerned and comes to hug me asking what is wrong. I try and tell him – nothing, everything, I don't know, but the tears just keep coming. I realise how much I have repressed over the last five weeks and maybe staying strong for everyone else is just too much for me sometimes. I know it is ridiculous, I have so much and there are so many people out there dying and living in hardship – I have everything to be positive about. I know Keith finds this difficult; he wants to fix it and there is nothing to fix, so I tell him he doesn't need to do anything apart from hold me and I know that I just need to let it out and get back on the bus. I try and accept that this is normal behaviour and everyone will be up and down – it seems that I am perfectly fine when I am just getting on with work and focusing but when people ask how I am and are nice to me it seems to really get to me. I am glad I went straight to my computer and didn't bother with make-up this morning. My first webinar is 1.30 p.m. so I have time to get my face cleaned up and back into super-positive mode.

I have been so busy this morning since I returned at 7.45 a.m. I haven't watched any news but I turn it on briefly. Captain Tom has raised over £27 million (it still becomes hard to fathom this amount of money). It always cheers me up to think of Captain Tom, the 99-year-old was guest of honour at the opening ceremony of the NHS Nightingale Hospital, Yorkshire and the Humber, in Harrogate, and appeared by video link in front of a crowd of around 100 people.

The audience at the Harrogate Convention Centre gave Captain Tom, who will turn 100 later this month, a standing ovation as they wished him a happy birthday.

I get to work and soon my focus takes away my edginess and I feel back in control again. We have already activated the idea for the furlough video and so I start to put together a presentation; it feels good to concentrate on something useful. I do a webinar to Saudi on resilience and the irony is not lost on me; here I am preaching to a group on how to manage their stress and emotions when four hours earlier I was having a complete breakdown! At 4.00 p.m. Sarah calls and we catch up. She never fails to lift my spirits and I think I am OK, until LJ and Elly do a group WhatsApp, and once again I fall apart. They try and coach me through it and I still can't tell them what the matter is, but I feel better talking to them – who would have thought my children would become such great coaches?

The briefing starts, with Dominic Raab at the helm and

the cautious optimism from this morning was a bit pre-emptive – the death rate, sadly, has risen again today – 873 fatalities, so a rise after the drop at the weekend. This means there is another chance we will not have reached a peak.

The big news today is that the vaccine is to be made available as fast ‘as humanly possible’. Trials are to begin this week. Matt Hancock is still standing by his target of testing 100,000 people per day, including NHS staff, who are not showing coronavirus symptoms and stated there was a plan in place to achieve this. Apparently, £42.5 million was ploughed into the jab.

The international figures are staggering. Worldwide more than 170,000 people have now died and 2.47 million have been infected.

In the US, Donald Trump has stated that he will suspend all immigration to the United States temporarily.

One fact that interested me is that MPs are set to approve plans for ‘virtual’ sittings of the House of Commons when it returns on Tuesday following the Easter recess. Easter recess? They were all on holiday? Seriously?

And Boris Johnson today has a call with Donald Trump and tells him that he is on the road to recovery from coronavirus – he will apparently be making a gradual return to work. Downing Street tells us that he discussed a post-Brexit trade deal and the need for an international response to the pandemic.

And a rousing finish from Mr Hancock, who tells us that we owe it to the people who have lost their lives not to throw away the progress made in fighting the disease and reiterates that they will not risk lives by relaxing the social distancing rules until the five tests are met.

TOTAL DEATHS – 17,337

Wednesday, April 22nd

Without question I feel better today – maybe I just needed the release, but I wake up feeling chirpy and well-rested; and excited! This morning I am going early to the shops, and not to the Co-op, I am going to The Range. We need a lot of household cleaning stuff, but I also want some compost as I have some seedlings that need to be potted and I wonder if they may have a few plants. We aren't really allowed to shop for plants as they are not essential items, but if they have some I am going to risk it. This is, without question, the most excited I have been for weeks. My plan is to walk there, which is a couple of miles to get my exercise, and then be there by 8.45 a.m. to queue to get in by 9.00 a.m. and Keith can pick me up. By 6.45 a.m. I am up and dressed and at my desk to get some things done before I go.

The debate this morning on GMB is an interesting one about the climate. I have been wondering about this a lot lately; the weather has been inexplicably brilliant almost ever since we started lockdown. Apart from a couple of days of rain it has pretty much been solid bright sunshine. Without question the birds have been louder and the skies clearer at night. I am sure that with factories closing down, less car journeys and flights there must be a change in air quality, I know I feel it when I walk as my lungs feel much clearer.

I do a bit of 'Googling' and it is true, evidence is showing that our atmosphere might just be a little healthier during this time. Satellite images released by the European Space Agency (ESA) have indicated that most European cities, including Paris and Milan, have experienced drops in atmospheric nitrous oxide and people in many countries are able to see horizons for the first time in their lives.

When you think about the fact that air pollution causes about 4.6 million premature deaths annually worldwide according to figures from the WHO and nitrogen oxide, a greenhouse gas that can cause respiratory problems and cancer was down 42%, then there is a chance that although so many people have died, long-term, many lives may have also been saved during this period.

And a lovely story, as humans take to the indoors indefinitely, animals have begun to encroach on urban areas and streets in search of a quick bite. In Wales, some sheep were snapped in the car park at McDonald's!

And some wonderful news – after more than a decade of trying to coax pandas Ying Ying and Le Le in Hong Kong to mate, they have finally consummated their union. I wonder if that's because there were no visitors to the zoo – I am sure the peace and quiet must have helped them in some way!

And for me, one of the most important changes is that both China and Vietnam have now placed a ban on the consumption of wild animals – there has been massive global pressure due to people blaming China for the outbreak.

There are signs coming through that Boris is close to returning and apparently, he will have his audience with the Queen this week – well there is a nice birthday present for her! Downing Street insists he is not yet working and that Dominic Raab is taking Prime Minister's Question Time. It is the first day of virtual parliament and pictures show him almost alone in the House of Commons with just the odd smattering of people in their seats.

There is more shocking news on the total deaths – if we really counted it accurately, apparently, it's likely to be more like 41,000; the care home figures have not been included, which is where the discrepancy lies – 41,000, I can't even register that number.

I walk to The Range, it's only two miles so it is an easy walk and I feel the most excited I have been in weeks – this is literally the first time I have been to a shop in nearly two weeks. As I arrive the car park is empty and there is a large artic delivering ... PLANTS! I stand outside the door and am first in line. This is something I have never experienced – being the only shopper in a store. I head for the plant section, which is completely bereft of plants apart from the new delivery and look longingly at the eight trolleys of Clingfilm-wrapped plants. I ask a member of staff if I can get into them – she tells me that they need to be checked in, and that will take an hour. I can't just sit out here for an hour but I thank her politely and put on my best disappointed look. Five minutes later she comes back and asks what I want and says she will get them for me. Keith picks me up, as I hold my trophy petunias high, and mutters about me finding jobs for him!

It is a good working day. I prepare for my big webinar tomorrow, get all of the scripting done for the video and the team have some success nailing down some work in August. Small steps but at least people are thinking about being open for business.

Dominic Raab takes the briefing and he looks absolutely exhausted. He is joined by Chief Medical Officer, Chris

Whitty, who delivers the bad news – we are not seeing the steep descent in new infections we were hoping for. Another 759 people have died in hospital in the UK. He confirms that it is likely there will be a high number of deaths in care homes.

Our hopes are dashed as we are told that there is an incredibly small chance of there being an effective vaccine, or even drugs, in the next calendar year.

We decide to go retro and watch *Erin Brockovich*. That girl has balls!

TOTAL DEATHS – 18,100

Thursday, 23rd April

St George's Day – for anyone who is marking any anniversaries at all anymore! A quick session in the gym before I wash my hair, put full make up on and get dressed in work clothes – how very exciting. And no, I am not going to work, I am recording videos today, so I take it as an opportunity to be smart and it feels really good.

My favourite man is on *GMB* – not you, Piers Morgan, not ever you, Piers Morgan, it is Captain Tom who has now raised over £28 million. He is as delightful as ever, with his daughter by his side repeating the questions to him to ensure that he has heard them all correctly. As always, I am humbled by this sweet man who is taking it all in his stride and so entertaining as he enters the last week before his 100th birthday. I can only hope I leave a small legacy for the world but his is just massive. Piers says he has a surprise for him, and they talk about the Pride of Britain Awards, which Tom absolutely loves. Cut to Carol Vorderman, who normally hosts the Awards, who does a lovely speech before giving the award to Tom and promising that later in the year she will present it personally to him. It is followed by an amazing video montage of people thanking him: stars, royalty and some gorgeous children – heart lifting. I honestly think he is the only person keeping me going at the moment. Tom is absolutely made up and so am I – I have to hold back the emotion as I have just put my mascara on. OK Piers, I am going to hand it to you, you did make this happen as they are your awards, so my thank you isn't even begrudging, it was a good thing to do. But don't think that means I am going to like you! Piers tells him that when it comes to the award, he will need to get himself a bodyguard as all the celebrities, royalty and people attending will be all over him wanting selfies. In true Tom style he says: "well if you get me one make it an attractive one!" In the end they agree that Susanna and Carol will be his bodyguards. Just priceless.

Recording the videos doesn't feel so good; my adrenaline is high, and I don't have much time, but Keith sets up the makeshift studio in the dining room and I start to manage my mental state. The first video is really tough as it is on *Managing Your Staff Through Furlough* – a subject I am not an expert on (well no one is!), so I have to learn my lines carefully. We are sending this out as a free resource to our clients and have consulted with our team who went through furlough to see how they felt and what they needed. That was highly illuminating; there were lots of things I hadn't considered, so I hope that my lessons will help others. It is such a difficult process and it affects everyone differently. Some people are relieved as it takes away the childcare and home-schooling problem. Others are angry, frustrated, guilty, worrying that they are not valued, jealous of other people and scared for their jobs. The second video is easier as I have already presented this three times, so I know the content well and that makes it easier to do it in one take.

We finish and I start to get ready for my big webinar at lunchtime (170 staff attending) but I listen to news in the background. Dogs may be trained to sniff out coronavirus.

Wow, can you picture that? You are off on your holiday, in the queue ready to board the plane, and the sniffer dog bounds over to you and you are escorted off for testing. Is that a picture of our future?

Parts of Britain are showing signs that they are getting back to work today despite the ongoing coronavirus lockdown, as builders lined up at construction sites and roads appear to be getting busier. I must admit I had noticed the roads were busier when I was walking the other day. Some B&Q stores are starting to reopen around the country, but a lot of the builders are failing to socially distance. I walked past three the other day working closely together to paint a wall.

The Webinar almost goes well – sound issues and people forgetting to mute were a hindrance with the first ten minutes, peppered with children shouting, dogs barking, an alarm going off and what sounded like someone snoring! Still, we made it through and there were a lot of thank yous at the end and some lessons learnt for next week for me.

Matt Hancock is in the chair again for the briefing joined by Sir Patrick Vallance, the Government's Chief Scientific Adviser, and Professor John Newton, Director of Health Improvement at Public Health England and the Government's national testing effort coordinator.

Sadly, the death rate has risen by 616 again today, less than yesterday but creeping closer and closer to the 20,000 figure. It is almost impossible to visualise that amount of people dying of a virus.

Apparently, the UK now has a 'clear exit route' due to the implementation of contact tracing. And he says that 18,000 people are being hired to work on contact tracing. I picture a mass of Private Investigators in grubby raincoats going to shops to talk to people about their customers! However, Hancock is still clear that they can only lift the lockdown when it is safe to do so, and when they can use a rigorous process of test, track and trace to keep the infection rate down. It seems we have reached peak – that would be a relief and it would be great to see the numbers go down.

He admits that the 10,000-tests-a-day figure is a demanding one but tells us that the capacity is being increased, indeed there is now the capacity to carry out 51,000 test per day and more people have access to tests. With a flourish he also announces that from today employers of essential workers can go online and book a test for their staff, and from tomorrow essential workers will be able to do this themselves. Results will be sent out by text. I don't really understand this, is it just to find out who has it and to send them home? Apparently, we are also going to see home-test kits being introduced and also mobile testing sites. The teaching union welcomed the announcement that they will get priority for testing as they will not open schools until this happens.

In the US the insanity goes up a notch with Trump seemingly to be clearly suffering from some form of brain damage, as he stuns people when he announces that people could receive injections of disinfectant to cure coronavirus! Even going as far as saying: "And then I see the disinfectant where it knocks it out in a minute, one minute! And is there a way we can do something like that by injection inside or almost a cleaning?" The task force response co-ordinator, Deborah Birx, stays silent and looks like she would rather be anywhere but there, but doctors then had to warn people about the danger of drinking disinfectant. Jaw-droppingly unbelievable. Whilst our government might not be giving us the answers, they are not endangering our health by suggesting ridiculous dangerous practices.

The clapping at 8.00 p.m. is even louder tonight; more fireworks and whooping and it sounds as if my next-door neighbour has a drum set – or at least a good set of pans. I can't see through the bushes, so I shout over to them, but I really enjoy the experience of celebrating the NHS.

We then have a family Zoom call and it is wonderful to see everybody. My brothers have a wicked sense of humour and it is an hour full of laughter and catching up with everyone to find out how it has been for them. As a family we generally only catch up a couple of times a year as we all lead such ridiculously busy lives and are not particularly local. With Elly and Ernie in Lincoln and Lawrence and Sophie in London, fixing dates to meet is a real challenge, so it is a real treat to all have a giggle together.

TOTAL DEATHS – 18,738

Friday, 24th April

I have noticed a pattern, that by Friday I don't want to jump out of bed at 6.00 a.m. and go in the gym, so I have decided to go with this and just allow myself to wake up when I feel like it and do a more relaxed exercise session; yoga, or stretching, which is incredibly good for my leg muscles and knee. I had a terrible night's sleep last night, with violent dreams of having coronavirus, and being put into a coma. It was terrifying and I woke up sweaty and shaky. I can't understand why, after all this time, that happened and why it was so vivid. It really unsettled me. I am so relieved when I wake up and then I doze again until 7.00 a.m. Today I put on a summer dress, the weather is so beautiful and I am bored of wearing jeans and tops – it makes me feel good to wear something different.

So, Boris is coming back to retake control of the crisis – maybe that means we will get some clarity. He has apparently been working most of the week and is fit enough to come back and take charge. Donald Trump described him as 'sharp and energetic' after a call with him yesterday. Some may question that he was ever sharp, but Trump seems to have his own narrative when it comes to his relationship with Boris.

The first two people were injected with the coronavirus vaccine today. In total 800 people have volunteered for the study. Half will receive the COVID-19 vaccine and half will receive a control vaccine – the volunteers will not know which vaccine they are getting. Amazingly, the vaccine was developed in under three months by a team at University of Oxford. The professor of vaccinology at the Jenner Institute, Sarah Gilbert, led the pre-clinical research. I cross everything that I have got that this might work.

Well, the testing that Matt Hancock announced last night that was available today has gone swimmingly! The testing site closed hours after being opened by the Government with an 'applications closed' message being shown as 5,000 home-testing kits were ordered in the first two minutes of the tests going live and 15,000 tests were booked to take place on Friday at drive-through sites. Matt Hancock had said that it would be as easy as booking a flight – perhaps that statement should be changed to as easy as getting a refund from a delayed EasyJet flight (and believe me I have tried). I expect Matt Hancock will be glad for Boris to come back and pick this up!

Europe has been absolutely decimated by the virus – although Sweden, who refused to lockdown is not as bad as us, they could still be behind our curve though. I wonder whether this will mean that people will ban Europeans from visiting their countries for a year until they are sure there is a vaccination that works.

A new face for the briefing today - Transport Secretary, Grant Shapps, who is joined by Dr Jenny Harries.

He tells us that the test website that had crashed so badly yesterday was to close and reopen with more slots, due to exceptional demand. This means that key workers can apply for tests at drive-through centres and he insisted that more slots would be available on Saturday morning.

16,000 bookings were made on Friday. Apparently, the Government were encouraged by the initial demand for tests and still says they are on track to hit the trajectory of 100,000 tests per day by the end of April. He also tells us that up to 18,000 home-testing kits per day will be available by the end of next week.

Apparently, Britain is likely to hit the grim milestone of 20,000 deaths due to coronavirus later on Saturday. This is likely to happen when the daily count is added to the current toll of 19,506 people who tested positive for the virus and died in hospital later today. The death rate from COVID-19 in hospitals across the United Kingdom increased on Friday by 684 in 24 hours.

Some terrible local news, twin sisters have died within three days of each other after testing positive for coronavirus. They both died in the local Southampton hospital within days of each other. Katy Davis and identical twin, Emma, were 37 and both were nurses. How dreadful for their family.

I go to the 'pub' with the team and then get ready for my Zoom call with the Isle of Wight Festival girls. We go every year to the festival as a group and are so disappointed not to be going so we look forward to a call. We had agreed to dress up in festival gear, so despite the beautiful sunshine I wear my rain gear and hood and put a straw hat on top of it. It is wonderful to see them all and we laugh like I haven't laughed in the last six weeks. It might also be the bottle of Prosecco I consume during the calls that makes me giggly, but whatever it was, it made me feel good to see all of my girlfriends and my daughter. After the call Keith and I go in the hot tub and later have dinner. We sit down to watch a film and I fall into a Prosecco-induced coma within seconds and sleep for three hours.

When I finally do go to bed, I tell Keith I am a bit nervous about going to sleep after my awful dream that I was in intensive care as it was so horrible. His response – "Don't worry, darling, I am sure you will be out by now!"

TOTAL DEATHS – 19,506

Buckingham Palace, London

Leicester Square, London

The Cut near Waterloo Station, London

Southbank, London

Southbank Centre, London

Inside Waterloo Station, London

Saturday, 25th April

I wake up after a badly disturbed night's sleep, no coronavirus dreams, just unable to sleep. That will teach me to drink! I suddenly have the urge to do the food shopping. I want to go to Aldi and buy something different, so I get up quickly and get ready – this is quite exciting. But it doesn't quite turn out as expected....

I get in my car, and oh the pleasure of being able to drive for the first time in over six weeks. It feels so liberating and I realise how much I've missed it. I guess that is the same with everything. You don't really know how much you miss something until you get it back. I toy with going to Asda or Aldi as they are close to each other, but as I drive past Asda I see so many people queueing that I decide to go to Aldi. There are about 20 people queueing, quietly and politely social distancing and I feel fairly comfortable. At the front of the queue a very nice man is handing out trolleys and disinfecting handles. Once in the store I feel like a kid in a sweetie shop; the shelves are full and I can get everything I want. They have lots of vegan options and I enjoy planning our meals for the week. The veg looks fresh and everyone keeps their distance. So far so good. I checkout and the cashier is behind a Perspex screen. She tells me that I can't pack my goods straight in to my bag, I have to put them in the trolley and then go and pack at the counter. I am happy to do this, I don't really care, I am just delighted to be out and shopping, and it makes the checkout very speedy as I throw everything back into the trolley. After I pay I thank her for coming into work, I really do respect the people who are out there keeping the world going and making sure we can have food. As I start packing, I see the next woman in the queue having an altercation with the cashier. She obviously didn't like the packing rule and was telling the cashier it was ridiculous as she didn't have so much shopping. The cashier stood her ground and the woman started to get nasty, telling her she had an attitude and was a 'jobsworth'. She calls over the manager to make a complaint. I have been watching from the side but suddenly I see red and I decide to intervene. I tell the manager that the cashier had been absolutely pleasant, and it was the woman who had been rude, she had simply been told the rules as I had. The cashier looked at me gratefully and the woman turns on me telling me I shouldn't get involved in things that aren't my business. Normally I avoid conflict but today I am incensed. The two guys packing either side of me at the counter also tell her what they think of her behaviour. She storms out of the shop and once again the cashier thanks me. I tell her she shouldn't have to put up with that level of abuse and she says she gets it all day. I pack and as I am leaving the woman brings her trolley back and is telling the trolly man outside loudly about the situation and how rude the cashier was and how she didn't get an apology. Obviously, he had passed his customer service training with flying colours and tries to calm her and says he will apologise on the cashier's behalf. I can't help myself and tell him that she shouldn't have an apology as she was the one abusing the cashier. Once again, she starts to have a go at me – so there it is, me, a 60-year-old woman, with two children, an expert in behavioural science and managing conflict having a verbal slanging match outside Aldi! What would my clients think if they could see me now? But fortunately, the queue is on my side and she realises she isn't going to get anywhere and so stomps off to her car. Perhaps I should send Keith next time? I come home and shamefacedly recount the incident to my children who thankfully wholeheartedly support me.

I decide to go in the gym and do some boxing. That feels good. The rest of the day is lovely, more beautiful sun and we spend hours in the garden, have lunch outside and I read this week's book.

Social media is going crazy with Trump's ridiculous statement yesterday and there are hundreds of comments and jokes circulating. A couple of my favourites on Twitter:

"Never normally do this, but are there any science doctors out there who can help me? I've run out of Toilet Duck to shoot up, will I get the same effect from freebasing Persil non-bio?"

But my real favourite was from Danny Baker who said: "Awake to find the President of the USA has floated the idea of injecting bleach into the body to cure coronavirus. Perhaps we might also inject alphabet soup into him to see if he can start forming coherent sentences!"

There is a real scramble for professionals in the US to insist that no one should inject with disinfectant. Apparently, the US president now plans to 'pare back' his daily briefings and instead of going on the offensive, he claims today that he was being sarcastic and cuts the briefing short!

Some good news comes through for once – in Merseyside a six-month-old baby who had contracted coronavirus has recovered – the baby had been born with a heart condition so it is even more amazing that she recovered, and nurses clapped and cheered in a very emotional moment as the baby was moved out of isolation after two weeks. We really need stories like that.

Priti Patel takes the briefing (still not warming to her) and says a further 813 people have died in hospital after testing positive for COVID-19. She is joined by Professor Powis who says the virus can spread from household to household so we can't forfeit the gains we have made by relaxing the rules. We have now exceeded that 20,000 death number, which is horribly shocking.

A journalist challenges them by saying that they had said they hoped the UK could have kept the death rate below 20,000 and asks whether the strategy should have been different. Professor Stephen Powis replies and says that every death is tragic and that even countries who thought they had got on top of it are starting to see new infections. He reinforces that we need to follow the guidelines and Priti Patel adds that we aren't out of the woods yet, despite the fact we are making progress.

At 5.00 p.m. our friend Tony Fletcher does his Saturday night concert on Facebook and we all tune in to watch – today he is doing it in the street with all his neighbours socially distancing – they must feel so lucky. But we set up speakers in the garden, transfer it to the TV and once again we feel close to our friends around the country who are all watching at the same time. I realise that we now have our weekend routine; Friday night pub with team, Festival Friday drinks, Saturday concert with Tony and Sunday night's quiz night. It hasn't taken us long to get institutionalised.

This time I manage to stay awake through tonight's film but wish I hadn't – complete and utter rubbish.

TOTAL DEATHS – 20,319

Sunday, 26th April

Today I should be doing the London Marathon and I think about how it would have been if I had done it – it has always been an ambition of mine to do the London Marathon and I really hope I get another opportunity. Sunday is my normal six-mile walk; another ritual that has been established, and I always like to be out before 8.00 a.m. when it is relatively quiet. I generally complete it in well under two hours and can be back before the streets become crazy with walkers and joggers. It is yet another beautiful day, it truly feels like someone up above decided that we had to have some compensation for the dreadful virus and turned up the dial on the sunshine. I cannot remember a spell of hot weather like this for years, either in spring or summer.

As I walk, I think about my friend Sue, I had noticed she had been a bit quiet online lately and last night she revealed on her Facebook page that she had been suffering with COVID-19 for three weeks. I feel guilty that I hadn't contacted her; she had told me that she had a bad cold when I last messaged her, but I didn't realise it had developed into the virus. Thankfully, she is recovered and getting stronger now. And then I feel a strange emotion – jealousy! I have no idea where it came from, but I suddenly felt she is lucky to have survived and not been in hospital and I wish that I had got it too in the same way. At least for now she can be free of the fear, and once she has recovered from the dreadful symptoms, she should be able to get on with her life without the nervousness of being around people. It is irrational I know and there is no evidence yet that you can't get it twice. However, there is also no evidence that you can. I don't know whether to be disturbed by my thinking or not.

I get home and the Andrew Marr Show is on and Nicola Sturgeon is being interviewed on older relatives – Scotland has been much clearer on the release strategy. One of her ministers had been very critical of our London ministers' responses about beginning to ease lockdown, calling it botched, shambolic, too slow, too late, too chaotic. She remains diplomatic and supportive of other governments. She tells Andrew that the measures she has in place are working but it is still too early to lift the measures.

Next up is Dominic Raab confirming that Boris is returning tomorrow. He is sincerely expressive about the 20,000 deaths and the heartbreak for the families but reiterates we are seeing the flattening of the peak and also capacity at hospitals. Andrew Marr challenges him on the amount of deaths suggesting it could be double that and Raab says that the data is being collected. He moves on to protection and he insists they are doing everything they can to get the PPE and he sidesteps the issue that they may have failed the NHS staff. I decide the weather is too nice to listen to government errors being rehashed again and remind myself of my promise not to listen to, or watch, news during the day unless it flashes up on my phone.

Keith's current obsession is with the lawn. He battles with it every year but this year it feels that it is his mission and he is feeding and watering it like a dervish. I am sure that after this hot spell of six weeks it won't be long before we are told there is a drought and however good he gets it we will still end up with a dried-out yellow carpet. I don't mention this and smile encouragingly as he stoically takes up his position again with his hosepipe. We all need our things to obsess about during the virus and this is his. He has worked like a Trojan on the garden, and apart from the lawn, it is looking absolutely amazing. Every job I have ever wanted done out there (and jobs I didn't even know needed doing), painting, transplanting, cutting back, new beds dug, has been completed – I take my breakfast outside and look at the beautiful wall of flowering rhododendrons and azaleas and the flourishing pot plants. I once again feel blessed. It must be a morning for feeling grateful as I also slowly savour my favourite poached eggs on toast and think how lucky we have been that we have not gone short of any food at all during the pandemic. It really has been no hardship at all to be at home for this period. I know that some people with children, and who live in flats, must be struggling no end but for those of us lucky enough to have gardens, this weather has made it feel quite joyous. The predictions for the weather are that it will break on Tuesday and the rain will come in; that could make it all feel very different. So, I savour the rest of the sun today. There are plenty of inside jobs to be done, but I help out in the garden and then finish reading my book. Some interesting learning in this one on growth mindset, failing fast and making mistakes.

The Government is still under huge pressure to reveal how we are going to come out of lockdown. Senior government ministers are keen for it be earlier rather than later to assist the economy to recover, but Boris stays firm and reiterates that he has told the country when we will come out – when we have passed the five tests.

In Spain millions of children are allowed out today for the first time in forty-two days as the Spanish police try some new control rules. Beaches were opened but only to children living less than one kilometre away. They still aren't allowed to play with other children outside their family group or go to playgrounds so it is pretty much the same as the UK, but we have been very fortunate that we have been allowed this all along.

The global death rate passes 200,000 today – I still can't compute that England's death rate is one tenth of the global rate, how did we get it so wrong?

The briefing today is held by George Eustice the Environment Secretary and Stephen Powis the Medical Director. Hospital deaths are at their lowest level since the end of March – finally some good news. Still 413 people had died in hospital, which is actually terrible news.

George Eustice says the rules will be reviewed again in a couple of weeks – so that probably takes us to the Thursday after next. Meanwhile, he says it would not be a good idea to release people from the current guidelines in case the curve has not truly flattened. I am predicting at least another month of lockdown after that taking us to the beginning of June with maybe some relaxing of the rules, but we will see. That would mean that we were over halfway through; I tell myself that I can do this.

We have dinner and prepare for our Sunday night pub quiz – routine, routine, routine! We lose again but it is very good fun!

TOTAL DEATHS – 20,732

Monday, 27th April
Official Lockdown, Week Six

It's the start of the sixth week in lockdown and another sunny one. My routine of an early morning virtual workout with my trainer, Olivia, helps to set me up for the week. I feel energised and positive and ready to go.

That mood soon leaves me as I put on the television and, try to avoid *GMB*, (I just can't face Piers this morning). But as I watch BBC this is just heart-breaking; they are doing a tribute to the people who died and seeing the faces behind the numbers, well there are no words for this. I well up again and can barely watch, pictures of vibrant people, at parties, weddings, cruises, family barbecues, cuddling family, all ages, denominations, this cruel illness is totally indiscriminate. They play videos of loved ones talking about how they didn't say goodbye, they didn't think they needed to, how amazing their relatives were and how they don't know whether they can live without them. I think of my own children; we are so close and whilst death itself doesn't frighten me, the thought of how they would cope without me is the worst. Out of respect for these people on the screen I keep watching and thinking about their losses and what a terrible grieving process they are going through. It is just unbearable.

I switch over to *GMB* to a lovely article about a little girl, Harmony, who had been raising money in the 2.6 Challenge yesterday. The London Marathon should have been happening and of course, along with other sporting events, was cancelled so people were urged to take part in different challenges. This little girl lost her arms and legs due to meningitis but had still completed the challenge by doing six things the doctors had said she wouldn't be able to do – running, handstands, swimming and other activities. She is incredible and raised £1,700 for charities. Wonderful news and Piers agrees to match the money she has put in. Good one, Piers, just occasionally you are human.

They start to interview the Health Minister and the subject again is testing – a lot of debate around the amount of testing that is going on and some emotive questioning from Piers "Why were you sending ticking time bombs back into care homes?" Ooh! that is a bit strong. He is pushing to find out why they are sending people back from hospitals into care homes. The Health Minister responds by saying that we are focusing the capacity of testing on where scientific advice told us to and we are now expanding the testing. But the interview is cut short as we are told that there is to be an address from the Prime Minister at No. 10, so the camera flicks over.

The door of No. 10 opens and Boris strides out, his fluffy hair longer and wilder than ever, but I am guessing a haircut was not a priority for him! He apologies for 'being away' and thanks the NHS, everyone in government for stepping up and also the country for showing the grit to stay in. He tells us that we are making progress and thanks to our good sense and collective national resolve we are preventing our NHS from being overwhelmed.

He describes the virus as an assailant or 'invisible mugger' and says that this is the time we can wrestle it to the floor and press home our advantage. Another strange analogy. But he also mentions that this is the time of maximum risk and that anyone who is thinking this is the time to give up the social distancing must not. He tells us that he understands our impatience and shares our anxiety about the economy but we need to avoid a second wave. He reaches a crescendo as he says that he refuses to throw this all away and asks us to maintain our patience and remember that despite all of the suffering, we have nearly succeeded. He reminds of the five tests and tells us that when these have been met is the time that we will move on to continuing to bring in the second phase, and one by one to fire up the engines of this great economy, but he can't tell us when. He tells us that he will be transparent and that we will, as ever, be relying on the science. He finishes by urging us to keep going and helping the NHS to save lives and as we as a country can show the same spirit and energy as Captain Tom Moore, who turns 100 this week. Yay, Captain Moore gets a mention.

At 9.00 a.m. one of my staff emails with good news – we have won a big contract for approximately £40,000. Sadly, it won't come to fruition until the end of the year, but even so, it is gives me faith that people are still buying and it lifts our spirits ready for our 10.00 a.m. call. And more good news from another client yesterday indicating that there will be work at the end of this if we can hang on in there.

In happier news, Captain Tom Moore is honoured with a postmark! Just wonderful.

And for fans of sausage rolls the news that Greggs has announced plans to start opening some of its outlets will no doubt be welcomed! A few fast-food restaurants opened.

News comes through that some countries are relaxing

regulations; Italy outlines plans to ease restrictions from the 4th of May after its lowest daily death rate. (I remember we are still three weeks behind Italy.) New Zealand is moving out of its toughest lockdown at midnight. Germany has made it mandatory to wear masks outside.

The day races past and it is 5.00p.m. but the Health Secretary Matt Hancock is taking the briefing rather than Boris. He talks about other illnesses and how people should still go to hospital and announces that as from tomorrow he will start to release the NHS for other things such as cancer care and important operations. I feel instantly relieved for Sarah, although she has still been receiving good treatment from the hospital during this period.

Again, he reinforces the reminder that lockdown is hard but that we don't want to see a second wave. He sounds strong and resolute, no doubt buoyed up by Boris's return. Sadly, it is revealed that 82 NHS staff and 16 care workers have died from the virus, but research is coming to light that BAME patients were more likely to become ill and die. The Health Secretary announces a 'life assurance scheme' for front-line NHS staff and said: "They have dedicated their lives to caring for others, and I have a deep personal sense of duty that we must care for their loved ones." Each family of staff affected will receive a £60,000 payment and he respectfully added that nothing would replace the loss for the family but that they want to support front-line staff.

The questions come thick and fast as usual with still a great emphasis on the tests and moving out of lockdown, but Chris Witty says we can't give an exact number and that the death rate needs to fall before releasing us from lockdown. A question comes about news that has emerged about people coming into the country being quarantined for fourteen days – Hancock responds by saying that given the current level of new cases in the UK, and low amounts of infections with no travel being allowed, we need to consider what happens when travel increases again as cases coming from people travelling internationally could increase the numbers.

My routine kicks in again – tonight is another episode of *Killing Eve*. We need something positive to look forward to every day – if you can describe a gory, psychologically twisted series about a manic psychopath positive!

TOTAL DEATHS – 21,092

Tuesday, 27th April

The rain has arrived as promised and it is heavy. I look at the BBC weather site and it looks like this could be set in for at least a week, with only a few days respite. This throws a whole new light on lockdown, not for me personally as I have so much work to do, but for those who don't and who have been enjoying the sun I think this will bring on a whole new level of cabin fever. I hope that this doesn't mean that people start to become casual about lockdown and start visiting each other. We are getting close to levelling the peak and we really need to stay strong now. I take one look outside and decide to give walking a miss, so go to the gym.

I come back in fully intending to go straight to the study and use some of this energy to work but get distracted in the kitchen. I have been promising I would make Keith bread pudding so decide it would be nice for him to wake up to the lovely cinnamon smell of it baking. I haven't entered into the big Lock Down Bake Off for two reasons; one I just don't have time, and two, we have tried not to have any sugary snacks in the house. I watch with admiration as people display their beautiful creations on social media, but my cooking is very much around healthy home-cooked meals. We have managed without chocolate and biscuits so far and I don't really want to start down that road, however, I feel he deserves a Delia type treat. As I get out the equipment I can really understand the obsession; there is something very satisfying about baking – however, I am not making a habit of it!

I open the post and there is a beautiful card from Sarah. It is so unexpected and touches me deeply – the front of it has pebbles with LOVE and HOPE engraved on them. The other side is decorated with a funny hand-drawn picture of us smiling, singing, drinking and enjoying the Isle of Wight. It reads:

"To my soulmate, just wanted to say how much I love you and how very proud I am of you. You are, as ever, being strong, hardworking and totally amazing. We will come through this 'shit'. All your dedication will shine through. Proud to call you my best friend. Love always."

I can barely contain my emotion; we have been friends for thirty-four years now and 'soulmate' says it all. No one has, or ever will, touch me or my life in the way that she has. I long to hug her and to spend a weekend talking rubbish and drinking wine. We are due to go to Juicy Oasis in August for a week (lots of talking but no drinking wine there!) I pray that we might be able to go there, it is our favourite place and truly is an oasis. I take a deep breath and start work.

Apparently, there is going to be a one-minute silence at 11.00 a.m. this morning in honour of the key workers who have died serving the country during coronavirus. I am sure there will be more to remember them, but I set my alarm to make sure that I take that time to think about them and their families. When it starts it is very moving as we see pictures from around the country of people both inside and outside of hospital standing silently, with heads bowed, observing the silence. It finishes with another clap.

I check in on Captain Tom – it is two days till his 100th birthday and he has received over 120,000 cards. His Spitfire birthday flypast from Biggin Hill has been jeopardised due to fears of crowds coming together but the RAF are going to do a flypast instead. He is still topping the charts with his single with Michael Ball and has smashed several Guinness World Records; one for the greatest single fundraising attempt. He has had murals painted of him and benches in his image delivered to him. How amazing.

BBC news pings and tells me that British Airways are going to make up to 12,000 workers redundant. They have made serious losses in the first quarter and of course they are going to be even worse in this quarter. British Airways has been my best friend over the last ten years and I have flown with them at least 10 times a year, and the idea of them going under is unthinkable, but they are predicting that customer demand will take several years to return so the restructuring and redundancy may affect many staff.

There is still no sign of Boris tonight, so Matt Hancock is taking the briefing with Professor Dame Angela McLean, and Professor John Newton from Public Health England, who is coordinator of the national testing effort. Hancock starts by referencing the one-minute silence this morning to remember the heroes of the NHS and key workers who lost their lives looking after us and says that it was a 'solemn moment of reflection'. He is not wrong.

He goes on to discuss the Government plan and reaffirm that it was working – evidenced by the fact that the NHS has 3,260 spare critical care beds. In terms of testing, yesterday 43,453 were carried out and in total 70,387. Sadly another 586 people have lost their lives, which is just dreadful.

He says 21,678 people have now died in hospital with

coronavirus – an increase of 586 since yesterday. He states that the proportion of coronavirus deaths in care homes is around a sixth of the total, however, that doesn't correlate with the figures published by the Office for National Statistics, which shows that for the week ending Friday, 17th April, almost a quarter of coronavirus deaths in England and Wales were in care homes. Well, tomorrow we should know as apparently the Government will publish daily figures for deaths in care homes and the community.

I finish work and Keith has updated our photo book. As an anniversary present last year, he collated memories from every big trip we had been on, with a note of the date as a memory and he has added our skiing holiday 2020 in La Tania. As I look through, I see he has also added a few pages entitled Lockdown – the pictures are all of the garden! I doubt whether we will record any further trips this year.

TOTAL DEATHS – 21,678

Wednesday, 29th April

I can't believe April is nearly all over. We arrived home from skiing on the 15th March and I have only left the house to shop four times since then apart from my morning walks. If you had told me then that we would stay in for this period I would never have believed it was possible, but now it is just normal and I can't imagine what it is like to have my freedom.

I am thoughtful as I do my walk this morning. I am thinking of writing a blog, probably the most difficult blog I have ever written, and this has been prompted by the news of the amount of deaths today. I feel that almost everyone is going to be touched by someone dying.

It is a blog to help companies consider how to support workers through the death of a colleague. I am not sure how many companies have guidelines for this but I have some incredibly sad previous experience of this. I was working for a client in Portsmouth back in 1999 delivering a training course for them, there was a knock at the door of the training room and I was asked to go to their head office in Slough immediately. They told me they thought that they had lost some staff in the Paddington Rail crash – a terrible crash where 31 people died and 417 were injured.

When I arrived in Slough they had just received news that 2 staff members had died and they were unsure of how to handle it. We worked through that terrible day, learning some lessons as we did so on how to support staff, helping them to process the news and start the grieving.

Sixteen years later I remember running to get a train at Waterloo and just flinging myself in a seat on the 5.35 p.m. to Southampton. I took a call from my colleague, John, from a company that we had gone into partnership with to deliver training in the Middle East. Each year we attended the exhibition in Dubai together and along with Trevor and Barry we had the most amazing fun. As I sat on the train I remember John's words telling me that he was sorry but Trevor had died. I couldn't compute it; Trevor who we had been in Dubai with just a few months ago. Trevor who had emailed me last week and who I was due to be going to a client with next week. Trevor the super-fit triathlete. It felt like he was joking but he wasn't. Trevor had been delivering training in a hotel and had gone to bed and just never woke up. The staff found him in bed the next morning a victim of sudden arrhythmic death syndrome. The shock was overpowering and it took me a long time to process it. I am now thinking of all the people in the UK who might have heard of colleagues dying but because they have been in lockdown will not have processed this properly. But when they return to work they will be faced with that massive void – the desk where the colleague used to sit, their mug in the kitchen cupboard, all the emails they recently sent, the projects that they were working on together. And it will be incredibly hard for them, particularly if continued social distancing doesn't allow them to grieve in the way we normally would. There will be no funeral for them to attend, no closure, they will have to work through this in their own time. I make a few notes and consider whether I want to write this.

I read in the news about one sad case yesterday – the Head of IT at ITV. Someone posted his last three tweets; the first one talking about being a new dad and how they were coping, the next one saying he was in hospital with COVID-19 and that it was awful and he had thought he was a 'goner' and then a final post from his brother telling the world he had passed away. And he is just one of many who will not be returning to their desk and their projects and colleagues. This is the heartbreak we are all going to have to cope with once the euphoria of being able to go back to life has died down, the grim reality of the damage the virus has really done. A sombre way to start the day so I don't even turn on the news this morning as I get dressed.

But then BIG breaking news – Boris Johnsons fiancée, Carrie Symonds, has given birth. I had no idea she was so close to the due date. He was apparently at the birth but then went back to work in Downing Street. It is a boy; well congratulations, Boris. Now I understand why he hasn't been at the briefings for the last couple of days! The baby is healthy, and they are both doing well. What a famous baby this young man is going to be. He apparently has five siblings – the news rather awkwardly reported it as: "He is known to have fathered five children!" Was that a suggestion that there could be some unknown ones? A quick Google does seem to suggest that he has been quite evasive in the past about how many he actually has!

Dominic Raab unsurprisingly takes the Prime Minister's Question Time and starts by saying that he was sure the whole House would want to send congratulations and very best wishes to Boris. He also wishes Captain Tom Moore a happy 100th birthday for tomorrow. I am already looking forward to the celebrations. Today he had 2 trains named after him – he really is the gift that keeps on giving.

My day is manic and stressful with calls and recording two videos. We completed the first video and then realised the lighting had been wrong so had to do the whole thing again. Still, in the greater scheme of things it is only a minor setback and we adjust the lighting and film again. Keith is getting much better at being patient with me fluffing my lines and needing to re-record (no eye rolling today) but the cat was less respectful, jumping on the table and rubbing against the tripod and purring loudly! I then write the blog and we will publish it tomorrow; it is horribly sad, but I hope it may help some people.

Dominic Raab leads the briefing and starts by telling us that the total deaths have risen to over 26,000 after care home deaths are included for the first time. Shocking! Professor Jonathan Van-Tam, the Deputy Chief Medical Officer for England, gives out the death figures and states that they are an improvement. It doesn't feel like one, as it has risen significantly due to the figures being added from care homes and the wider community, so it has jumped to over 26,000. This doesn't mean it has been a surge as the new deaths recorded happened between the 2nd March and 28th April.

Raab reminds us of the five tests to be met before lockdown and states that the fifth is the most important and gives us a stark reminder that Germany has seen a rise in cases since they eased lockdown. Raab says whilst there are some encouraging signs he is going to wait until he gets advice from the Scientific Advisory Group for Emergencies (SAGE).

There has been a poll by Opinium for Amnesty between 24th and 27th April, which showed that 2 in 3 people in the UK believe the Government has performed poorly in providing PPE and a further 78% felt that the Government had not been fully transparent in the way it communicated with the public.

Another journalist asks: "How will social distancing work in a school setting? Will home education have to continue into next year?" There is an acknowledgement of how hard it is but they are still adamant it was the right thing to do to close schools. Another challenger asks whether it is even possible for young people to stay two metres apart and Van-Tam confirms that would be difficult.

So not much to report really. I FaceTime Elly for a chat and get my list ready for another crazy day of working very hard for very little money tomorrow!

TOTAL DEATHS – 26,097

Victoria Station South, London

Outside Waterloo Station, London

Waterloo Station, London

Archbishops Park near St Thomas's Hospital, London

Horse Guards Road and St James Park, London

Covent Garden, London

Thursday, 29th April

It's Captain Tom's 100th birthday. But it isn't Captain Tom's birthday, it is COLONEL Tom's Birthday. He has been given an honorary promotion for his birthday in recognition of the incredible work he has done. The head of the British Army, General Sir Mark Carleton-Smith, appointed him as the first Honorary Colonel of the Foundation College, Harrogate, and the Queen sent him a message. *GMB* is all about Colonel Tom today with his fund sitting at just under £30 million this morning – Piers gives it a push to try and get over the £30 million point whilst the programme is on. Two flypasts are happening today, and as we watch, the Battle of Britain Memorial Flight it is just so moving. The money is one thing, but he is just our symbol of goodness, kindness, altruism and hope; it shows what an ordinary person can do when they set some goals. *GMB* also broadcasts other messages to him; one from Boris, which is fun but formal, but my favourite is from Harmony, who is also fundraising. What an adorable little girl she is; a beautiful bundle of energy and her fundraising is now over £60,000 despite her having no limbs. News shows the new trains being revealed; I bet they now wished they had waited another day so that they could have named them

Colonel rather than Captain! Michael Ball appears and sings 'Happy Birthday' and Tom's face is the most delightful picture, he makes me think of my dad and I suddenly am overcome with emotion thinking of him.

I have a good gym session and then get ready for a morning of recording and webinars. This morning Grumpy Rob will be making a comeback in a short satiric video – previously we had recorded and sent out 6 videos of Grumpy Rob answering questions about how to cope in isolation and it had been really well received. So today we are recording a broken unshaven Grumpy Rob, compulsively eating chocolate, drinking whisky and banished to living in the shed by his family! After the sombre and difficult post, I wrote yesterday on dealing with a colleagues' death I thought it would be good to do something a bit lighter, and Rob and I always have fun when we do the comedy videos. He is a great actor and makes it so easy. Following that I have a very serious morning of podcasts for my speech at the virtual Association for Coaching Conference, and then a webinar to almost 200 people at one of our biggest clients. Today the subject is about families working together from home – and I am really looking forward to this, the psychology of behaviour is my favourite topic.

Boris bounds into the briefing today like an exuberant puppy. He still sounds a bit breathy (unless of course he had run down the corridor). He is flanked by Whitty and Vallance (at a distance of course!) He apologies for not being there and thanks everyone, particularly the NHS for bringing him back and supporting him with a much 'happier' hospital situation yesterday.

First the figures: 901,905 tests for coronavirus have now been carried out in the UK including 81,611 tests yesterday, 171,253 people have tested positive, that's an increase of 6,032 cases since yesterday.

He again says that they are committed to overcoming the challenges, getting the PPE to the right people, and references the frustrations around the number of tests carried out. He assures us that they are all throwing everything at it, night and day, to get this right but still recognises the challenges of the front-line staff. The message again is that our efforts to stay at home are working and have been proved to work. He says we have avoided an uncontrollable and catastrophic pandemic with over 500,000 deaths. He confirms we have passed the peak and are on the downward slide. Apparently, he tells us, we have lots of reasons to be hopeful. I process this for a second; I was almost about to nod gratefully when I just realised what he has said – that we have avoided the tragedies other countries have suffered. I digest this and then start to feel angry. What utter crap. It is estimated that we are going to have a death rate that is the one of the worst in the world. How can he say that we have avoided a catastrophic pandemic? We are living it.

Boris Johnson then says he will be setting out a comprehensive plan as to how we will get the economy back on track, and the children back to school, and how we can continue to supress the disease and restart the economy. He reinforced the key tests we must satisfy before we can come out of lockdown. The fifth is the most important, and it is important that the measures we take do not risk a second spike. He keeps reiterating that we have come through the peak and that it could have been much worse, but it is vital that we don't lose control. He refers to it as going through an alpine tunnel with the sunlight on the other side and uses one of those strange 'Boris analogies' about not losing control and running slap into an even bigger mountain. Apparently, in order not to do this we have to ensure that the R rate does not get back above 1. I am not entirely clear on how the R and the 1 works, but thankfully he shows a clip about the tests from the Government. It talks about decreasing the rate of infection, the R, which is the average number of people one infected person passes the virus on to. To beat it we need to keep the R rate as low as possible, i.e. under 1, which is what slows the spread down and gets it under control. At its peak in March it apparently was around 3, but since social distancing we have reduced it to below 1. However, we have only just passed the peak of the virus and we need to keep it under 1. It was a clear and useful video – I get it now. He then hands over to Patrick for the figures. The figures show the steady, but painfully slow downward trend – it is still hard to fathom what is really going on out there. Being shut away for so long I can understand why in America they stop believing it is really dangerous and want to go back to work. If it wasn't for the news our lives wouldn't be touched by it at all. But it is very real.

There were more challenges to the fact that the Government had ordered lockdown too late and Boris defends the fact that he feels the UK did the 'right thing at the right time'. He is asked what lessons he may have learnt from the fact the UK has the worst death rate in Europe. He hedges around the collation of data and finally says that, broadly speaking, he thinks that they did the 'right thing at the right time'.

When questioned on the national debt and the fact that it is rising by hundreds of billions, and asked how much risk there was, he assures us that he thinks the economy will bounce back strongly. He flirts with the term austerity and says it won't be part of his approach. I have to be honest I would like something more than a 'think the economy will bounce back' – it would be good to have something firmer than that.

I go into the lounge and Keith has the CD player on shuffle; he is very into retro vinyl and has a record deck but also still has a 300-CD piece of kit. Normally, I huff and sigh at it but tonight it is nice; tunes that take me back to the 80s, to the Isle of Wight Festival and to when the children were born. We make dinner together and play Scrabble whilst we eat. Before I know it 8.00 p.m. has arrived. I find a particularly good wooden salad spoon with a metal end, and a pot that is incredibly loud to bang. Once again, the noise is louder and more determined.

Another day in the Big Lockdown House is over.

TOTAL DEATHS – 26,711

Friday, 1st May

Is it really Friday again? And we have made it to May. Another incredibly busy week and my routine is holding out. I am still getting up at around 6.00 a.m., an hour of exercise and get dressed, half an hour for writing and reflection, a full day's work between 9.00 a.m. and 5.00 p.m., another half an hours' writing whilst I listen to the briefing and then dinner. Not once, can I honestly say, have I been bored during this whole period. In fact, there are still some things that I haven't sorted out yet that I want to, and whilst I know in my head that the lockdown will be going on for at least another month, I still feel the urge to get everything done and finished. What does that make me? I'm not sure why, but I know that I will feel better.

I decide to go to Aldi before work. I park up around 8.00 a.m. and this time have a successful shopping trip. The queue is short, the shoppers are respectful, and I manage not to get into any fights!

I am home within forty-five minutes – that is one of the benefits of Aldi, there is not much to look at so you are in and out quickly, unless of course you are having a major altercation with a random stranger!

I sit at my desk and my calendar reminder pops up.

Amongst the recently added coaching sessions is a reminder that I was supposed to be flying to Greece today. This was part of my sixtieth-year holiday celebration plans. I stop for a second and dream about what it would be like to be at the BA lounge, to be packed up and anticipating ten days of sun, sea and sightseeing. I try not to dwell on it; I had long ago come to terms with the fact we would not be going to Greece, but the next booked holiday in July is the really big one. Instead of having a big party I decided I wanted to have a wonderful birthday celebration with the children and their partners in Mauritius. It is highly unlikely we will go but it hasn't been cancelled yet. I think of the lovely wardrobe of summer dresses I had collected in the sales ready for the holiday and feel resigned to the fact that we won't go – it's the only way to avoid disappointment. I read an article on air travel that suggests that it would be impossible to enforce social distancing at airports. John Holland-Kaye, the CEO of Heathrow, said that airports will have to introduce health screening and passengers would have to wear masks. Sadly, there have been three General Municipal Boilermakers Union (GMB) members working at Heathrow who have lost their lives to the virus. But I wonder if that could ever work? If people are on long haul they will need to eat and even taking the mask off for fifteen minutes would put themselves and others at risk unless they are only going to allow one passenger per row, which would make travel hideously expensive. However, the chief of Ryanair, Michael O'Leary, backed the call for temperature checks and wearing face masks through the airport. Indeed, people in Asia have been doing it ever since SARS hit. EasyJet have openly said that it was possible to leave the middle seat empty on planes when they resume flights. The GMB are already voicing concerns over safety of staff since 2 planes arrived at the same time and only one conveyer belt had been allocated. How the hell did that happen? The airports are almost empty so to make a mistake that allowed 500 people to be collecting luggage all at once is unbelievable.

The country is in a frenzy waiting for Boris to reveal the plan to ease out of lockdown next week. An article in the *Mail* suggests that many Brits do not want to leave lockdown. There are lots of different methodologies being discussed including staff working alternative days or weeks, wearing PPE when in canteens (if they open at all) and face coverings on public transport, but people are still uneasy. I am one of them and whilst I am desperate to get business back to normal and want the economy to bounce back, I'm seriously concerned that it is too early and we might catch the virus.

At lunchtime, the BBC news says that the Government is likely to 'come close' to its target of 100,000 UK coronavirus tests, according to the Communities Secretary, Robert Jenrick. If that is true, I would imagine Matt Hancock would be breathing a sigh of relief. Yesterday Diane Abbot had called for his resignation over the failure to meet targets.

Matt Hancock takes the briefing with Professor John Newton, who is the co-ordinator of the UK coronavirus testing programme, and Professor Stephen Powis. The general focus is the fact that they have indeed provided 122,000 coronavirus tests on the last day of April (as promised). Hancock looks relieved and announces it was an ambitious target, but testing is necessary to get Britain back on its feet. Further interrogation suggests that this doesn't mean 122,000 people were tested, that was the number of tests dispatched. The press are accusing the Government of fiddling the figures.

The death rate has jumped after another 739 people died today. This feels like a rise again, but this now includes deaths in care homes so the actual total deaths in hospitals is 427, which is lower.

Finally, a bit of light relief in the day – my Friday night call with my best friends that we call the Isle of Wight Festival call. My daughter has produced an amazing quiz based on artists who attended the Isle of Wight and it is a call full of hilarity and memories. I am so grateful for an hour's respite, and probably equally grateful for the gin that I consumed during the call, which took the edge off my anxiety and allowed me to slide onto the couch and slip into a delicious sleep on the sofa halfway through another film.

TOTAL DEATHS – 27,510

Saturday, 2nd May

I watch the morning news. One of my ridiculous fascinations at the moment is the deterioration of everyone's hair. Who knew we were so reliant on our hairdressers? For the men who have a good head of hair their style is heading for something reminiscent of an 80s bouffant, and for the women, the fringes are covering eyes, the balayage's are growing out and the roots are getting longer. It feels far easier to relate to the newsreaders as normal people. I am going to need to experiment with some 'up dos' for the rest of the lockdown although my fingers are twitching for the scissors. One of my best friends is my hairdresser and I was teasing her with my scissors on the Zoom call last night and she was begging me not to do it. I will be cutting Keith's hair today so that might get me on a roll!

In the sporting world, the debate continues as to whether the Premier League can complete the football season amid the pandemic. There have been lengthy debates including discussions about logistics, locking down grounds and creating a safe environment. They are also looking at neutral venues and protocols around testing. In a statement the League reconfirmed their commitment to finishing the 2019–20 season and welcomed government support. Call me heartless (and I know the majority of the male population will) but this feels so unimportant in the grand scheme of things. I do know that so many people are missing their sports and there are some big financial implications, but I would hate for this to distract from the more important factors that we need to be dealing with.

In another report, there is talk of taking BAME NHS staff away from the front line to reduce the death rate from COVID-19, which seems to have been disproportionately high in this group. In the *Guardian* last week, a report revealed that 63% of the first 106 health and social care workers who had died from the virus were black or Asian. The reasons are not entirely clear yet but this will be worth exploring.

I am still feeling a bit lost and empty today – I can feel I am on my emotional bridge, ready to teeter off to either side and I know that I need to manage this. There is no particular reason, as there often isn't, but just a dark and anxious feeling. Thankfully, the weather looks better, albeit a little chilly, so I decide to spend as much time in the sunshine as I can this weekend. Due to the weather, I haven't been outside apart from one walk and one visit to the shops, so maybe I am low in Vitamin D! I am also going to make some juices today to try and boost my immune system. I think of plenty of jobs I can do to keep myself busy (most of them that I have been procrastinating on a long time). Somehow, I think having too much time to think could be a rocky road today.

True to my word I have a really busy day sorting out an old filing cabinet that hasn't been culled since 2003, cleaning the decking and cooking and before I can blink it is 5.00 p.m. and Tony is doing his Saturday night live concert.

I check in on today's news. Boris Johnson and Carrie Symonds have named their boy Wilfred Lawrie Nicholas.

He is named after their grandfathers and two doctors who treated Mr Johnson whilst he was in hospital, which is quite a tribute to how serious it really was. The first published picture suggests he has inherited his father's hair!

Matt Hancock is up again for the briefing, and still lots of defensiveness about the testing debacle following accusations of fiddling the numbers. Jenny Harries acknowledges that the peak has been passed but there is still a lot of work to do – the death count today was 621, so it is not dropping significantly.

Robert Jenrick joins Hancock and announces £76 million to support most vulnerable people. Whilst this is great to hear that they are doing this and looking to support victims of domestic abuse, I just can't help wondering where all this money is coming from. Jenrick also tackles the subject of returning children to school recognising that there are some children who are vulnerable and not receiving the right level of home schooling.

The future of the aviation industry was questioned at the briefing with Rolls Royce considering thousands of job cuts, following announcements this week that BA and Ryanair were also looking at large cuts. Apparently, the industry could take several years to recover to pre-virus levels.

There is still a question of whether you can catch coronavirus twice and this was posed by a member of the public tonight. Dr Harries says that the WHO doesn't feel that they have enough information to be clear enough yet. If only we could confirm that we couldn't, that would make a massive difference in terms of returning to normality.

I open a bottle of Gavi with dinner, which hits the spot well, and try to avoid drinking the whole bottle.

TOTAL DEATHS – 27,880

Sunday, 3rd May

I sleep until nearly 8.00 a.m. – I am getting better at this lying-in thing! But still once I am awake, I am awake, so I get up and go for my usual six-mile walk. After ten minutes it starts to rain and I consider giving up but then decide, I don't mind the gentle drizzle, and decide to carry on. Before I know it, I am in my stride and lost in my thoughts. My mood is still low and I hope that the walk will lift it. I try to work out why I am feeling so low and I can't put my finger on it, so I turn my thoughts to work. As I walk I realise that we could put our Women's Development Programme online. Why not? It is an international programme anyway and we could break down the modules into small parts. I have always thought that we couldn't do it online but now I start to see it differently. Pounding the pavements, I work it through in my head and I can see the possibilities. It would take some work, but I make a mental note to talk it through with the team tomorrow. When I get lost in work it really helps my mood.

We are all social distancing well today and there are not too many people out due to the weather, so I smile and say hello to people as I walk. Apparently, we have mirror neurons, which mean we can be contagious with our moods, so I wonder if their smiling back would help me. I decide to conduct an experiment and see how many I can get to smile and say good morning. I notice there are three main categories; the Bright and Chirpies – happy to smile at anyone and actively seeking eye contact, the Not Normally Sociable – who look as if they don't want to engage but at the last minute decide to risk it, and the Fully Focused – those who are in their zone and will avert eye contact at all costs! I wonder how many I can engage and I start to find a strategy. For the dog walkers, if you smile at the dog first they will always engage, same with babies in prams, easy to infect the parents. For the walkers you need to start smiling to yourself a while before you get to them or you won't get their attention. Couples running were a definite no – they strode straight by, as did most joggers, apart from the odd woman on her own. I reckon I have about a 70% hit rate! I am not sure what that experiment proved to me, but it was fun trying! The walk feels a really easy one today, I am definitely ready to walk further and can't wait until they allow us to drive and walk so that I can do a 10 miler. I don't feel confident at all that the London Marathon will go ahead in October but at least if I keep my times up and keep my muscles going, I should be fit for next year. Plus, it gives me a target and I need targets at the moment.

An article in the *Daily Mail* reports some dreadful news from Russia: a third doctor plunges from a COVID-19 hospital window after complaining about the pressures that medics were facing and apparently being forced to work even though he had been tested positive. He is in a grave situation with head injuries. Russia have recorded a sharp rise in infections with a massive leap in the death toll from 58 to 1280 – Moscow is the hotspot in Russia. Two other senior women doctors also have died after falling from hospital windows.

Gove is taking the briefing tonight with Powys supporting. Lots of praise from Gove to Hancock in his 'amazing success in increasing testing', which he felt would increase confidence in the Government as they move into the next phase of lockdown. There have been an additional 631 deaths today.

He tells us that the Government is consulting with employers and trade unions about the guidelines, and if and when the guidelines are eased they are done in a way that makes British people's sacrifices worth it. 'If'? What a strange thing to say. 'When' is what we want to hear. He says that it will be a phased approach that makes sure everyone understands the guidance about working safely and that there would be no sudden return to the 'old normal'. He mentions that there were possibilities it could be re-imposed in a localised way but gives us no idea of what that might mean.

There is a question over whether we needed the Nightingale Hospitals and Professor Powis insists they were absolutely 100% not built in error after a reported low capacity of patients. He says it would have been foolish not to plan for extra capacity and it was 'good news' that the Nightingales' capacity was not required. He suggests that the peak was around mid-April.

I finish some work and we have dinner before the Sunday night quiz. Another weekend gone, and hopefully another week closer to freedom. If only we truly knew when freedom would be and could tick the days off on a calendar.

TOTAL DEATHS – 28,131

Monday, 4th May
Official Lockdown, Week Seven

I am up early ready for my virtual PT session. I think that my mood is beginning to lift; it is hard to tell but I feel a bit lighter and more positive today. It is damp and chilly and as I sit to put my trainers on I watch the birds in the garden – I had put some bread out on the table and my pair of robins are joined on the table by the most beautiful little blue tit, almost in conference. After the session we check my heart rate on the Fitbit App and it has improved considerably over the last five weeks, now settling at 61 bpm resting. Fitbit also tells me that my VO2 Max score is 32.5 which is 'Very Good' and 'Excellent' (for women your age!) Your age? They had to ruin it! I check my phone and once again Facebook tortures me with memories on Time Hop. But today is a wonderful memory; six years ago I had posted a video of my children from the last VE Day celebration twenty-five years ago and it cheers me up no end to watch my gorgeous little toddlers on their tricycles in a wonderful street party. How very different today is, and we are all trying to think of how to celebrate VE Day on Friday virtually and remotely.

But one country that won't be worrying about this is Belarus. I saw a news article last night that showed people in Belarus continuing to defy the measures and going about their normal daily life without any rules about social gatherings. They are still going to football matches, and despite a rise in infections and advice from the WHO, they remain defiant. Even more incredulous is the advice from their President, Alexander Lukashenko. He spoke in a packed church and said: "I've proceeded with one simple wisdom borne from our people – when things are hard it's best not to change our way of life." But even more incredible is that last month he advised people to drink more vodka to help protect against the virus. Dear God, where do they get these people from? Well at least that is less dangerous than drinking disinfectant!

I watch *GMB* but no Piers Morgan this morning; he apparently has mild symptom so is not risking infecting others. Ben Shephard takes his place with Susanna and the mood is lighter. Apparently, there have been 1,645 complaints about Piers in just five days (making it almost 4,000 in total), due to his interviewing style throughout this period – people have described him as 'bullying', particularly in his interview with Helen Whately and his ongoing interviews with Matt Hancock. However, the complaints were not upheld – apparently broadcasters are 'able to hold those making political decisions to account'. I am sure he is very proud.

And for those of us who were Remainers, some proof that the EU works. A senior Brussels official has said that we would have suffered food shortages during the pandemic if we had not had the EU single market. Apparently, we were lucky that we hadn't already crashed out when coronavirus struck. Apparently, 6.3million workers are now furloughed, costing £8 billion – which is just staggering. No-one has mentioned the Brexit word for weeks but this in combination with the virus really feels like it will be the demise of our economy.

Matt Hancock with Professor Van-Tam take the briefing and Hancock states that the UK is now in a position to carry out a test, track and trace programme to identify and track those with symptoms with a trial starting on the Isle of Wight on Tuesday, and all residents will be asked to download it. This will allow the Government to take a more targeted approach to the lockdown but still contain the virus. He reminds us that we still have to keep going with the lockdown guidance rules.

Earlier we had heard that Boris will set out the new strategy on how the lockdown will be eased on Sunday although Nicola Sturgeon has already said that it is very likely the Government will continue their lockdown after the review on Thursday. Rumours have suggested that the UK plans a staggered workday for commuters along with new hygiene rules and potentially screens between workers. However, organisations are still very nervous about the impact of organisations not paying sufficient attention to safety regulations if the lockdown is eased sooner.

Van-Tam starts to go through the charts and reiterates the five tests for deciding whether we will change the lockdown rule. He says it is clear that we are past the peak. He recognises that there are still clear challenges on PPE but that we are in a good position on testing. He reminds us that we have to be confident that we will not risk another peak and that is a deep and scientific discussion.

At 5.30 p.m. I realise I have barely left my desk and decide I need a distraction. I find that distraction in my dear Keith's hair and he looks at me nervously as I come out brandishing my new hairdressing scissors. He says that the sharp metal comb hurts as I attack his sideburns with gusto, so I don't do a great job; a few patches here and there but it is definitely better.

We have dinner and then I remember it is *Killing Eve* tonight – an hour of escapism.

TOTAL DEATHS – 28,734

Tuesday, 5th May

I get up early and go hill walking. Not beautiful scenic hill walking as I can't drive anywhere, but just up the roads around me. There are a few hills that are a bit of a challenge, so I decide to tackle those this morning. I had more deep and disturbing dreams last night but this time I can't quite remember them, maybe that is a blessing. As I walk, I allow my unconscious brain to launch; it is my favourite time for coming up with ideas and processing things and today it has an absolute classic for me. I realise that I am not practising what I preach. I spend my life teaching people to create new neural pathways and only ever to use positive language so that the brain will give you the state that it wants and I think back to some of the texts and messages I have sent to people who ask how I am doing. I have told them how dreadful the impact of the virus has been on the business, our fight for survival or the fears I have for the future of the business. I consider what impact that will be having on my 'state' – one of desperation and anxiety and negativity. I need to really change my thinking and a song comes on Spotify that really resonates with me – I am not sure who the artist is and I don't recognise the song, but as they sing about losing everything and how that would mean you have nothing more to lose, the lyrics resonate with me.

I suddenly realise that this is the paradigm shift I need – without sounding dramatic, we have almost lost everything, all of our training has been cancelled, so we do have nothing more to lose. Which means we can view this as a start-up – we can really embrace what it takes to build up a business and design it in the way we want to and I am lucky enough to have some good people to help me to do this. This excites me and I realise this is where my dark moments and anxiety have come from, trying to hold on to everything we have. I just need to let it go and to start again. I did it once and I can do this now. Life does carry on and if we stay positive and strong, we will succeed.

GMB is light this morning with Piers off for a week – he doesn't have COVID-19, but he is going to stay off for a week to let the symptoms pass. Ben Shephard and Susanna continue with the lovely Doctor Hilary. An interesting debate about obesity and COVID-19 catches my attention. The mortality rate is increased by 40% if you are overweight, apparently it is something to do with the fat cells being less able to fight the disease than healthy cells.

Then there is an interview with Ethan Eardsley and his parents. Ethan is a young lad with Cerebral Palsy and he is walking up and down his road to raise money for people who need it, who have lost loved ones to COVID-19 and have to pay for funerals. Sadly, he lost his great aunt and so he is trying to raise £15,000 before his 10th birthday by doing 100 laps as he was inspired by Captain Tom and wanted to be part of his 'army'. He has raised £2,000 so far and Ben Shephard does a wonderful interview with him on *GMB*; he is such a sweetie. I am sure that this will help his cause. I am right, within thirty minutes they have an update and he has now raised £31,100. I love how the country gets behind these heroes.

My thoughts turn to the NHS and the people who have

died serving us and I wonder what proportion of them did not have the right PPE. This is triggered by the Italian doctors who have attempted (and succeeded) at taking their own lives due to the pressure. I think about a normal company and what the consequences would be if people had died at work due to not having the correct equipment. There would be a public enquiry and a huge compensation payout. People would down tools and refuse to work until the situation was made safe and the right amount of equipment was bought in. But for the NHS they are required to simply mourn their colleagues whilst they carry on in the same situations. If a doctor causes harm then they have to declare it honestly and face the consequences, shouldn't it be the same for the Government? Or is there going to be a big cover up?

I leave those thoughts to focus on work and do another big webinar and a good call with a client – my approach of reinventing ourselves seems to be working and they are really interested in what we can offer virtually. Their view is that it will be unlikely they will do any classroom-based training until 2021. If that is the view of clients, then we have to make the virtual stuff work.

Raab is up for the briefing again this evening and tells us they are continuing to see evidence of the flattening of the peak of the virus. He says the next stage won't be easy. With you on that Dom, but this stage hasn't exactly been a breeze! Deputy Chief Scientific Adviser Angela McLean goes through the charts. One thing troubling her is the increase in use of motor cars. I agree, when I go out walking it is definitely getting busier. She also notes that visits to parks are increasing and other data backs up the idea that people are going out more. I am not sure how they know that; I haven't seen anyone around Southampton Common with a clicker counting us in and out!

Deaths have been falling since the 24th April, although deaths in care homes were still rising and she admits we need to get to grips with why this is. There have been 693 more deaths today as we head close to the 30,000 marker and we are now the country with the highest death rate in Europe. Until today it had been Italy. Raab calls it a massive tragedy but says that international comparisons might be inaccurate.

Testing has reached 84,806 today, again less than the promised 100,000, which it actually hasn't passed since the 1st May. The figures show that 194,990 people have tested positive, which is an increase of 4,406 from twenty-four hours ago. That is still a huge amount of people out there with it so those people who are leaving their homes more need to think carefully.

Raab takes questions from the public and the first question is about how we can learn from the pandemic and he is humble in his reply saying they all want to learn lessons and that they had been given a timely reminder of the need to 'level up' the country as it has taught us to appreciate key workers. Well, the proof of the pudding and all that stuff.

Nothing much to feel too positive about there tonight. Keith comes home after doing the food shopping and has done another 'drive by' to the hairdressers to collect some hair colour for me. He is doing a bit of work at the salon and tells me that Kate had been in there getting it ready for reopening. I know a lot of people who are going to be extremely glad to hear that!

TOTAL DEATHS – 29,427

Wednesday, 6th May

I am awake early feeling quite chirpy this morning, but not as chirpy as my resident robin. He is waiting for me as I go to the gym this morning, hopping around the grass picking at the grass seeds. As I start my workout he flies over and positions himself on the post outside of the door looking directly in; he is so incredibly brave. I go out on the decking to see him, forgetting I am not Snow White, and he flies off but it makes my day to see him! I wonder if there is a nest and babies?

I look forward to *GMB*, Ben Shephard and Susanna are much more cohesive and although they are still ensuring the interviews are challenging, I don't have to put up with the Piers Pantomime. I watch a lovely story about a mother and daughter being reunited after the mother was in a coma for four weeks after contracting coronavirus – Susanna asks many questions and mentions Kate Garraway's husband; they are searching for any hopeful news that they can give her. I haven't heard a recent update, so I suspect there is no change and again I feel horribly sad for her family.

There are calls for a public enquiry into whether the Government acted early enough and whether we went into lockdown at the right time. With the official figures apparently now showing over 32,000 deaths and the UK having the highest deaths in Europe I agree that there are questions to be asked. Should we have done something earlier? Were we too casual in early March? Apparently, Boris Johnson was continuing to shake hands even as some scientists were advising the Government to end hugging and handshakes in early March. In a paper released from SAGE on the 3rd March there was a strong signal being sent about good hand hygiene in stopping the spread of the disease, but he continued to ignore it. Forget lessons being learnt from this experience, were they really culpable for our country losing more people than we should have done?

And then, a massive scandal is reported, the senior government scientist, Professor Neil Ferguson, whose advice led Britain into lockdown, has resigned after it was discovered that he allegedly allowed his married lover to visit him! He had been dubbed Professor Lockdown, and for all of those members of the public who have been missing their boyfriends and girlfriends and partners and complying with the rules, this must be incredibly infuriating. There is a debate with a psychologist who was saying that it is really important for families to be able to get together as soon as possible; she says that she has never been so concerned about the mental health of people and that going forward fears hugely for suicide rates.

Over £100 million has been raised for the NHS fund – 30% of that from Colonel Tom but also credit to the other people who had attempted fund raising events – climbing stairs and hundreds of other activities.

Ahead of Sunday, predictions are beginning to emerge about what the relaxation of the lockdown rules will mean. If shops are allowed to open it could mean that changing rooms are closed and customers are encouraged to shop alone. Potentially out-of-town outlets may be prioritised for opening. Some DIY stores have already opened. Retailers will be hoping for a bounceback and trying to shift bargains, but will people want to go shopping?

Will we be able to see our loved ones? For me this is the critical one. The Government are looking at whether a small group of friends could meet in a group or 'bubble', but this still could cause a risk to vulnerable groups, so, whilst it would be hugely welcomed it would terrify me that it would cause a second spike.

Our workplaces will no doubt change irrevocably and already I am talking to many companies about what this could look like. Whilst there are many ideas about staggering shifts, putting screens up in open plan areas, one-way walking routes for staff, canteen closures, etc., there is still a big issue about the use of toilets.

Public transport will be incredibly difficult so I don't see myself going to London on the train for many months and if I did it looks as if there will be severely reduced services.

Schools and universities may be able to make a phased return but they would need to really be sure they could keep pupils and teachers safe, so they would have to consider limiting class sizes, groups of pupils attending on different days, redesigning classrooms and staggering break times, so whatever the answer it will mean continued disruption for parents. There is still a level of uncertainty over whether it will be possible for students to go to universities in September or whether everything will be online. That would be a completely different experience for them and I wonder how that would affect fees.

But this is all speculation and I know that we will all be glued to our televisions on Sunday for the Prime Minister's briefing to hear what the rules are going to be.

In other news, rumours are that Rishi Sunak is preparing to wind down the furlough scheme from July in order to ensure that people don't get 'addicted' to it. What a strange statement! But of course, it needs to wind down, as the idea is to get people back to work, and we certainly want our furloughed people back to work as soon as we can.

Boris Johnson was back in the Commons facing quite a grilling from Kier Starmer for the first time today. There were questions regarding the tracing app with fears that 'malicious' fake alerts could be generated by the new NHS contact-tracing app, and also privacy, which could render the app unusable. The trial is due to start tomorrow but this puts a big question mark above it.

The day is another busy day of calls and webinars with some more good ideas coming out from the team on how we can reshape and come up with new products. Our income is still grim, but we are working hard on sales calls, so I remain hopeful.

The briefing tonight is taken by Robert Jenrick, Yvonne Doyle, Director of Health Protection for Public Health England and a first appearance for Nikki Kanani, Medical Director of Primary Care for the NHS.

He starts in the typically grim tradition of these daily briefings with the figures that are so dreadful to hear – we have exceeded the 30,000 figure with deaths up 649 from yesterday, although the number of deaths involving COVID-19 that have been registered stands at 32,898.

Once again the Government has to admit to failing to hit the target of 100,000 coronavirus tests per day for the 4th day running with only 69,463 tests yesterday – it has only actually hit the target on two days and that felt like a bit of a fudge.

Nikki sounds understandably nervous and talks about how difficult it is for her personally but wanted to reassure people that the NHS is still here for us and then it is over to Yvonne for the slides. Transport usage is still down but less so for motor vehicles again. New cases have increased on the slide quite considerably, but this is down to more testing, which is apparently what we want. The amount of people in hospital has declined. But less good news on the deaths, very tragic but it is coming down and it is a rolling average, so we are seeing a slow decline.

Apparently, tonight we have the last supermoon of 2020, a flower moon, so I decide to change our evening routine, which has got a bit predictable! I have a webinar at 6.30 to 7.30 p.m. so after that I think we will take to the hot tub to enjoy a bit of star gazing. I have already changed next week's evening routine by booking calls with all of our friends in the evenings. We don't watch much television but generally after dinner we will sit on the sofa and watch a film every night and I feel the need for change.

The moon is indeed beautiful.

TOTAL DEATHS – 30,076

Thursday, 7th May

I wake up at 7.00 a.m. this morning, a bank holiday treat, and have allowed myself a rest day from the gym. I glance at my phone and see a message from my best friend, Sarah. It is simply saying that she won't be joining the girls' call tonight but as I read it my heart tells me that something is wrong. After all these years of friendship my intuition is never wrong. I often feel the need to phone her or she feels the need to phone me, and it is always just at a moment when something is happening and we need each other, so I trust my intuition and call her. She sobs into the phone. Her mother is dying and has very little time left. She is in a care home and has Alzheimer's and has been gradually deteriorating over the last year. Sarah, despite her cancer, has been visiting her almost every day for the last year until lockdown happened and has been trying to stay in contact with her by phone but it is difficult. Her level of understanding and recognition of Sarah varies from day to day and she has also been suffering from water infections, which have made her quite aggressive. Along with Sarah's cancer this has been a particularly difficult situation. I have watched Sarah get more and more worn out trying to deal with it and it has worried me tremendously. We both knew that her mother didn't have long and sadly with Alzheimer's patients you know that they don't want to be that way, but it doesn't make the process any easier. People talk about the blessed relief for the sufferer but for the carer the whole situation is riddled with guilt, fear and uncertainty, yearning for the person who was, knowing that they will never be that person again and wanting to do the best for them. We sob together on the phone; she is concerned that when she saw her the other day she said that she would bake a cake and be back and now she can't go back to say goodbye to her. Knowing that it could be any time now this is really hard for her. We agree that might be better as her mother may slip peacefully away without the fear of death. Who knows? There are no right answers in this situation, but it breaks my heart I can't just be there and hug her. Over the last thirty-two years both of us had issues with our mothers but they had played such a massive part of our lives. I tell her that I will get to her as soon as the lockdown allows and we will have our own memorial. But I find it hard to concentrate as I can't stop thinking about her.

I try and focus on work but some news grabs my attention. Matt Hancock has had a fall from grace and certainly my opinion has changed about him considerably. I had never been sure about him but now I have truly seen another side of him – a bitter and manipulative view which is really unpleasant. As a coach to women I spend a lot of time talking to them about gravitas and tone and how to present points in an adult way that keeps people connected, staying warm and powerful and it really galls me when women are accused of being overly strong or emotional and bossy. When you know that, if a man had spoken in that way he would be considered passionate and challenging. The news reports on the debate in the Commons where a Labour MP (Shadow Health Minister Dr Rosena Allin-

Khan) who has continued to work as an A and E doctor, was publicly put down by Hancock and accused of using the wrong tone in her questioning. She asked Hancock first about the Government's failure to test front-line workers for COVID-19 and also whether the lack of testing has cost lives and many families being torn apart in grief.

He told her to take a leaf out of the Shadow Secretary's book in terms of tone. WTAF? I can't believe what I am hearing. Her challenge was absolutely valid and her comment resonates with what much of the country is feeling, and she is seeing these tragedies first hand, but to publicly patronise her and suggest she speaks more like a man is outrageous, condescending and verging on sexist. I watch the video several times to see if I am missing something, but I see nothing but a sombre and knowledgeable tone, and if anything, far more respectful than other journalists such as Robert Peston. Personally, I would have been a lot harsher and have seen many exchanges where childish taunts and antagonising language are thrown around by the boys on the benches. You can almost see from his body language he is lying.

I honestly feel outraged and feel that he should resign. To tell a practising doctor during a pandemic to watch her tone is disgraceful. Did she touch a nerve and was it that he did not want to hear the truth, or is he just egotistical?

I spend the morning on webinars and calls. The weather outside is beautiful and I find it hard to concentrate on work; it all feels so pointless today. Finally, I set up my office outside, under the big umbrella on the table, and the sunlight and cool breeze help me to refocus.

Dominic Raab starts the briefing with Jenny Harries – I find it difficult to watch him tonight after the episode in the Commons. The grim news continues; 539 people died having tested positive. It is very much a holding press conference. He reminds us that three weeks ago he set out five tests and now there were calls to ease up on the restrictions and people wanted information, and he reminded us that this wouldn't happen until Sunday.

However, the update is that the R level is between 0.5 and 0.9 and the rate of infections and deaths are falling but the virus is not beaten yet. He mentions that it is time to think about the next phase and how we will live and work whilst maintaining social distancing. He tells us that the Prime Minister has been directing ministers to look at the roadmap and there will be detailed guidance to inform us all. They have apparently set milestones, some which we might be able to implement immediately, and others might take longer. He does warn us that anyone seen flaunting the guidelines will be dealt with!

Jenny reveals the slides – 82% have apparently only left their homes for the right reasons – well done us! 44% of adults working from home – changed from 12% last year. Testing is not going well (not Hancock's words) with targets being missed for the 5th consecutive day, but apparently a technical hitch in the lab over the weekend! This number is a combination of tests carried out on the day but also those sent to individuals, which may not have been returned. Yesterday, Boris Johnson ramped up the pledge saying that 200,000 tests would be carried out a day by the end of this month. I wonder if they had a conversation about it.

My son phones me to say the offer on his house in London has been accepted and he is instructing solicitors. I pray this goes through as he really needs something positive to focus on, and as it is empty, if it all went smoothly, we could exchange in six weeks.

I cook dinner and get ready for the girls' quiz night. If I am honest, I am not in the mood either; my daughter had asked if I wanted to cancel it, but it will do me good and

I can't wait to have a drink. The call is fun and the girls are upbeat – the quiz is hilarious and it is wonderful to be connected with them all, including my friend Lauren in California. We have been through so much together over the years, this is just another challenge for us all. We break at 8.00 p.m. to all go outside and clap and we think of Sarah and what she is going through, so very mixed emotions. When it is over Keith and I sit in the hot tub for an hour watching the full moon again.

TOTAL DEATHS – 30,159

Friday, 8th May
Bank Holiday , VE Day

A post-workout pot of tea, some delicious poached eggs with avocado on toast and some time to sit and write in the garden. That's how I roll. The day is beautiful and I sleep till 7.30 a.m. – waking at 6.00 a.m. with that delicious moment of knowing I can go back to sleep. It is ridiculous – I no longer have the pressure of getting up for early trains and rushing around early. I could sleep till whenever I wanted, no one watches the hours I work or what I am doing but I have made a commitment to myself to exercise every morning and work full days and I am sticking to it. I realise that I have hooked into the only thing that I can control, and somehow I feel that if I let go of it, I would let go of everything. It is almost obsessive and very unlike me.

I message Sarah – she is still waiting for news and still incredibly anxious – I feel it and feel so frustrated I cannot help her. Hopefully, my flowers will arrive tomorrow, not that it changes anything but at least she will have something physical to look at and know I am thinking of her.

So, today is VE day, Victory in Europe Day, which marks the day in 1945 when Britain and its allies accepted the unconditional surrender of Nazi Germany, bringing the war in Europe to an end. Massive celebrations have been planned and booked for this day, and the unprecedented step of moving the May bank holiday to the Friday was taken, and then it was all cancelled due to coronavirus. But we still want to mark the day in whatever way we can during lockdown. At 11.00 a.m. we have a two-minute silence to think of all those brave people who saved our country, a bit like all those brave people who are saving us now. The Prince of Wales and the Duchess of Cornwall lead a two-minute silence and as I bow my head to contemplate, one of my neighbours revs up a lawn mower. I consider going to find them and telling them to stop but by the time I did the two minutes would be over. So disrespectful. The commemorations began with a flypast over London by the Royal Air Force display team, the Red Arrows, whilst RAF Typhoon jets flew over Cardiff, Edinburgh and Belfast. There is also a lone piper playing near Balmoral at a war memorial and a gun salute from Edinburgh Castle marking the beginning and end of the silence. However, the event was notable for its lack of crowds; this would normally be a packed event.

There is a plan of events for anyone who wants to join in the VE commemorations:

10:50: A service in Westminster sees Commons Speaker, Sir Lindsay Hoyle, lay a wreath on behalf of the House of Commons. Lord West laid a wreath on behalf of the Lords.

11:00: A national moment of remembrance and a two-minute silence.

14:45: BBC One will play extracts from Churchill's victory speech to the nation announcing the end of the war in Europe is broadcast.

14:55: Solo buglers, trumpeters and cornet players were invited to play the 'Last Post' from their homes.

15:00: The country is invited to stand up and raise a toast as Churchill's speech was broadcast – the suggested toast from the BBC is: 'To those who gave so much, we thank you'.

20:00: Another BBC One special will feature Welsh soprano, Katherine Jenkins, actor, Adrian Lester and singer, Beverley Knight. We are invited to sing along to a rendition of wartime classic 'We'll Meet Again'.

21:00: The BBC will broadcast the Queen's pre-recorded address.

21:30: Spotlights will light up the sky in Portsmouth to recall the experience of blackouts during the war. The local council says the lights are also to remind people that lighter times will come again. We are also encouraged to go out and light up the sky.

The day is celebrated in many ways by the nation – Facebook shows photos of street parties all over the country, there is bunting, champagne and cream teas. People dress up and sing and share food, supposedly abiding by the rules, but there are also photos of people at parties not social distancing. One report on the news from a street in Portsmouth shows a mass of people and even though the presenter said they were social distancing the picture told a different story.

At 15:00, the same time that Winston Churchill addressed the nation on 8th May 1945, BBC One broadcasts his words: "We may allow ourselves a brief period of rejoicing, but let us not forget for a moment the toils and efforts that lie ahead."

Not one to miss a Churchill moment, Boris Johnson also addresses the nation referring to the virus outbreak, saying: "It demands the same spirit of national endeavour as shown during wartime." He continues by recognising we couldn't have the parades and street celebrations of the past, but he still wants to recognise that we owe everything we most value to the generation who won the Second World War.

Later we hear from the Queen who addresses us from the White Drawing Room at Windsor Castle, where she too is in lockdown with Prince Philip, who is amazingly 98. Visible on her desk was a photo of her father in his Admiral of the Fleet uniform with RAF Wings. There was also another photograph behind her of herself as a teenager with her father, mother and sister, with Winston Churchill on the balcony of Buckingham Palace on VE Day in 1945. She was due to be at Westminster Cathedral today and I bet she was wishing she could be out there today with London full of cheering crowds, but maybe this will make it even more memorable for us. I remember back to the 50-year VE celebrations when Elly was 3 and LJ was 5 and we had a massive street party. I made a huge cake and iced it as a Union Jack. I marvel at where the years have gone.

Once again, our Queen addresses us. She says:

> *"I speak to you today at the same hour as my father did, exactly 75 years ago."*
>
> *"His message then was a salute to the men and women at home and abroad who had sacrificed so much in pursuit of what he rightly called a great deliverance."*
>
> *"The War had been a total war; it had affected everyone, and no one was immune from its impact. Whether it be the men and women called up to*

serve; families separated from each other; or people asked to take up new roles and skills to support the war effort, all had a part to play. At the start, the outlook seemed bleak, the end distant, the outcome uncertain."

She talks about her sister and her on that day and then finishes with reassuring words:

"Today it may seem hard that we cannot mark this special anniversary as we would wish. Instead we remember from our homes and our doorsteps."

"But our streets are not empty; they are filled with the love and the care that we have for each other."

"And when I look at our country today and see what we are willing to do to protect and support one another, I say with pride that we are still a nation those brave soldiers, sailors and airmen would recognise and admire."

"I send my warmest good wishes to you all."

There is a lovely programme on the television about Colonel Tom Moore and his contribution during the War. Again, I am incredulous – he truly was and is a hero.

But, coronavirus is still relentless, despite the celebrations there is still the sadness of over another 600 deaths.

TOTAL DEATHS – 31,241

Saturday, 9th May

My sleep has been disturbed and fragmented and I wake at 5.00 a.m. In my dreams Sarah and I were young again and she was living in her house with her parents in Bournemouth. She was 18 and I went to her house to get ready to go out on a Friday night. Her mother brought us food whilst we were getting ready; a typical mum thing to make sure we did not just go out and drink on an empty stomach. Her father was downstairs in his chair watching television. Her mother is trying to tell me something but I didn't understand, and then the dream raced on and I am somewhere else, and I think I could see my dad in the distance. I try to find him but it was foggy and I couldn't see anything through the grey mist. I wake up sweating and disorientated. I try to get back to sleep but just doze fitfully

When I wake again at 7.30 a.m. I looked at my phone. Sarah had texted. Her mum had passed away that morning at 5.15 a.m. I feel so sad for her but wondered about the strange and crazy dream. Was that just because she had been on my mind for the last two days or was it the spirit world trying to connect with me? I imagine the dream meant that Annie was telling me to look after Sarah as she left – who knows? But whatever the case I will look after her. Apart from my children she is the only person I would fight or die for. Her text says she is not in a place to talk so I can only message her back. Once again, the temptation to just get in the car and go to her is so strong, but I will be putting her at risk too. I want to hug her so badly and sit with her during this terrible time. Having lost both parents, I know how surreal these days are following the death and particularly as she can't busy herself with funeral arrangements or having a stream of visitors. We both know that it was the best thing for her mum, she had no quality of life at all, but that does not make the reality any easier to cope with. I feel inadequate and horribly sad. Hopefully, the flowers I had ordered on Thursday will arrive today.

No hangover for me today; after a large glass of wine with our VE celebration dinner in the garden I stopped drinking, so I am ready to work out my frustrations in a hard session this morning. I have signed up for extra PT sessions and this morning is a small group session with Olivia and Elly joining from Lincoln. It is lovely to see her on screen and I thank God for Zoom once again.

Sarah texts with a picture of the flowers; I apparently made her cry again. Not my intention but I think she meant it in a good supported way.

After the session I get on with some jobs in the garden. There isn't a huge amount to do but I like to have achieved something – my strange compulsive obsession that I appear to have adopted.

To take my mind off Sarah I am contemplating a few big questions. How can we be sure that there will not be a second wave of coronavirus? Can we catch it again? And will a vaccine work? These three questions are important to me in knowing how I will feel about coming out of lockdown. I do some research and certainly the 1918 pandemic that killed more than 50 million people came in multiple waves

– with the latter being more severe than other waves. In subsequent flu pandemics, apparently, this has been the case too. Without question, this is the worst pandemic we have had for a hundred years. Greater hygiene is obviously helping us, but even so, if there were a second wave how many more people could die? And without a vaccine and no widespread immunity we could be in deep trouble.

There appears to be strong feelings amongst scientists that second waves occur after the capacity for treatment and isolation becomes exhausted. The concern for our economy that is driving strong calls for lockdowns to be eased and the frustration of isolation could be a threat, unless the susceptibility of the population to the disease falls below a certain threshold or we get a vaccine. We already know that won't happen quickly, and as we are still not entirely clear on the real rate of infection, it feels like there is still a high risk that we are vulnerable to resurgence – and we already can see more people out and about and on the roads.

So, can we catch it again and will this happen every winter? My research is a bit fruitless as we seem to know very little. I read about our immune system, which seems to come in two parts, the first part being ready to go and leap into action as soon as it detects something and releases chemicals and white blood cells that can destroy infected cells. However, it appears that this system is not specific to coronavirus, apparently it will not learn and won't give us immunity to the virus. So, what we need is the adaptive immune response to kick in – this part includes cells that produce targeted antibodies that can stick to it to try and stop it. We also need something called T cells. I Google T cells and it tells me they are also called T lymphocytes that originate in the bone marrow and mature in the thymus (look at me getting all scientific!) They are sent to peripheral tissues or circulate in the blood and once stimulated by the appropriate antigen they secrete chemical messengers called Cytokines, which stimulate the production of antibodies. But this takes time and studies suggest that it is around ten days to target the coronavirus and for the sickest patients to develop the strongest immune response. Now I understand why patients must shield. Apparently, if the adaptive immune response is powerful enough then it could leave a lasting memory of the infection that will give protection in the future. So, the question for me is that if someone only had mild symptoms will they develop a sufficient adaptive immune response? And all the more reason to keep my immune system healthy, which I have to say it feels it at the moment due to lots of juicing, plant-based foods, sleep and exercise.

Science has never interested me but now it affects me personally I am immersed! I research how long immunity lasts and apparently it is like our own memory, it remembers some infections clearly but can forget some. For example, measles is highly memorable, and one bout gives lifelong immunity. The problem with coronavirus is that is has not been around long enough to know how long immunity lasts, so we can only take clues from six other bad viruses including SARS and MERS in which antibodies have been detected a year later. In summary, it seems the question is not so much whether we can become immune but more how long for? I can see now why the Government is nervous about using immunity passports to get us out of lockdown; it could cause a dangerous false sense of security.

Transport Secretary Grant Shapps takes the briefing and announces 346 more deaths today – this is probably under reported as this often happens at the weekend, however, it is almost half of the 621 fatalities announced last week. The Government has missed its target for 100,000 tests daily for the 7th day in a row. Professor Van-Tam joins him and says that he is confident the reproduction R rate is below one. Well, it might be for now but as pictures come in from around the country of people out at beaches and in parks, and after yesterday's street parties, I would not be surprised if there wasn't a whole new wave of infections. They call them Covidiots – those who still refuse to see the danger. Van-Tam cautions that we need to be very cautious and careful about what happens next. Yep, that definitely feels that people are being cautious and careful.

After dinner we decide to search for a new TV series to watch – with it looking like lockdown being at least another month we can easily get through 30 episodes of something!

Sunday, 9th May

I wake up early as normal but manage to sleep until 7.30 a.m.

I decide this week I want to ramp my walking up to at least eight miles. I also need to do a week's shopping so I work out a way that I can walk to the supermarket and Keith can pick me up with the shopping. As I walk, I think about Sarah and I think of something practical I can do. When I get home, I write a poem about Alzheimer's and email it to her. I also know that she loves memories and if I can find enough pictures of her mum and her beloved dad, I can make them into a photobook. I know she will treasure having something to look at and remember her mum. I only have a couple of photos from her wedding, but I search her Facebook and consider whether I could ask her son, Thomas.

When I get home I watch some news. Airlines are talking about a 14-day quarantine for people coming into the country. This really does feel like the proverbial horse has bolted – surely if we had done this from the minute we locked down, like other countries did, we would not have suffered the deaths that we did.

The testing debacle is still raging on – I had put a lot of hope in tests and today I had a call with a friend. She lives with two other women, both of who are in the nursing profession. Apparently, they have all had coronavirus. The first lady to get it tested positive. My friend does not work for the NHS so couldn't get a test but had exactly the same symptoms. The third friend also had the same symptoms and got tested but it came back negative. When she recounted her experience of the test, they apparently did not push the swab right to the back of her throat and only swabbed the entrance to her nose. Some research shows me that there are many questions about testing including the comment: "there are throat swabs and then there are throat swabs – is it a dangle or a good rub?" There has also been some discussion around whether doctors testing people's throats at the back are looking in the wrong place, as this is a deep lung infection rather than a nose or throat infection. Surely the test should be done when the person is coughing and bringing up some virus to detect? There is also a question over storage; if the samples are not correctly stored and handled the test may not work.

Stories in several countries suggest people are having up to six negative results before finally being diagnosed and other tests have proved defective. So, regardless of how many tests are achieved, do they really help? I feel my lifeline slipping away.

There is a new strapline to replace Stay at Home; Stay Alert – Control the Virus. Scotland is quite keen to let us know that they were not party to this decision and that it lacks clarity, to the extent they will not be changing this in Scotland. I agree, perhaps we should be saying 'Isolate or Intubate' – maybe that will focus the minds.

And then it is 7.00 p.m. and the moment the UK has been waiting for – the briefing from the Prime Minister. Boris comes to us from inside No. 10 sounding strong, focused and resolute. He starts with the typically rousing speech and thanks to everyone that we have begun to expect but then says something that really jars with me.

> *"Because you understand that as things stand, and as the experience of every other country has shown, it's the only way to defeat the coronavirus – the most vicious threat this country has faced in my lifetime."*

> *"And though the death toll has been tragic, and the suffering immense, and though we grieve for all those we have lost, it is a fact that by adopting those measures we prevented this country from being engulfed by what could have been a catastrophe in which the reasonable worst-case scenario was half a million fatalities."*

Did I hear that? Prevented a catastrophe? Worst-case scenario was 500,000? Really? I am sure that I heard early conversations saying they wanted to contain it under 20,000 and I am sure all of those who have lost loved ones will not feel that we prevented a catastrophe?

He continues: "We must control the virus and save lives," and bangs on about how much we have all lost. He tells us that he wants to provide a plan to beat the virus and provide a sketch of a roadmap of what is to come and when, and how, on what basis we will go ahead. He says he will be presenting more details in Parliament tomorrow and taking questions from the public in the evening. I am sure he will be mobbed. He adds that he has consulted across the political spectrum, across all four nations of the UK. He tells us that though different parts of the country are experiencing the pandemic at different rates there is a strong resolve to defeat this together. Not so sure about that Boris, Nicola Sturgeon seems to feel differently.

He goes on to remind us again that we cannot move

forward unless we meet the 5 tests. He also tells us that it is a conditional plan; whilst the death rate is coming down if they see things change, they will immediately resort to previous lockdown. He reminds people of the R rating. It is below 1 but only just, although it has been up to 4. We must keep it under 1. He also mentions 2 more things we must do; reverse the deaths in care homes and have a world-beating system for testing people and tracing their contacts. He recognises that we have done a lot on this but that we have so much more to do.

He says we have not met the five conditions so now is not the time to end the lockdown. First is a change of emphasis – and he is going to announce the first, careful steps to ease the lockdown.

He then announces the plan to ease the lockdown.

Step One

He starts with: “And the first step is a change of emphasis that we hope that people will act on this week.” These words worry me a bit as people won’t understand a ‘change of emphasis’ – they understand ‘rules’.

He tells us:

> *“We said that you should work from home if you can, and only go to work if you must.”*
>
> *“We now need to stress that anyone who can’t work from home, for instance those in construction or manufacturing, should be actively encouraged to go to work.”*
>
> *“And we want it to be safe for you to get to work, so you should avoid public transport if possible – because we must and will maintain social distancing, and capacity will therefore be limited.”*

So how will they get to work then? He immediately answered me by saying: "Go to work by car or even better, by walking or cycling."

Next is exercise, and from this Wednesday people can take more, and even unlimited amounts of outdoor exercise. He even says we can sit in the sun and play sports but only with members of our own households. I can already imagine the number of picnics and football games in the parks tomorrow.

He insists that they will enforce fines if people are seen breaking social distancing. If we fulfil these conditions in the next few weeks and *if* the R continues to go down, then other changes may come in. He goes on to explain what might happen in June and July.

Step Two

At the earliest by 1st June – after half term – he tells us that they believe they may be in a position to begin the phased reopening of shops and to get primary pupils back into schools, in stages, beginning with Reception, Year 1 and Year 6.

This is to try and let secondary pupils facing exams next week get at least some time with their teachers.

He stresses again that all of this is conditional, it all depends on a series of big 'ifs' and that it depends on the whole country to follow the advice, keep social distancing and to keep the R down.

Step Three

By early July, if and only if, the numbers support it, we will hope to open some of the hospitality and other places, but only if they are safe and socially distanced.

He also says that to prevent reinfection from abroad he is now serving notice that people arriving by air will be quarantined coming in but there is no date on this. Just about eight weeks too late Boris. He states clearly again that everything we do will be driven by science, data and public health. Well, if that truly was the case then we should have stopped shipping in planes full of fruit pickers and allowing anyone to enter our borders without checking in any way.

He reiterates that he will be monitoring progress and if there are problems they will not hesitate to put on the brakes. He tells us we have been 'coming down the mountain' but adds that sometimes that can be the dangerous bit.

He finishes by telling us about all the wonderful efforts everyone has been making and revs up to a breathy crescendo as he goes through the list of people to thank, to the point that I wonder if someone has speeded up the autocue!

This is not what people were expecting – nothing about when they will be able to see family members again and there are so many different messages both from the UK and in England and this is not going to be helpful to people to know what they can do. Facebook explodes with posts from people with the confusion and messages from people who are working out how to stretch the rules.

I am filled with terror at the thought of what is going to happen tomorrow – we are going to hit a second wave faster than we can blink. My newly found 'respect' for Boris has very quickly disappeared.

TOTAL DEATHS – 31,855

Monday, 11th May
Official Lockdown, Week Eight

Boris has thrown the country into chaos and confusion and I have a water infection. Not a great start to the week. The water infection is due to the stress of the weekend; I used to suffer a lot when I was stressed and I was only thinking the other day how I had been clear for a while but this one is bad. I down cranberry and medication and drink three bottles of water. At 8.00 a.m. Sarah phones me and we have a long chat about how she is feeling, and she takes me through the dreadful time she had over the weekend, talking to her mother via FaceTime in her last hours. Normally in this type of situation her days would be filled with arranging the funeral and clearing out her mother's possessions, but she can do nothing but sit at home and grieve. My heart breaks for her.

I have to cancel my PT session so get straight to work although I am in a lot of pain and am not able to sit still for long. Piers is back with a bang this morning after his COVID-19 symptoms and having a week off. He had been tested but thankfully he was negative. Well, he certainly has come back to a complete storm and he is relentless. And today I must agree with everything he says. He absolutely slams the announcement from last night branding it 'complete nonsense', particularly the new 'stay alert' slogan. He says exactly what I was thinking, that we are given a 7.00 p.m. Sunday night slot to watch the PM's address, expecting to get loads of detail, which clears everything up, and instead you get a whole load of (in his words) "Flim flam, bluster, and his bellicose fist-pumping rhetoric."

Susanna adds she was hoping for them to give some detail of when she can see her family again. She says that we all needed a bit of comfort or hope that we could see a friend. I know I certainly do. But Piers was mostly seething about an update from Dominic Raab. During an interview with the BBC he suggests that people could visit their parents at the same time as long as they maintain social distancing. It was since clarified by the Government, who said that you could see only one parent at a time. So how does that work, one of them has to go in another room?

Piers says: "When Dominic Raab initially said you could see one parent, then he upgraded it on the *Today* programme to both parents with a two-metre distance, the Government has now clarified – you can't. You can only see one." The Government had to apologise to the general public for getting the guidelines wrong.

Labour leader, Keir Starmer, declares that the statement has raised more questions than answers and voices concerns that England, Scotland, Wales and Northern Ireland could end up pulling in different directions. He says that: "The Prime Minister appears to be effectively telling millions of people to go back to work without a clear plan for safety or guidance as to how to get there without using public transport. What the country wanted tonight was clarity and consensus, but we haven't got either of those."

However, in a video last night, Matt Lucas, Little Britain star, summed up the mood of the nation with an incredibly hilarious, and very accurate impersonation of Boris saying: "So we are saying don't go to work, go to work, don't take public transport, don't go to work. Stay indoors if you can work from home, go to work, don't go to work. Go outside, don't go outside. And then we will or won't something or other." Nailed it Matt!

Despite the complete and utter ridiculousness of this chaotic pantomime, the underlying fear is that people will just do their own thing, and this will cause us more problems.

At lunchtime we now get the guidance that from Wednesday we should aim to wear face coverings on public transport and in shops. Again, horse, stable, door! Apparently, we might need to wear these on public transport for the next couple of years until a cure is found! However, they are not going to fine people who don't wear them. I order some on Amazon before they turn into a ridiculous price again.

A glimmer of hope for the sports fans. No professional sport will take place, even behind closed doors, before 1st June, but after that they may be allowed to be played without crowds.

The briefing tonight is at 7.00 p.m. – a bigger platform for our Churchillian 'wannabe'. So, will we get more clarity or more guff? Whitty and Valance are his wing-men tonight. They have published more details on the plan, but the leaders of Scotland, Ireland and Wales have pretty much rejected it, going with their own plan. He starts with the figures 1,921,770 people tested, 223,060 tested positive, which is an increase of over 3,000. 11,401 people are in hospital.

He repeats pretty much what he said last night. He adds that his advice to people and the updated messaging is now to 'Stay Alert, Control the Virus'. That means for many people staying at home, working from home, limiting contact with other people, limiting distance to two metres, wearing a face covering, and if anyone has symptoms everyone needs to self-isolate. Apparently, if we all stay alert and follow the rules, we can keep the R down and continue to save lives.

First question from the public: "Can we see people at the park – what if they are already there, do we have to leave?" Boris says you can go to the park on your own to exercise or with people from your household but if it is someone outside of your household it should just be you and them and keeping two metres apart. He looks desperately at Chris Whitty who explains they are trying to allow small steps.

Another question about schools: "How do you propose that people go back to work if there are no schools open for them at the moment? His response is that we are hoping to open primary schools' Year 1 and 6, and then bumbles around for a while until he eventually hesitantly says you should speak with your employers. If you don't have access to childcare or can't get them back, it is only fair to regard that as an inability to get back to work, and he feels sure that employers will agree with that. No discussion as to whether they will get paid. Not much help there really!

Another question from the public: "Yesterday you left the nation with more questions than answers, why have you been so vague about which businesses can open. When will we get clarity?" Boris replies with a big thank you to her for the 'excellent question' (bet he hated her for asking it!) and then neatly sidestepped it.

The first journalist is more challenging and asks why people could go and see each other but grandparents could not look after children – she also said that some workplaces were not ready to go back to work. And with a cheeky final question asks if Whitty and Valance approved the 'Stay Alert' message change! Boris does not answer that one but passes over to Patrick. Patrick does not really answer but just uses the word 'alert' a lot. Chris fudges it by saying they have been involved in everything but neither he nor Patrick are communications experts.

I can't be bothered to listen anymore; I am just going to stay in for another three weeks.

TOTAL DEATHS – 32,065

Tuesday, 11th May

I am up early and marching, yes marching. I am full of energy, inspiration and positivity today. After speaking to Sarah yesterday and hearing her voice and knowing that she is OK my anxiety is reduced. We still have to go through the grieving process, but I always worry when she is anxious and stressed, as I know this is not good for her cancer. As I speed-walk around the Common, I think again about the business and am now looking forward to having a day on sales, hitting the phones, reconnecting with clients and getting some business in. As I think about the future of the business and how much I have enjoyed being at home I realise that my life probably will never return to the crazy travelling that I was doing; all of the frantic early starts to get to London to deliver long courses. I feel that all of the clients who were very anti non-face-to-face training are starting to change their views and if we can prove that it can work then maybe I really can achieve better balance in the future. It's a bit like working from home. All of those companies, who always said that it was impossible for staff to work from home but have needed to, will have to reconsider flexible working and the reasons they give for insisting people come into the offices. For that reason, it is quite exciting to consider the future and the possibilities. I get home feeling energised and immediately see a couple of messages from people wanting to talk about some virtual sessions. You see, you just have to ask the universe and it delivers!

The country is still confused about the messages from last night and there are major discussions on *GMB* about what does it mean? How will they police it? And does anyone really understand what we can and can't do?

I think that the very sad thing is though that we are a disunited kingdom today, no longer a United Kingdom since Nicola Sturgeon has said that they will not take up the new slogan preferring to keep the 'Stay at Home'. In England we can now play tennis, work out in the park and sunbathe if we keep social distancing but in Scotland and Wales we can't. Nicola is still issuing strong and clear messages but how will the people in those countries feel in the next week or so when they see what the UK is doing.

A rather amusing argument ensues between Piers Morgan and Edwina Curry – the challenge is around cleaners. Piers bellows at her: "So, I can have a cleaner in my house providing they socially distance. Does that mean I can have my son as a cleaner in my house? No, it is breaking the rules!" Fair point I suppose. And then guests were left wondering whether one of the guests, Tobias Ellwood, an MP, disappeared from a live link without notice. Was it Wi-Fi or had he walked off in frustration at the hammering he was getting over the clarity of the new rules? He had been trying to defend Boris and say that he had been clear and when Piers launched at him, they ended up shouting over each other and as it got more agitated, he disappeared. Several government ministers have now boycotted *GMB* over the car crash interviews, although Matt Hancock later chose to appear on *This Morning* with a far more relaxed interview with Holly and Phillip.

The EasyJet boss comes on to run the gauntlet with Piers and insists that he will be flying us on holiday in July to Spain and Portugal. He says that we will have our temperature taken at the airport and we will have to wear masks for the whole flight. But if that means we can travel I am very happy to comply with that. Sarah and I are due to go to Portugal in August so that sounds hopeful. He challenges the 14-day quarantine issue and says it will be impossible to enforce this.

We hear that Chancellor Rishi Sunak is about to start the winding down of the furlough scheme, which is due to run out at the end of June and is costing us £14 billion a month. Some of the hard-hit industries fear widespread job losses if the support package is removed but rumours are it will be a gradual winding down.

Boris does not appear at the briefing tonight. I wonder if that is anything to do with the fact that the death toll is 627; a massive rise from yesterday. Business Secretary Alok Sharma is in the firing line, assisted by Professor Powys and Sara Albon, CEO of Health and Safety Executive. The figures show over 2,700,146 tests have been taken, including 85,293 yesterday. Nearly 3,400 cases have tested positive since yesterday, worryingly, that figure does not seem to be going down. There has been 672 fatalities. Once again, we are told that we need to stay alert and control the virus.

Sharma reminds us of the 5 levels of alert, which determine the amount of social distancing that will remain in place. Since 23rd March we have been at Level 4, with high and rising COVID-19 but apparently, we are now in a position to move to evel 3 in small steps.

I realise that my book has already got to 87,000 words – how did that happen in nine weeks? I am writing around 1,300 words a day and if lockdown continues for another couple of months, and if I keep going like this, it is going to be a ridiculous size. Time for some serious editing! Well there is the proof for me. One hour's writing a day for three months and you can produce a book!

It is a nice evening, so we have dinner outside tonight.

TOTAL DEATHS – 32,692

Wednesday, 13th May

Today is the first day of easing the lockdown so I just want to check that we all understand the rules because yesterday looked like chaos outside and on the news. So, all together now:

- I can go to the park and meet one other member of another household, if we promise to keep 2 metres apart, but if I know two people, I have to choose one. Hopefully, I will have a favourite. If the other person wants to see me do, I see them the next day? If the favourite doesn't feel like meeting me can I choose the other person?
- I can have a cleaner in my house, but I can't allow a family member to clean my house.
- If you are 4 you are able to go to school in June, but if you are a university student (fully paid up for tuition and accommodation that you haven't seen for two months) you can't go. When you go back to school (i.e. the 4-year-olds) you may not touch anything or anyone and have to maintain social distancing. (This

is ideal because 4-year-olds are great at sitting still and not touching people or things.)

- I can take my young child to a school to mix with 15 other children, but I can't let my mother or aunt look after them if they don't live in my house.
- I must go to work if I can, but if I can stay at home and work, I should do this. Whatever, I shouldn't use public transport – but I can exercise and watch the empty buses drive past.
- I can go to work with my colleagues and sit 2 metres apart, but I can't sit with them in their garden or at the park if I have already met one person from another household.
- I can now go out and exercise as much as I like; I can play tennis or golf (can I sail?) but only with people from my household. What if they don't play tennis? Can I choose the one person from the other household, or possibly the other one who wasn't my favourite? You can meet at the park with a personal trainer and exercise but if 2 people from another household you know join the session you have to go – or ask one of them to go?
- I can drive as far as I like to go out and exercise providing it isn't Wales or Scotland.
- If you are over 70 or at risk, you can pretty much stay at home forever. But the slogan isn't 'Stay at Home' it is 'Stay Alert' so, if you are an alert over-70 can you go out?

- We all can stay alert – we are not sure what we should stay alert for or to but so long as we stay alert, we will all be safe. But if you break the stay at home rule you might be fined, so be careful. What if we don't stay alert, will we be fined for that?

I hope that has clarified for anyone who didn't understand! I truly just had that conversation in my head – I feel delirious; lockdown fever must be taking hold. As I said, I am just going to stay home but I am sure that the Covidiots are going to stretch those boundaries.

Kier Starmer and Boris have a head-to-head today after Starmer accuses Boris of misleading MPs over care homes. Starmer says that they were told right up until 12th March that it was very unlikely anyone would become infected in a care home. Boris denies that the advice had said that and accuses Starmer of being selectively misleading. I am with you, Starmer; we cannot brush over the chronic and sad death toll in the care homes and I am sure there will be a major investigation.

Housing Secretary Roger Jenrick leads the briefing today. Over 87,000 people were tested yesterday – missed the target again. There were an additional 494 deaths.

He reminds us of what has been done already, establishing a new COVID-19 alert level system based on the R value and the number of cases. This alert level determines the amount of social distancing measures in place. He tells us that throughout lockdown we have been at Level 4, meaning that the virus is rising. Through the measures, we have bought the level down to 3 and will carefully modify the measures and gradually ease the lockdown.

Today we are told we are allowed to move to a new house – fingers crossed for LJ then! There is new governance today, which means that now you can view houses and show homes. Hang on! So, you can go and view someone's house but you can't go to your parents'? Ahh, he announces open houses are not allowed! Well I am not sure how many people are going to want people to bring any viruses through the house and have to disinfect the house every time. But still it does allow some movement.

Over to Jenny Harries for the slides – testing 87,000 plus taking the test total to well over 2 million. Apparently, we have capacity well over that, which will take us forward. She tells us that they recognise these are only laboratory confirmed cases. She shows us lots of flattened curves on the charts – the number of people in hospital with the virus is 15% lower than a week ago.

Questions come through from the public. The first question from someone in theatre and performing arts who asks if the Government will pledge to protect these industries. Jenrick nods sagely and demonstrates concern for this sector. He reminds them of the support package, i.e. the furlough scheme, the self-employed treasury schemes, but there is nothing new.

The next question is about families meeting up in 'clusters' or 'bubbles' – when will this happen? A reminder is given that you can meet up with one person if you maintain social distancing and then back over to Jenny to answer about the longer term. Jenny fields it well and states that she knows those who are isolating would love to see people for their mental health. But she tells us it is very technical – if you have large families, that could end up with a large family gathering. So, no real answer yet, but quite rightly so.

TOTAL DEATHS – 33,186

Thursday, 14th May

Another incredibly sunny morning; this has to be the best weather for years and years. Could it possibly be a sign of the shutdown around the world or is it just a co-incidence? My walk is lovely through the woods and I take a different route back looking at the houses and thinking about the people living in them. Some people have gone to town looking after their gardens, and for others the weeds are almost covering the doors, as if they haven't even opened them for weeks.

Today there is a lot of debate about the dreadful story of the woman who was spat on and later died of coronavirus. Belly Mujinga was a railway ticket office worker and died after the man spat at her and claimed he had the virus. Another colleague was also assaulted at the same time and both of them fell ill. Belly had underlying respiratory problems and was admitted to hospital and put on a ventilator. The attack was described as despicable and British Transport Police are trying to trace the man. I wonder if this is the new murder crime of the future; not guaranteed to kill but certainly could scare a lot of people, and for police and people trying to keep order this is going to be terrifying.

There is a big debate on *GMB* about the care home scandal. Were people really being sent back to care homes with COVID-19? One care home owner talks about how they lost 13 people in their 'family' in one week and then had to take people in as they would have gone under if they hadn't with no support. It really does feel like care homes were afterthoughts. *GMB* is a bit light this morning as ministers are still boycotting appearing on the show!

I get started on work. This week we are having a magnified sales attempt and we are all trying to get through to as many clients as possible and see what we can bring in. Yesterday I managed to achieve the grand total of £4,000 – but that is worth celebrating! Every penny is vital at the moment. But we had a good staff meeting and find that we are starting to open some new markets. We all seem to have our heads around the fact that this is now the way forward and we are a virtual learning organisation. Personally, I had a frustrating day yesterday as my laptop wasn't coping well at all; it had double vision and juddered and whirred like a crazy thing and became so hot that it was impossible to use. Sounds a bit like me on a bad day! Apparently, it is a result of all the Zoom calls, and as I needed a new laptop, £550 of my hard-earned sales has to go towards a new laptop. We cannot risk it crashing whilst we working towards becoming virtual experts!

Globally the number of people who have been confirmed to lose their lives from COVID-19 is close to 300,000 with 1.5 million recovered. I can't get my head around that number. I know people are lost in tragedies and in the third world, but this was flu, how could this have happened?

Sarah texts me to tell me her mother's cremation is on Tuesday. I tell her that I am going to block that out in my diary so that I can be thinking of her and if she wants to message me, she can. She is going to go and sit on the bench dedicated to her father and think of her. I am so sad and desperately want to be with her.

The briefing today is by the Transport Secretary, Grant Shapps, joined by Professor Jonathan Van-Tam this evening. First, the figures, and today he proudly announces testing has apparently hit an all-time high. Over 126,000 tests carried out yesterday; a 45% rise from the day before and the highest to date. Still quite a way to go to reach the target of 200,000 by the end of the month, as announced by Boris. There is still confusion around whether this is tests or testing capacity, which is about the theoretical number of tests and not the actual. An increase of 3,406 cases tested positive and 11,000 people in hospital, which is down from last week. Sadly, a further 428 people have died with COVID-19. Again, more tragedy for the families, although that is a drop from yesterday.

The first question from the public is around universities and what will happen with the students due to go to university in July – should they pay? Students will be thousands of pounds worse off and will miss out on the student experience if they do not physically return to university. I totally agree; why should they start paying for student accommodation if they are not using it?

There is a lot of discussion about the new antibody test and when it will be rolled out and who will get it. Shapps describes it as 'very exciting' and a very reliable antibody test. Apparently, this will be rolled out rapidly as soon as it is practical, first with hospitals and care workers. However, it will take time to understand whether having the antibodies protects us against infection. So, once again, we are back to the immunity issue. If we can't work out immunity, I have to question whether it is actually worth doing an antibody test.

The clapping at 8.00 p.m. is louder than ever. As I clap I think of all the workers and the toll the last two months must have taken on them and their families, and I feel angry again at the idiots who can't just be patient and keep everyone safe so we can all come out of this together. I know it is only a minority but that is all it takes to spread it. They are not giving a moments thought to the people they may infect, just considering that they are probably young and fit enough to be immune.

TOTAL DEATHS – 33,614

Friday, 15th May

It is insane that it is Friday again and the week has passed so quickly. My routine is still as strong as it was on day one and I think that is why the days don't drag. I would never have believed I could be so disciplined, and as I exercise and get dressed I wonder if I will be able to carry this forward to my life after lockdown. That's what I think I will call it LAL – not LOL, LAL. Not the 'New Normal 'because my life was never normal in the first place.

Again, *GMB* is a quiet and relaxed affair without Piers Morgan. I wonder if they will furlough him now that no guests will come on the show to talk to him!

There is a debate over the schools reopening. The National Association of Head Teachers has significant concerns about the expectations the Government is putting out that children would be able to return to school before the academic year ends. They stated that the proposals to send certain children back before this academic year would be impractical and unworkable in most schools.

This is a major blow to employers and also to parents, as this would free up parents to go to school, but they are right to insist it cannot happen until it is safe for them to do it. Another debate follows about British transport workers and keeping them safe. Yes, this is critical, we need to do this, particularly after the news yesterday about the death of Belly.

It's a busy day today, starting with coaching at 9.00 a.m. and straight on to a meeting at 11.00 a.m. and then a presentation to be written for a conference that I am speaking at, plus a whole host of emails and issues to be addressed. Unfortunately, amidst all this my new laptop is being updated and it takes up a phenomenal amount of time this afternoon.

Sad and worrying news comes through about a midwife, Safaa Alam, who passed away aged thirty in Birmingham after contracting coronavirus. She was thirty and my future daughter in law Sophie is a midwife around that age. I look at her picture – a beautiful girl who people described as passionate about her job. And even worse, she died just three weeks after the death of her family too. I hear so many stories where multiple people are affected and it really is so heart-breaking, to lose one person is devastating, but two.

And before I can blink, it is time for the weekly pub call. Before the pub we have an update on what has been a phenomenal week of sales and calls. The whole team have pitched in and there are lots of possibilities and hopeful signs coming in from clients.

Matt Hancock, Jenny Harries and Dr Nikita Kanani lead the briefing tonight.

Apparently, we are bringing the R down cautiously and are now ready to start moving to Level 3 and start to restore freedom to the country. He reminds us that we have initiated the first step but reiterates that this weekend he hopes that people can enjoy the good weather without taking risks.

A question on nurses pay rises comes in – will they now be seen as having a highly skilled profession and get an increase? Hancock says that he totally agrees with this and says last year they got a pay rise of 15% but now is not the time to enter into a pay negotiation. I think I read somewhere that nurses were paid around £25,000 a year at the moment, which seems ridiculously low. I for one, once this is all over, will expect them to be handsomely rewarded for what they did. But then I guess it is the same as army cadets, I don't think they get paid much either and yet when push comes to shove, they are the people out front protecting us. Silent warriors, all of them, who is going to fight for them?

Interestingly, Transport for London is to raise the congestion charge by 30% to secure a bail-out from the Government of £1.6 billion after it took a large hit of 90%. How is that supposed to encourage people to travel by car rather than public transport? Free travel is also being suspended for under 18s and for the over 60s, or those with a disability during peak hour.

We have the Friday night girls Zoom call and it is hilarious – we have an amazing quiz with lots of laughs and it is lovely to see everyone. This is what life is really all about; support, friendship and laughter and we are so lucky to have each other and all be safe and well. It is also wonderful to have my daughter and her best friends on the call too – so I finish the call feeling blessed. Once again, my gin and tonic was just a tad too large and it isn't long before I fall asleep on the sofa.

TOTAL DEATHS – 33,998

Saturday, 16th May

As always, I wake at 6.00 a.m. I try to go back to sleep and have just nodded off again when the alarm goes at 8.00 a.m. This morning we have an online group PT session, so I go up to the gym to get ready and get warmed up. I love the group sessions as I push myself much harder and my daughter also joins, so it is fun to do it together.

The weather today is slightly cloudy and cooler but still some sun is peeking through and I consider what people will be doing today. The public have been urged to think twice before heading to England's beaches and country parks, but I am betting that they will all be out and about, and I wonder if they will be social distancing. I see lots of people on Facebook talking about going to meet people and I just can't help thinking that if I was to go and meet with one of my friends, particularly Sarah, I wouldn't be able to resist giving them a hug. I guess we will find out over the next few weeks. Yesterday, I had an idea that we could go out this weekend and take a picnic to the park early evening for a change, but today I don't want to, I feel really nervous and anxious about going out. We can have dinner here in the garden instead. There will be plenty of time to go out when this is all over. For a second I wonder if I am becoming agoraphobic.

A dreadfully sad article comes up about a funeral for a nurse and his parents – apparently, they all died within weeks of each other after contracting coronavirus. Keith Dunnington was 54 and had been a nurse for over thirty years, he died at his parents' home and then both his mother and father died days later. Nurses, doctors, emergency services and well-wishers lined the streets to pay a very moving tribute to the nurse. Perhaps everyone thinking of flouting the rules this weekend should read this article and think about how they could infect the whole family.

But no, far from thinking about flouting the rules a group of protestors have gathered in Hyde Park in London to protest against the lockdown. They carry banners suggesting that the lockdown was a hoax to get more control and one protestor tells the news agency: "I never thought I would see, in my generation, the suppressing of civil rights over a fake virus!" What?? The police are booed as they lead away a protestor and guess who it is? Piers Corbyn, the brother of Jeremy Corbyn. He had taken a megaphone and was proclaiming that coronavirus and 5G were linked and calling it a pack of lies to 'brainwash you and keep you in order'. Apparently, they say that the Coronavirus Act that has gone through Parliament has made changes that infringe our freedom. They blame it all on the press and suggest the figures reported on cases and deaths are untrue and the actual risk of dying was minimal. And, would you believe, the very place I was thinking of going to for a picnic, Southampton Common, also had a protest there.

In lighter news, today it should have been the Eurovision Song Contest. It would have been another year of 'nil points' for us due to Brexit and in fact I am sure that people might have given us minus points if they could, so no loss for us but I feel for the people who had been selected to sing. Apparently, there will be an alternative event to celebrate the acts that were due to take place and the best songs from the past. Deep joy!

As I watch the news it is as I feared; crazily busy on the roads with police stopping day trippers heading for Brighton. Apparently, millions of people defied the pleas to stay away and headed South. So, what will this mean for us in three weeks?

Today's press briefing is chaired by Education Secretary, Gavin Williamson aided by Dr Jenny Harries. A further 468 people have sadly died today and I feel the UK is creeping towards the 40,000 mark.

The briefing is very much focused on the reopening of schools. Williamson once again reiterates that primary and secondary school pupils could be ready to return in just two weeks – they are looking at Reception and Years 1, 6, 10 and 12 to return. For Years 10 and 12 they may come back 'on a limited' basis. This is to help them to plan for exams next year. He insists that the Government are looking at the best scientific advice with children at the very heart of everything. He warns that there was a consequence to schools not opening and that children would miss out.

We watch our Saturday evening live concert in the hot tub with a drink and I head to the sofa to play with my new laptop. Another Saturday night gone.

TOTAL DEATHS – 34,466

Sunday, 17th May

This time last year I was in Vegas. My Time Hop on Facebook shows me that I was at the MGM Hotel in Vegas delivering a coaching culture programme to 650 managers with an amazing team of people. It was the most incredible event, which took some military precision to organise, and we had the best time in the evenings and afterwards. How could that be just a year ago? It was just one of many amazing trips I had last year to Dubai, Saudi, Lisbon, and many other countries. I don't think my life will ever be like that again. And I try to decide if it is a good thing. There was excitement and fun but there was also a lot of stress and packing, sitting in airports, unhealthy food, late night dinners and burning the candle at both ends. I hope that in the future I will still travel but maybe for pleasure and at a less frenetic rate. I still haven't quite got my head around the fact that we possibly won't have a holiday this year, but maybe, if we can't fly, we can go somewhere nice in the UK. Even the idea of a weekend in a lovely hotel in the lakes sounds amazing now.

I go out early for my Sunday walk and think about this and what my life might be like in the future. I want to do more speaking although the thought of standing up in front of a large group of people again seems alien to me. The week before we went skiing and came back to lockdown I did six presentations to large audiences and I felt so confident but it has been two months now and I have no idea how long it will be before I can do it again. I seriously hope I don't lose my mojo.

I watch the news and there is some data about who is catching coronavirus. Apparently, it is unlikely that children will get it but it is unknown whether they can spread it.

Today Zoom has finally creaked and groaned under the strain, with a very public issue during the briefing tonight. Journalists were unable to ask questions live on screen due to the technical issues, so they had to submit written questions! I am not surprised; I have been wonderfully impressed at how robust Zoom has been. I hope that they manage to sort it out as I have a major week of calls.

Alok Sharma takes the briefing and tells us that today there have been 170 deaths, this is the lowest since lockdown began. This is almost 100 fewer than the 268 reported a week ago. Still horribly sad for all of the families but if that is true then we can be hopeful. However, I don't feel that hopeful as often the numbers on Sundays and Mondays are lower. However, the infection rate in the UK has gone up and is close to the point where the virus starts spreading rapidly. It is now between 0.7 and 1.0 and needs to stay under one in order to be under control. We are still to discover the effect of the changes to the lockdown from last week. The number of new cases is still falling but not as quickly as in the past.

The Government also announces that the clinical trial for a COVID-19 vaccine at the University of Oxford is progressing well and announces that there will be £93 million to speed up a new vaccine research lab. This is on top of the £47 million already invested in the vaccine.

AstraZeneca have apparently finalised a global licensing agreement with Oxford and the Government, which means that if the trial is successful, 30 million doses will be available for the UK by this September. Sharma guarantees that the UK will be at the front of the queue for getting the vaccine. That does sound ambitious and it is very confusing as some days we hear that a vaccine is a year away, some days we hear that we can't produce one at all and today we hear 'maybe September'.

TOTAL DEATHS – 34,636

Monday, 18th May
Official Lockdown, Week Nine

It's Monday morning and I am feeling rested and ready for the week. I have a great workout- it just goes to show what two months of discipline can do. I feel a bit cross with myself as I had always made so many excuses for why I couldn't do it but perhaps if I had really made it important I would have done it. That's the thing isn't it, whether things are a priority and I had never made it a priority

Well, it will be interesting to watch Piers today as the proverbial has really hit the fan! A petition asking for him to be sacked gets 50,000 signatures branding him 'one of our country's most heinous public figures'. According to the *Mirror*, the petition was started following thousands of complaints that were filed to Ofcom about the combative interviews he had conducted and also what they describe as 'ITV letting hate crimes on transphobia and discrimination over gender identity play out'.

Certainly he is less abrasive today with his panel as they discuss whether it safe to go back to school and the view is very much that we are not in a position for the 1st June and that other countries are doing it differently, i.e. 6 children to a class, and that is possible to socially distance, but with 10 or above it is impossible. A study[2] suggests children in wealthier households are studying significantly more at home than their poorer counterparts, adding to worries about a growing divide.

Some happier news comes through on ITV; young Ethan Beardow, the boy with cerebral palsy who, inspired by Colonel Tom, took on a 10,000-metre challenge before his 10th birthday is getting a treat. They join him at the Etihad Stadium, Manchester, the stadium of his beloved football team. He is an absolute delight; he has raised over £50,000 and is so excited to be on television. He receives a football goody-bag and is told that when games resume, he can come back and be a mascot. I start to well up; these types of stories keep us going through these terrible times.

Public transport is starting to crank up slowly again and we are told that we will see crowd-control measures at major stations from Monday. There will be security guards on duty and limits on platform and carriage capacity implemented. Sorry to appear monotonous but isn't that a bit late?

There is still massive criticism of the Government, particularly of the fact that early on in the crisis they said that they were locking down care homes but clearly didn't, their lateness in acting, the fact that they seem to keep changing their advice and Piers suggests that we are following the worst scientific advice ever. However, we are not the only country who are disappointed with their government. In Belgium, the Prime Minister, Sophie Wilmes, was greeted by staff at a hospital in Brussels on Saturday with a silent protest. A clip shows that as the cars arrived the waiting staff lining the road to the hospital all turned their backs. Wow, that is powerful. According to local press the protest called for increased acknowledgement of their efforts and against a decree that stated they wanted to recruit unqualified staff. I wonder what would be an appropriate protest for our NHS?

Raab appears for tonight's meeting. But where is Boris? We have not seen anything of him since Sunday's announcement and I wonder if he is on paternity leave? Or is he doing a Trump and hiding from the press? The figures for deaths have dropped to 170, although the figures are typically lower than the other five days of the week due to fluctuations in reporting. However, the death toll in the UK still remains the highest in Europe

During the briefing, Raab is asked if the Government could commit to having the new tracing app ready for the return to school on the 1st June. He says that he can't commit even though at one stage the Government had said they wanted it up and running by then, and simply tells us that it is still the intention to roll it out. He couldn't be more precise as to when, but they are making pretty good progress. Very vague.

He is joined by Jonathan Van-Tam who reports on the app and stresses it will only be part of the tracing scheme, the rest is the tried and tested methodology used by Public Health England. Raab uses the words 'roadmap with maximum conditionality' – wow, that is a real catch-all and seems to translate into the fact that no one really knows what could happen and when because there are too many variables!

There have been claims that many coronavirus cases (potentially up to 200,000) have been missed, as, until today, loss of smell was not listed as a symptom. There were questions about why it had not been formally listed before but Van-Tam counters with the fact that most infected people with loss of smell would have had other symptoms.

He did accept that the coronavirus test results needed to be processed faster.

Van-Tam also said that the Government was currently considering plans for whether people from different households could be allowed to meet up as part of a so-called 'bubble'. If they do, I do hope that they do this after the bank holiday weekend. It is set to be a scorcher and it could mean people giving up on the guidelines completely.

Some worrying news from Van-Tam that the autumn and winter may provide even better conditions for COVID-19. Is that when we will get our second wave I wonder? That is my worst nightmare, that we get ourselves back to work, starting to earn and then three months later a second wave knocks us back again, I am not sure whether our economy can take that.

But in more encouraging news, the first results from the vaccine human trials are looking positive with eight volunteers showing that they are producing an antibody response on a par with that seen in people who have had the disease. More importantly, the vaccine has been deemed safe for use in humans.

After a wonderful Skype with a client I haven't spoken to in a few years, and a nice dinner, we settle down to *Killing Eve*.

TOTAL DEATHS – 34,636

Tuesday, 19th May

Yesterday was a good day and I felt that as a team we achieved a lot, so I wake up feeling positive. We had an energising meeting, lots of sales calls booked and some interest in some of our new products plus a few concrete bookings. I feel determined this morning as I wake up early and go for my walk. I also managed to prep some scripts for my filming session tomorrow, so I feel a bit more in control of my workload.

But it is Sarah's mum's funeral this morning. I consider whether I should just go there, but she has said she wants to be alone, so I take her at her word and text her to arrange to meet for a walk the Saturday after next. She has her radiotherapy injection on Thursday and is normally wiped out for a few days, so if we wait a week, we should be able to have a socially distanced walk and chat. I cannot wait to see her, but I know it is going to be hugely emotional and so hard not to give her a cuddle.

An article I read last night is playing on my mind and it was really making me wonder how the whole approach to the virus has been dealt with – it is something that has been troubling me for a long time and I have tried to be supportive of the Government, but have I been blind? The article was titled 'MPs call for release of government scientific advice' and it was urging the Government to publish scientific advice that underpinned the key decisions that had been made in combatting the virus. An influential committee of MPs, led by Conservative MP, William Wragg, who chairs the Public Administration and Constitution Affairs Committee, wrote to the Prime Minister following criticism over the secrecy around the expert advice the Government receives. The Government are always talking about following the science and for the most part I have blindly agreed that we should, but am I right to think that?

The article in the *British Medical Journal* states that the Government seemed to be confident that they were well-prepared when coronavirus swept East Asia. Their initial response, which provided the-four-pronged plan of 3rd March, to contain, delay, research and mitigate was originally supported by all UK countries and apparently backed by science. Since then we have discovered that the UK's response was neither well-prepared nor adequate. On 30th January, the WHO declared a public health emergency and urged governments to prepare for the spread of the disease, but the article suggests the UK ignored these warnings.

Apparently, it further documents that by 11th March, Italy had taken decisive action and was in full lockdown, followed closely by Spain and France, but SAGE rejected lockdown believing that the population would not accept it. Patrick Vallance chaired SAGE. A day later the Government apparently inexplicably announced a move from the containment phase in its strategy to the delay phase. Chris Whitty explained it was no longer necessary to identify all new cases and that testing capacity across the UK would be 'pivoted' to hospital patients, NHS111 and teams working on contact tracing became confused and overwhelmed. The standard containment approach recommended by WHO of find, test, treat and isolate, which had worked well in countries that were being successful in suppressing the viral spread, was abandoned. No restrictions were put on entry via ports and airports and no future plans prepared for community case finding, testing and contract tracing. Procurement and delivery of testing resources was ineffective. On 19th March the status of COVID-19 was downgraded from Level 4 to Level 3, which enabled the required standard of PPE to be lowered for staff in hospitals and to nurse patients in non-infectious disease settings. At the same time, the *BMJ* alleges a reckless policy of discharging older patients from hospitals to care homes without testing allowed the virus to spread. Apparently, Vallance initially rejected measures for stopping mass gatherings and closing schools and floated an approach to build up some degree of herd immunity. When subsequent modelling estimated that 250,000 people might die, but social distancing could limit it to about 20,000, a sharp reversal of policy followed. By the time we formally announced a lockdown almost 2 months of potential preparation and prevention time had been squandered. Evidence now seems to suggest that if we had intervened earlier, as in the case of Italy, we could have reduced viral transmission by about half and saved many lives. The fact that politicians were allowed to attend SAGE meetings has been highly questionable and negated the independence of SAGE.

The conclusions from the article were everything that I had been thinking over the last few weeks but seeing them in writing in this way is very worrying. Can we trust or believe anything that we are being told now? Have huge amounts of people lost their lives needlessly? I can't stop these thoughts coming into my head.

My day is busy with calls and meetings – a great potential collaboration with another organisation and some catch-ups with clients. It is beautiful sunshine outside but until 3.30p.m. I don't even get to stick my head outside of the door and decide to take my phone call in the scorching heat.

I book a walk with a friend on Sunday; the first time I will drive my car, meet someone and walk. The most time I will have spent away from my husband in ten weeks. It feels exciting and scary but something to look forward to.

Environment Secretary, George Eustace, takes the briefing tonight. *Where is Boris*? He is joined by the Ministry of Defence's Chief Scientific Adviscr, Angela McLean. In recent days only two people have been at the briefing; I bet they all love this part of the job. I can picture them running for cover as someone shouts round the office: "Who wants to take the bullets for Boris tonight?"

A further 545 deaths are announced today sadly, although Angela tells us that apparently deaths are falling. 10,000 people are still in hospital and being treated, so there is still a horribly scary chance of hitting the 40,000 mark. A quarter of the deaths have been in care homes. Those people in care homes who can understand the implications of the virus must be living in terror.

With regard to tests, 89,740 tests provided – again, still short of the Government's promise of 100,000 daily, so there is no way they are going to make it to 200,000 by the end of the month. And we need so many more. Really disappointing.

Farmers will need more help to harvest crops and urged furloughed staff to help and earn some more income! Apparently, unemployment has gone up by 50,000. But as Eustace called for workers to take up fruit picking as a second job the recruitment website crashed, and visitors were met with a 'service unavailable' message.

Some difficult questions from journalists, particularly going back to the 12th March and the decision to stop the programme of test and trace. Yep, with you there. Some very fudged answers on that one.

I finish work late today as my work is piling up and my brain is still mulling over all of the data.

TOTAL DEATHS – 35,341

Wednesday, 19th May

I get up at 6.00 a.m., go straight in the gym and hit the desk early – yesterday had been crazy, in a very good way. There was an explosion of activity and sales and calls, which filled me with hope and also anxiety, as there is so much to be done and followed up on. It feels like suddenly we have some momentum going and clients are changing from worrying about the virus to thinking about the future and what needs to happen, which is really hopeful. We are still not actually taking a lot of money but I don't expect to at the moment, there is always a timeline between discussions about programmes and actually delivering, but it appears, with virtual learning, that timeline is shortened. At last a benefit! When you don't have to book rooms for people suddenly things become a lot easier! For the first time in two months I can really see how we might have a future.

Piers is still sulking about the 21-day boycott of the *GMB* programme. Yesterday he lashed out at Cabinet Minister Therese Coffey for her comments that she was 'proud of the Government's testing during the coronavirus pandemic' – ranting that it was scandalous. Halfway through a conversation with Doctor Hilary about President Trump taking an unproven drug (yes really, but don't pretend you are surprised!) to prevent coronavirus he interrupted the flow, when he noticed that Therese had been interviewed on *BBC Breakfast*. "That must have hurt!" he rages, "she has just said we can look back on our testing, how we increased capacity with pride". He goes on to brand testing as a spectacular failure and slams down his tablet in a childish fit.

Today's interviews include some good news stories of someone who has recovered after forty-two days in a coma, an interview with Jean-Claude Van Damme about keep fit videos, but most importantly, an interview with the national treasure, Colonel Tom Moore who has been knighted following a nomination from the Prime Minister. *Sir* Tom Moore – what a star! The only ranting Piers can do is to comment on ministers in the news, show extracts from the BBC and rehash retrospective comments that people have made. Piers is very pleasant and actually quite fun – I wonder if this is the real him or whether he has been told to tone it down so that ministers will stop boycotting the show.

Today I am filming more videos for the Association for Coaching Conference, where I am a speaker, so Keith sets up the camera and lights. It makes a change for him from gardening! His obsession with the lawn is continuing and as I look out it appears as if a gangland murder is about to take place! There are three large sheets of polythene spread out on the grass –he is giving the grass a 'greenhouse' treatment and each day peers hopefully underneath to see if it is growing. Thankfully, it is! The sun is blazing down again, the hottest day of the year to date and pictures flood in of beauty spots and beaches packed with families enjoying the sunshine. I feel physically sick when I see them.

Trump is still insisting that taking hydroxychloroquine will save him from coronavirus. He is also continuing his attack on the WHO, giving it thirty days to make unspecified reforms or to lose out on US funding.

And after a full day of filming, meetings and coaching sessions it is 5.00 p.m. again and once again no sign of Boris. However, he was in the Commons today, being challenged by Kier Starmer over the absence of a tracing system since March.

Oliver Dowden, the Culture Secretary, takes the podium with Professor Stephen Powis and tells us that 363 more people have died in the UK. He adds that for the first time since March there are fewer than 10,000 people in hospital with coronavirus. That still seems a massive amount. However, according to Public Health England there have been zero new cases in the last twenty-four hours and Dowden concludes this is encouraging as are the test results with 177,000 conducted yesterday. Conducted! That doesn't mean 177,000 people were tested, those are the figures we really want to hear but that seems so difficult to get a straight answer on.

Dowd is asked if he would recommend that people use antibody tests that can be bought commercially and he issues a caution. In particular he would not want people to think that if they test positive for the antibody, they do not need to take precautions.

Apart from answering a question about the free TV licences for the over 75s he neatly sidesteps the rest of the interrogation with words such as, "being kept under review", "when it is safe", "if it is the right thing to do".

So, apart from some very sad additional deaths, nothing to report here.

I can't believe another day has gone. I have a great call with a friend Anthea who has returned from Dubai. We have known each other for over 20 years and had many adventures in Dubai and South Africa over the years but now she is living a nomadic existence, unable to return to South Africa and is currently camping in her mother's garden to isolate for two weeks. Is this what it has come to!!

Apart from that it is yet another uneventful evening and I realise that whilst I sit on the sofa and write (or sleep), my interest in watching television is really waning. Could that be because I spend all my day looking at the monitor on Zoom calls?

TOTAL DEATHS – 35,704

Thursday, 20th May

It's another early start, my diary is jampacked with meetings today, so I am not going to get much actual work done. When I get up at 6.00 a.m. it is tempting to go straight to my desk and start work, but I stop myself. That is old behaviours and the new habits I have are to commit to exercise and stick to it, and so I do.

I am shocked by the increase of cars around; it is almost as if it is a normal rush-hour period – has everyone apart from me gone back to work? As I walk, I think about our sales meeting last night. There has been a massive amount of activity from us all, with lots of hopeful conversations and proposals, but as Gemma, our voice of reason tells us, we still need to show her the money! I do feel far more positive about the future and that we may get some business but at the moment the confirmed bookings are still scarily low. We mustn't lose heart and need to keep going. God it feels like an uphill struggle.

It gets to 5.00 p.m. and Priti Patel, the Home Secretary, is on screen, joined by Paul Lincoln, Director General of Border Force and Patrick Vallance. With the required sobriety from the Government, she tells us that deaths today are 351. I have never been a fan of Priti Patel, but I try to watch objectively. She talks about the quarantine issue and that it is the right time to quarantine people as the number of people increases at the airport. Quarantining the new arrivals entering the country will have a much bigger impact, potentially causing a second wave. This feels like a justification of why they didn't do it earlier. She says that the Government doesn't underestimate how hard it will be for families to take these steps, but this is how we will save lives.

It will be tough; people will be required to go into quarantine for fourteen days and provide personal details so that they can be traced to ensure that they comply. She says that they know that the majority of people will comply, but she recognises there will be a small amount of people who will be reckless and she states strongly that the Government will not allow them to put us at risk. Apparently, they will begin to conduct spot checks by mid-June and those who refuse to comply will not be allowed entry. They will be empowering the police to issue fixed penalty notices and potentially prosecution for not complying. Strong stuff. And for people like me whose job is to travel (or was to) it makes it impossible to work and travel. I am not bothered as I believe that those days are over for now.

She hands over to Paul Lincoln to provide an operational update. He pays tribute to the role that Border Force has been busy fighting contraband, including drugs hidden in face mask shipments! Unbelievable! They also have been stopping counterfeit COVID-19 tests. He talks about future plans for travellers.

1. Ramping up communications so everyone knows changes.

2. Contact details, travel plans and where they will be isolating for fourteen days.

3. At the border there will be spot checks.
4. Passengers will then be required to go their place of isolation.
5. Fixed penalties of £100 for not filling in the form and £1,000 for not complying with isolation.

Again, a very stern message about enforcement. I guess that means that tourism and travel is completely out now!

Patrick shows us slides; the R – it is still 0.7 – 1.0, below 1 in every area of the UK but potentially quite close to the 1, so the virus is either flat or declining in most areas. The estimated number of new COVID-19 infections is 61,000 per week at the moment, which is roughly 1 in a 1,000. The epidemic is shrinking, and the numbers are coming down, the lower it is the easier it is to test and trace.

Testing today was 140,497 and 3,287 cases confirmed. So, the testing has ramped up quite considerably.

Priti Patel finishes by remembering the victims of the Manchester bombing and also Lee Rigby who lost his life. So much sadness now and then. I have forgotten what it is like to have lovely news and talk about fun things and future plans.

I take a large vodka to the hot tub.

TOTAL DEATHS – 36,393

Saturday, 22nd May

Another bank holiday weekend and another irony with the weather. This is the first time I can remember in years that both May bank holidays have been bright enduring sunshine; it really does feel remarkably strange that the weather chose this entire period to remain so beautiful. Although, there may be a few showers this morning which will make Keith extremely happy for his lawn. Each day I think it can't last but the 10-day forecast is showing blazing sun continuing. However, this won't be like the Summer of '76 that I remember from our childhood where the heatwave was the key thing we will remember.

I brace myself for the idiots who will be having parties and barbecues as I plan my stay-at-home weekend. The women who founded the Clap for Carers says that it is time for the applause to end on Thursday and suggested that it should become an annual event. She said that the public had shown their appreciation and it was now up to ministers to reward key workers. Dutch born Londoner, Annemarie Plas, who was credited as being the person to start the accolade, spoke on Jeremy Vine's BBC2 show yesterday and said it would be 'beautiful' to stop after the 10th week and move to an annual event. I think this is probably due to some of the backlash of criticism of people holding VE parties and being seen at the weekend across beaches and beauty spots, and she later hinted that the political narrative it is attracting is starting to change and she didn't want the clap to be negative.

I set up for our Zoom workout at 9.00 a.m. It is a wonderful thing to be able to do it with Elly, even through a laptop screen. After the workout I cook breakfast and we carry on talking and have a wonderful catch-up. We take each other for tours around the gardens to see what is growing and after we finish we do a long group chat with LJ. I send them a little money to treat themselves to something – I am not spending anything at weekends, so I like to surprise them. LJ is still struggling to sort out his mortgage and I wanted to cheer him up, but it is sounding more hopeful. If we could get this sorted through during the lockdown it would be amazing. I Whatsapp chat to them whilst I cook tapas for our Zoom party. LJ writes that he wishes we could all be together in the garden having some lovely food together and it makes me well up. Just the simple pleasure of a BBQ and my family around the dinner table, which I took for granted last year, feels so far away. And for Elly, even further in the future, as she would need to stay over and until we are allowed to do that with family, we can't. But I tell them that I hope it might only be a few weeks before we are allowed to meet family members in the home or garden.

The debate over Dominic Cummings has reared its head again with criticism that the top aide to the Prime Minister breached lockdown rules by travelling hundreds of miles and driving to his parents' house when he should be self-isolating. The Chief Adviser was seen in his parents' garden during the visit, but Downing Street has defended him and insisted that this was in line with lockdown rules. They denied that he was spoken to by the police. This has enraged

Piers Morgan who tweeted that if Boris Johnson does not fire him today, he will drive down to see his parents (from a 2 metre distance) for the first time in twelve weeks. Piers, is absolutely furious, and I definitely agree on this one, bearing in mind the discussion I had with my children over breakfast. We agreed we were determined to stay strong until it is safe enough and the rules are relaxed before we meet, so it is pretty irresponsible of Cummings. It has caused a real Twitter storm and I think it is unlikely he will last the day. Alistair Campbell publicly accuses Dominic Cummings of 'utter hypocrisy' and tells the BBC that he thought anyone who had been fined for making a long trip during lockdown could now ask for their money back now that the Government had backed Cummings!

I scroll through the news and apparently spitting attacks on police have risen during the pandemic by 14%, which had understandably made police officers very wary whilst on patrol.

At lunchtime France reveals reciprocal plans for UK arrivals, so if we go to France we will have to quarantine for two weeks. Airlines have said that quarantine rules would effectively kill air travel.

I go to do some garage clearing, watched over by an anxious Keith. This is his domain and he is terrified I will start throwing out his stuff. He is a borderline cable hoarder and there are boxes of electronics and leads kept for that 'just in case' moment! I miss the afternoon briefing but no surprise, so did Boris. Even if he had been booked for today there is no way that he would have faced the journalists baying for Cummings's blood.

I watch later and the short straw is drawn by Grant Shapps accompanied by Jenny Harries. It will be interesting to see what the formidable lady makes of the Government's insistence that Cummings did the right thing.

Shapps reports the numbers as usual and there is an increase of 282 fatalities. He announces £283 million to start moving public transport back to a full timetable. However, he reminds us; those who can still work from home should, and those who can't should still avoid all forms of public transport. Does that include government ministers I wonder? He goes on to tell us that even a fully restored transport service will only be capable of carrying, at best, one fifth of normal capacity to allow for social distancing.

Jenny does the slides and reminds us of the rules. "Using parks is good for mental and physical health but please observe social distancing – stay two metres away from people from outside your household and only meet one person at a time." She adds that 86% of adults have left their homes in accordance with national guidance, i.e. for essentials or exercise. How could they possibly know that?

The slides show that the steady, slow downward trend in hospital admissions in England continues, and across the four nations. The percentage of mechanical ventilator beds occupied by patients with COVID-19 is also falling. The only positive note on the number of deaths is that it is starting to come down on average, Harries tells us.

So, the moment we have all been waiting for – question time. And there it is, the first one from the journalists.

Question: *"Is the advice to parents now that if you don't have extended family nearby, even when you're ill with COVID-19 symptoms, you're allowed to leave your home, travel many miles across the country and isolate closer to your extended family?"*

Harries says: "The scientific and medical advice is to take symptomatic people out of the public domain. The advice is very clear: you self-isolate at home and your household self-isolates with you. If there is a safeguarding issue, for example with an elderly or clinically vulnerable individual or a sick child, there needs to be some sort of safeguard in place."

Shapps hurriedly says: "If younger members of the family can assist then that might be the best place for you to settle and stay while you're ill." (He clearly got the memo from Boris earlier along with the rest of the cabinet.)

Harries adds: "People need to come out of circulation and self-isolate the minute they have symptoms, and stay out of circulation." That's it, Jenny, stand firm.

Next question: *"Did the Prime Minister know that* Dominic Cummings *had travelled more than 250 miles during lockdown, and did he approve this?"*

Shapps says the important thing is that everyone remains in the same place whilst they're locked down, which is what Cummings did – he stayed put and didn't come out again until he was feeling better.

And another killer question: *"When have you said it was all right to resort to other family members if parents are unable to look after small children because one of them has symptoms?"*

Harries says that the public health advice is to take yourself out of society if you have symptoms. If two adults are ill and unable to cope for a small dependent, the guidance has a common-sense element, which accounts for such safeguarding issues like this.

And there is no let-up: *"Are you saying that anyone who becomes ill with the virus they can go closer to relatives no matter how far away that is?"*

Shapps hedges round this saying the rules have subsequently changed anyway. "People can now travel, if you're not symptomatic, any distance to exercise. If you're symptomatic, you have to get yourself locked down in the most practical way," he says. "This will be different depending on different family circumstances," he adds.

And so, it continues with Shapps vehemently defending Cummings and Harries sticking with the company line.

Apart from when asked, *"What are the risks of travelling if you have the virus and would you recommend it?"* she responds by saying, "If people have symptoms, they should self-isolate immediately and stay in their homes. The only exception to this is around risk, i.e. the issue of safeguarding for children or adults."

So, will he stay, or will he go? He clearly has angered the UK by his actions. We need to hear from Boris on this one.

I shower and wash my hair, even though we are not going out it feels nice to clean up a bit for our Zoom call and we have the most amazing evening with our friends Fran and Paul and Kate and Ian. I set the table for our tapas feast and even though it isn't a real dinner party it is nice to eat together. It is one of those nights where we laugh till we nearly cry, particularly when Kate asks me: "Is it just me or is it hot in here?" Priceless. I drink too much but still nowhere near as much as I might normally. Thank God for friends.

TOTAL DEATHS – 36,675

Sunday, 24th May

Today I have my first 'walk date'. The first time I will have significant long-term contact with another human being (apart from Keith) in eleven weeks and I am so excited. My 'date' is Trudy Simmons, who runs the Hampshire Business Women's Group and we go for a long, leafy walk around the beautiful village of Shawford, near Winchester. We have similar interests and backgrounds, and whilst we had messaged before, this was the first time we had met personally. It was wonderful to meet someone new, hear their story and just generally chew over life. The 5 miles pass in a flash. Plus, it meant I got to drive my car and gave it a well-needed run up the motorway. It was so wonderful to be in the car, although it did take me a few minutes to remember where all the buttons were! As we get back to the car I see a beautiful horse coming down the grassy hill and through the gate. I was so taken by the horse I didn't even notice that it had a police officer riding it and she stopped to chat with us. She was patrolling the picture book village of Shawford; I wonder whether she rode up to people's doors and checked if they were having a BBQ in the back garden. Can you imagine how much that would freak someone out if a horse's head appeared over the back gate as you were cracking open the beers? I remember how I used to love horse riding and vow that when this is all over, I will go out to the New Forest and ride again.

On the way home I put the roof down on my car and turn the music up. My spirits really feel lifted today and the weather is lovely, so I plan to spend a lot of it in the garden reading and thinking. I start to think about the last twelve weeks and what I have learnt and how it has really changed my approach to life and wonder how the future will be. I have so appreciated my home and garden, and my husband. As I sit in the garden writing, he is mowing his beloved lawn with the cat chasing him around and I watch, giggling. Maisie is so nosy; she won't leave him alone. I suddenly realise that I have never mowed the lawn since I met him, he just quietly gets on with things and lets me get on with my work. I feel so lucky to have him and I realise I have always been too busy to really appreciate his qualities, his quiet non-assuming self-sufficiency, (I really could not cope with a needy man!), how practical he is, how clean and tidy he is, and how satisfied he is with the small things in life. That is probably the most important factor for a lockdown partner! There is no drama, no highs and lows, just a quiet, steady comfort, who is always ready for a hug. I realise how important it has been for my career over the last 9 years that he was happy for me to travel the world and not be around, never questioning or challenging how little time I spent with him, but just being here to support me, welcome me home and make sure I had everything I needed. Am I going soft in my old age? I think of people who are in narcissistic and abusive relationships – how are people with partners like that coping? After three months they could have lost every shred of confidence that they had. There is going to be a lot of therapy needed after this.

I enjoy the day, sitting in the sun listening to TED talks and pottering in the garden. I then have a compulsive urge to clean the house and steam everything that moves!

Late afternoon, I tune in to the Government briefing, this should be interesting! Boris strides out with even more attitude, and before he even opens his mouth I know what he is going to say. He is like a headmaster addressing assembly and he tells us in no uncertain terms that he is supporting Dominic Cummings. He starts by saying: "I want to begin by answering the big question – are we asking you to do something whilst the Government flouts the rules? And the answer is no." He tells us that because he takes this so seriously, he has had numerous discussions with Cummings and has concluded that travelling to find the right childcare, following the instincts of every father, he would not mark him down. He even says that he has heard some allegations and they are absolutely untrue. Well, there you go – he is not going to take action; I hope he is ready for the consequences. All I can think is that Cummings must have some hold over him.

Then the figures: Over 3 million tests have been done; 259,559 people have tested positive, which is an increase of over 2000; 8,951 are in hospital with the virus, which is down by 11% from last week, and 118 people have sadly died since yesterday. He tells us that we mourn them and resolves to get this country back on its feet. He reminds us of his roadmap of 5 tests and confirms that he believes we can go to step 2 by the 1st June and open schools, recognising that not all will be ready. By the 15th June we can open some secondary schools to help students prepare for exams. He stressed we are making good progress but must continue to stay alert and control the virus.

The questions start and the journalists all press for the same thing, some quite challenging – if Dominic Cummings breached three lockdown rules, was in a confined space with someone with symptoms and went to a second home and you believe he behaved honourable, can people in the same situation do the same? Boris defends him vehemently, repeating what he said earlier, hedging around any specific questions and shutting them down.

Big mistake!

We have a really nice evening with dinner and even do the Saturday quiz sitting outside in the garden.

TOTAL DEATHS – 36,793

Monday, 25th May
Bank Holiday
Official Lockdown, Week Ten

The day dawns with perfect bank holiday weather. Clear skies and a light breeze. On a normal bank holiday everyone would swoop South to the beaches, and I wonder how many will. Particularly after what is happening with Cummings.

The country is enraged, doctors are threatening to resign, people have reported him to the police and Durham Constabulary have been asked to establish the facts around what happened. Scientists warn Johnson that backing Cummings has 'fatally undermined' COVID-19 response and even bishops turn on Boris with a suggestion that the C of E may refuse to work with Government in the pandemic after he has broken the trust of the nation. They even went as far as saying he has gone the 'full Trump'.

James O'Brien, British radio presenter and podcaster, said it all, as he powerfully read out two letters, one written by the Prime Minister to the public and another written in 1982 to his father, Stanley Johnson, by his university master who said: "I think he honestly believes it is churlish of us not to regard him as an exception, one who should be free of the network of obligations, which binds everyone else." James told the public:

> *"Last night the Prime Minister made a fool of every single human being who did what he asked of us. He made a mug of every father, every daughter, every son, every brother, every sister, every nurse, every doctor, every teacher, every paramedic, who have done their best in incredibly trying circumstances to pull together. To prioritise the national interest over personal inconvenience and even misery, Boris Johnson stood before me, and before you, last night and demonstrated categorically that he still believes it is churlish of us not to regard him as an exception, one who should be free of the network of obligation that binds everyone else."*

A report from the Faculty of Public Health has said that the Government's response has undermined essential public health messaging and that it supported, at the very least, an inquiry into the matter. Serious stuff.

I abandon the news for a fun workout with Elly on Zoom and breakfast in the garden.

The day is wonderful, just peace in the garden listening to the birds, listening to podcasts and relaxing. At 5.00 p.m. I have another walk date with my friend Sue, and as I go to get changed I see that Dominic Cummings is about to do a press conference. Really? And in the Rose Garden at No. 10. What? The last time I remember the Rose Garden being used was when David Cameron and Nick Clegg announced the coalition in 2010. I put my headphones in and listen as I walk to the Common.

The interview is a car crash for many reasons; it starts thirty minutes late (fair enough for a busy Prime Minister but not for an adviser). I picture the scene inside No. 10 –

what was going on behind the scenes, was he suffering from nerves, were they making amendments to his script or were they still deciding whether it was a good idea? Whichever, they got it badly wrong. Cummings finally appears, starts with a nervous "Hi,' and "sorry I am late," (which is the only apology that we got) and then, as he starts his monologue, it sounds like someone is playing the bagpipes or using an air horn behind him. This goes on for the first ten minutes as he reads through his detailed statement. He walks us through a day-by-day account explaining how his wife was symptomatic and so was he, there were protests outside his house (umm, weren't we in lockdown?) and threats on Twitter and therefore he decided to go to his father's smallholding to lock down. He insists that he drove straight there without speaking to anyone or stopping for toilet breaks and locked down in a house in his father's land, which was apart from the other houses where his family lives. His reasoning was that if he and his wife both had COVID-19 then he would have someone to look after his son, i.e. his sister and niece. He did not phone the PM as Boris had COVID-19 and 'had an enormous amount on his plate'. They apparently locked down in the cottage and a week later his son was taken ill and had to be blue-lighted to the hospital. He was too ill, so his wife went with his son. The next morning his son was released and so he drove to the hospital to pick him up. A week later he thought he might be ready to go back to work (fifteen days after first symptoms) but was struggling with his eyesight so asked his wife to come with him to do a test drive to see if he was OK to drive for five hours. Bizarrely, they took their son for this test drive. That for me is the weirdest thing, that you would worry about whether you were safe to drive and go out with your son in the car for a test drive. They drove to Barnard Castle, but he felt sick, so they got out of the car and sat by the river, which is where they were seen by someone. On the way back their son needed the toilet (even though he hadn't needed to go on the 260-mile drive) so they stopped at some woods where they all got out and were seen by someone else. The journalists showed no mercy and his story was pulled to pieces by every question. He said that he did not regret it and did not apologise even though pushed on several occasions by the media. He said he did not offer to resign and had not considered it. The response from the journalists and public was still one of horror and disgust, particularly people who have lost loved ones to the virus.

It really was one of the most extraordinary political moments of our time.

Boris then appears at 7.00 p.m. for the press conference. He gives people notice of the changes he plans to make as we move into the next phase of lifting the lockdown, beginning with a summary of those announced yesterday for schools to reopen.

He then announces that outdoor markets and car showrooms will be able to reopen from the 1st June (with proper measures) with a further wave starting on the 15th June that will include department stores. He says the open nature of such places means they represent a lower risk than indoor places.

Professor Yvonne Doyle of Public Health England delivers the numbers. I get the impression she would rather be anywhere rather than in the briefing room today. She reminds us of the importance of keeping the R number below 1. She says it is around 0.7.

The figures showed that 121 people had sadly died today.

Of course, the questions from the media were all about Dominic Cummings and Boris gets increasingly more irritated, evading each question and referring them to Cummings's speech.

When asked if Cummings was safe in his job, Boris says that he cannot guarantee anything, but he claims he does not believe anyone within Downing Street has done anything to detract from official messaging.

The Prime Minister is asked if he is standing by Cummings because he cannot deal with the pressures of his office without him and whether the whole affair is detracting from the vital official messaging.

Boris repeats he will not add anything to Cummings's earlier statement and agrees that official messaging is all-important.

Twitter explodes with indignation and disgust. People are baying for the PM's blood. It is all too much, and this isn't going away.

I need a lie down.

TOTAL DEATHS – 36,914

Tuesday, 26th May

Back to work and I have to say that was one of the best weekends since the lockdown. It was lovely to relax and to see a couple of people; we had so much fun on our quiz and tapas party, I took some time out for personal development and I also did some more sorting and cleaning around the house. I am really beginning to appreciate what it feels like to have weekends off. It used to be that I delivered training throughout the week and the weekend was the time when I caught up on emails and design work. How did I do that? The importance of totally clearing your mind has really hit me now and I am determined that I am going to do everything I can to maintain this when I return to work.

I am aching this morning after all the exercise yesterday and so I decide to do just do some stretches to ease the muscles out. I turn on *GMB* and as expected the news is all about Cummings – thankfully, Piers isn't on today as I think he would have combusted with rage if his Twitter feed is anything to go by. The public have not changed their mind; according to a poll, 70% still want Cummings to resign or be fired. Apparently, this morning the leaders of the political parties will be debating this. It is like an excruciating chess game. Now that Boris has laid out his stall and supported

Cummings, if he does a U-turn he will end up with more than egg on his face, and if he does nothing he faces the whole of the country rebelling against the rules. So, I don't think Boris will fire him, if anything he will be 'persuaded' to resign. As they say, a day in politics can be pretty long.

In the rest of the news there are pictures of Covidiots at beaches in groups of up to 20 clearly not social distancing. The police were called and they were told to be more sensible. Around the country there were other reports of crowds converging to beauty spots.

Shops and car showrooms are getting ready to open and talking about how they are going to ensure social distancing – it is not going to be easy and I really do wonder about who will want to go shopping. I certainly will not be going into any shops for a good couple of months unless I absolutely have to, but I am sure there are people who have missed their Saturday shopping expeditions. Car dealerships say that they are prepared, and it will mean that people have to do test drives on their own – that should be interesting. I wonder if they will have to leave children as collateral!

The scientist behind the UK's leading virus-tracking project has said that two major sporting events held in March caused 'increased suffering and death' – absolutely, watching the scenes at Goodwood and at the rugby there is no way that a large proportion of those didn't end up with COVID-19 and some may have died.

Some news from around the world, and Trump must be disappointed today as the WHO has suspended trials of hydroxychloroquine, the anti-malarial drug as a possible COVID-19 treatment amid safety fears!

Good news for Ireland as it reported no new virus deaths on Monday for the first time since mid-March – I cannot wait for us to announce that.

Spain has said that it will no longer quarantine foreign

visitors after the 1st July and airlines such as easyJet, Jet2 and Ryanair have announced that they plan to resume some flights from airports across Europe soon.

But the main thing people are thinking about is the fact that potentially we will be able to meet in gardens, in 'social bubbles' within the next couple of weeks for BBQs or gatherings. That feels hugely exciting and I am thinking of ways that I might be able to do that and get Elly down too. We have a small flat that we rent out locally, which is empty at the moment, and I wonder if we could use that for her to stay in and have a family BBQ. The thought of it is too exciting but I decide not to get my hopes up just in case something happens.

Matt Hancock strides out for the briefing looking resolute with Professor John Newton. He goes straight into the updated 109,000 tests yesterday, still way short of the end of the month promise, and 134 people died in the last twenty-four hours, and whilst still horribly sad, this shows a consistent drop and the lowest number for six weeks.

He tells us proudly that we are past the peak, flattening the curve, we have protected the NHS and we must keep our resolve. He thanked everyone over the bank holiday weekend who stuck to the social distancing rules. No mention of those who didn't!

The next update is R&D and he tells us that we are leading the way on clinical trials. The recovery trial is the world's largest trial of COVID-19 treatments. He announces a new trial for selected NHS patients, which has already shown that it can shorten treatment by four days and tells us this is probably the most significant discovery to date.

Over to Newton, and then the first questions tonight are from the public.

"Why can't we visit relatives when we are now sending children back to school?"

He appears empathetic (or just grateful it is not a Cummings question) and mentions the changes that are going to be made mid-June and that they are looking at how they can manage to do that in a safe way.

The media then launch straight into the topical subject of Dominic Cummings. Hancock defends Cummings but says: "I can understand why reasonable people would disagree." I noticed this yesterday from Johnson and Cummings – the reference to reasonable people, how strange! He is pressed to admit it is doing damage and undermining what the Government is trying to do but still continues with the defence. So over to Robert Peston, who, in his inimitable style, reminds Hancock that he and his wife also both tested positive and have three children but stayed home, and asked what the difference was. Hancock sounds abrupt as he announces that the difference was that they had childcare and Peston was shut down very quickly. Hancock's patience appears very thin as more questions come through. He says he understands how people may feel angry and is sorry that they would feel that way but feels we need to work out what we need to do next rather than focusing on this. He reminds them that he was at the podium when the guidelines were laid out, which said, if you have adults who are unable to look after a small child, that is exceptional circumstances. Another one quickly dismissed. The last question is about the fear of a second wave and people flooding into small local areas and bringing the virus. They ask what tools they will be given to prevent this, including PPE. Hancock says that there have been some problems with PPE and they have been acting as fast as they can to do something about this. The Secretary of State is much happier to answer this and says he has been talking to the local MP in Barrow in Furness and if there are flare-ups in future there will be local lockdowns.

And here endeth another day in the big lockdown house. My excitement for the evening is deleting a few emails and watching an unmemorable film.

TOTAL DEATHS – 37,048

Wednesday, 27th May

I get up early and have a great workout session with Olivia. I can now easily do 20 press ups and BPM is down to 59 – it is the fittest I have ever been, and that was one of my goals for my sixtieth year, so I feel as if I have achieved it.

I switch on *GMB* as I get ready for work and three items catch my attention on the news this morning.

First, the sad news that two people died in the sea in Cornwall at the weekend. Apparently, people were going crazy in the sea over the weekend and the RNLI were unable to cope. They were pushing back at the Government and saying that they were told that the beaches would not be open so soon, and they had not had sufficient time to put in place the measures that they needed for social distancing and were calling for the beaches to be closed again. This is ridiculous – how did the Government not check with the RNLI that they were ready before allowing this to happen? Of course they need time, if they are taking a boat out to drag idiots out of the water how are they supposed to keep their distance?

Second, an interesting report asking whether the countries who have female leaders had handled the crisis better. Certainly, some of the countries have had lower death rates, such as Germany (8,498 deaths), New Zealand (21 deaths), Iceland, Scotland, with Angela Merkel, Jacinda Arden (who is apparently one of the most popular leaders in New Zealand for a hundred years), Sanna Main (who is only 34 and has 4 female-led parties and who has had 10% less deaths than Sweden) and Tsai Ing-Wen in Taiwan being cited as great leaders during the pandemic. The panel were questioning whether this was because they listened better, were more empathetic and more considered. Boris Johnson's sister, Rachel, was one of the females being interviewed who was actually quite critical of the seemingly all-male approach at No. 10. The argument continued to consider whether Margaret Thatcher or Theresa May would have done a better job. One of the comments was about how women would have preferred to see their mother rather than go to a garden centre (I substitute hairdresser in that context!) I don't know whether it is because they are female or whether it is just that they are great leaders, but it is always refreshing to see women role models emerge.

The interview naturally turned to asking Rachel about Dominic Cummings and Rachel revealed she is worried about Boris as he makes huge decisions, but did say: "As my brother said, nobody has his unconditional support. I mean, I think if I had been Cummings, I would have admitted I had messed up, got on the front foot and said I apologise to all of those who followed my messages."

Finally, a lovely piece appears about an ICU nurse who has worked for forty years in one particular hospital and was nursed back to health on the ICU ward she managed. Sue Snelson was seen leaving with a guard of honour after recovering from twelve days in ICU with the virus. The nursing sister talking about it could barely speak through her tears, as she said it was the worst twelve days of her career after working with Sue and being a friend. It is hard to imagine what that must be like; nursing your own friend on a daily basis and not knowing whether she would pull through, and to be almost dying on the ward you have managed for years; such an irony.

Boris Johnson is going to come under fire today about the Government's handling of the pandemic. No doubt there will be lots of questions about his senior aide, Cummings, as anger refuses to abate. More than 35 Tory MPs have now called for either a resignation or for him to be fired. Yesterday, during Question Time, Secretary of State Hancock was asked if all penalty fines imposed on families travelling for childcare would be reviewed. Apparently 13,445 fines have been handed out for breaching lockdown rules in England up to 11th May. Most of them have been for not abiding by the restrictions on movement introduced towards the end of March, according to the National Police Chiefs' Council, but that doesn't indicate how many people were fined for reasons such as those cited by Dominic Cummings. Just 137 fines were handed out by the Durham Constabulary in the period up to the 11th May.

It is yet another crazy work day for me with back-to-back Zoom calls, and some hair excitement! Keith has gone to do some work at Kate's hairdressing salon, which means he can pick up some hair colour, and just as I am finishing my last call at 5.30 p.m. he arrives back with some ready-mixed colour – my roots are looking so dreadful that I feel disproportionately happy about this. I sit outside and listen to the briefing whilst he carefully paints the colour through my parting; a skill he never thought he would have to perfect!

Tonight at the briefing we are treated to a two-part session. First, Boris being grilled by the Liaison Committee, a panel of 37 MPs who chair various select committees, on a whole variety of questions. This is the only commons committee that can question the PM, and this was his first appearance before the committee since he became PM last July. The session was followed by the normal daily briefing with Hancock.

The first session sees Boris challenged with questions on austerity, the impact of the lack of women on government decisions, whether the Government will be maintaining the Triple Lock for pensions as promised in the manifesto, whether the Government can guarantee there will be no rises in tax, when track and trace will be up and running and whether it will be compulsory for people to stay at home. He is artfully vague about all of the questions.

Then he is pressed on a question regarding Cummings asking him to outline which of the allegations in the press were untrue and he responds by saying:

"I have nothing to add. I have repeatedly said to other distinguished members of this committee what my strong belief is, although I understand people's frustrations and indignation with this whole business. I think what the country wants is for us to focus on how to go forward on the test and trace scheme, how to protect their jobs and how to beat the virus."

Another pointed question is thrown at him: "Why did we, in the UK, not start quarantining people coming from abroad earlier?"

He tells us: "The scientific advice was not clear it would make a difference; we are doing it now to stop re-infection".

Well there you go, it's all perfectly clear now. So over to Matt, joined by Van-Tam.

Hancock quickly reports on the figures. Sadly, an additional 412 deaths and quite a jump on yesterday. As always, he tells us we mourn them and will not forget. It really does feel like a perfunctory platitude particularly as the total number is edging every nearer to the 40,000, which is incomprehensible. However, he reiterates, we have passed the peak, flattened the curve and protected the NHS.

But he announces proudly, tomorrow they will roll out the Test and Trace initiative. Hancock states that this will be an incredibly important milestone. He tells us that this will mean we can start to replace lockdown with individual isolation. He describes breaking the chain of the virus until it gradually disappears. He pays tribute to Dido Harding, who led the work, and her team. But the problem is, will people comply if they are contacted, or will the Dominic Cummings scandal mean that people feel they don't have to?

I chew this over as we have another exciting evening on the couch!

TOTAL DEATHS – 37,460

Thursday, 28th May

Another beautiful sunny day in our run of good luck with the weather, so I go walking at 6.30 a.m. and have an early morning phone call with Sarah. She is still off her chemo tablets for another month, but she has a pain in her rib where the cancer is. I try not to worry, and she is upbeat as it could be many other things, but it still preys on my mind. It is good to hear her voice and feel her positivity. I will see her in a couple of weeks, which will be wonderful. I get showered and dressed quickly as I have a lot to get through this morning. Today I have the urge to put on a dress for the first time in ages and it feels good to wear something different. I even put perfume on; very sassy!

The news says that pubs might be opening next month and it really feels as if we are starting to move towards some form of normality. The big questions on everyone's lips is: could Test and Trace be the system that changes our lives after nine weeks of lockdown as Boris has indicated? Apparently, there will be a 25,000-strong team who will shortly begin texting, emailing and calling anyone who tests positive with the virus to find out who they have been in contact with. I wonder how this works if you have been in a shop? Or sitting in a park? Scotland is also launching today, and Northern Ireland is already up and running with Wales starting in early June. However, it will depend on how quickly contacts can be found and whether we all comply with the rules, so it is not a magic bullet, but it is a move in the right direction, providing everyone doesn't think that they can just go back to normal now that it is in place. Scotland will start to release lockdown by allowing people into outdoor spaces today.

Yesterday we had a call about the holiday to Mauritius and had to make a decision on whether to go or not. Apparently, BA needed to ticket yesterday so we had to say yes or no. Why they would be insisting on ticketing a flight for July yesterday when the Government had still not approved any non-essential flights is beyond me, but if we said yes and went ahead and then couldn't fly we would have to take vouchers for six of us, which we didn't really want to do. It is hard to predict; will we be able to fly in July? Will we be allowed into Mauritius and will we have to quarantine on the way back? So, we said no and lost our tickets for now and will just watch what happens over the next couple of weeks. We can move our booking up until September so there is still an outside chance we will go. Considering what other people have had to suffer it is no big deal and if we go, we go.

I start on my calls and have a wonderful meeting with the F: Entrepreneur ladies, listening to what they have been doing and how they have been pivoting their businesses. It is so inspiring to be part of a group like this and I feel grateful for our support group, even if we can't get together officially.

Yet another busy day for me, I just don't know where the days go to and I don't achieve anywhere near as much as I had hoped. I was hoping to have a free weekend but it looks like I will have to do some work – I want to be careful that I don't slip back into old habits, it would be easy for me at the moment to work every hour of the day but I have realised how important it is for me to shut off. I stop briefly for some home-made soup at lunchtime and LJ calls for a catch-up. Still no news on the mortgage offer but we keep everything crossed that they might be able to move in early July.

At 5.00 p.m. the briefing comes on and this time we see Boris. This must mean some easing of the lockdown as he normally only turns up to deliver favourable news these days.

He goes through the latest data on tests, positive cases and deaths, and reminds us that five tests must be met before adjusting the lockdown. It feels like he is taking us through our school report.

- Protect the NHS's ability to cope. The data shows, on 26th May, 475 people in England were admitted to hospital with coronavirus, down from a peak of 3,121 on 2nd April, so this first test is being met. Tick one.

- See a sustained, consistent fall in daily deaths. According to the seven-day rolling average the UK's daily death rate stands at 256 as of today, and therefore the second test is being met. Tick two.

- The rate of infection is decreasing to manageable levels across the board. Today's count shows 1,887 cases confirmed and therefore the Government is satisfied this test has been met. Tick three.

- Operational challenges, including testing capacity and PPE, are in supply for future demand. Apparently, we have now reached 161,214 tests per day and PPE supplies have been boosted. I guess it depends on how you are counting this, but Boris thinks it has been met. Tick four.

- Any adjustments to current measures must not risk a second peak of infections that could overwhelm the NHS. Boris tells us that he will set out further details on schools, social contact and retail. Apparently, different parts of the UK are moving at different speeds with this. Tick, sort of, five. We wait with bated breath. And then he says the news we (or certainly I) have been waiting for – groups of up to six people can meet outside in England from Monday.

It feels so exciting; from Monday, up to six people will be able to meet outside, providing members of different households continue to stay two metres apart. We can do this in gardens and other private outdoor spaces, although we must still maintain social distancing. Barbecues will be allowed providing we are all scrupulous about washing our hands. This is fine, I have a very big garden and it means I can see both my children and their partners. I am beyond excited and can barely wait for the briefing to finish to message the children. He also says we cannot have overnight stays yet, but I have a plan. My gym is a log cabin and if required my daughter could stay in there, we could take a mattress up. Boris tells us that these changes mean friends and family will start to meet loved ones in what would be a 'long awaited and joyful moment'. You aren't kidding, I can barely contain myself.

He then goes on to announce that shops will begin to reopen. We knew this was happening – outdoor retail and car showrooms first and then on the 15th June other non-essential retail, providing we are still meeting the five tests and all shops have Covid-secured themselves. As we had previously been told, schools can reopen to some pupils from Monday; nurseries, Reception, Year 1 and Year 6 will be first. A fortnight later, on the 15th June, secondary schools will begin to provide face-to-face contact time for Years 10 and 12.

Questions about Dominic Cummings are quickly shut down and Johnson says the police said they would take no action. He curtly says that he intends to draw a line under the matter.

There is a question about local lockdowns, which are quite possible, and what measures will be put in place for anyone who could potentially lose their income in this situation. Johnson reminds them of the furlough scheme and other loan schemes. He adds that nobody should be penalised for doing the right thing.

Johnson adds that measures will be re-imposed if there are local flare-ups and he hopes that in the coming weeks we will be able to do more to return to a normal way of life, providing the scientific data confirms it is safe. It is very likely there will be local outbreaks and where necessary measures will be re-imposed.

I break my 'no alcohol before Friday' rule and have a gin and tonic to celebrate and arrange to have a BBQ in two weeks with the children. Much as I would love to do it immediately, I just want to make sure it is as safe as possible, and I have waited this long, another fourteen days is nothing.

We do, what is supposed to be the 10th and final clap for NHS, just as emotional as the others. In Manchester tonight people took to their doorsteps, balconies and gardens to have a mass lockdown singalong. They were lucky enough to be joined by stars including Liam Gallagher, Mark Owen, and Tim Booth with a moving rendition of hits such as 'Shine' by Take That, 'Sit Down' by James, and 'Search for the Hero' by M People, at the 'Together in One Voice' event. The singing was led by local choirs and streamed live online with an introduction from musicians including Mike Pickering from M People, Tom Walker, Liam Fray and Emeli Sandé. However, the most moving moment was when Tim Booth introduced the James anthem 'Sit Down' and told us how he sung the hit to his father-in-law over FaceTime just an hour before he died from COVID-19 last month. Amidst the excitement of releasing lockdown may we never forget all of those people who will not have loved ones to be reunited with and who have been lost through this terrible pandemic. Cue tears, never far away.

Friday, 29th May

I wake up very early and remember the news from yesterday. We can start seeing other people in our gardens, and I still can't quite process it. I have got so used to not going out and not having people round that the thought of doing it fills me with such excitement, but I am scared to get my hopes up in case something changes. In my head, I have already started planning the first family BBQ. It is one of my great joys, cooking for my family and friends, and it is the thing I have missed most (apart from my family and friends of course). I think of my friends in the Middle East; I have always admired the principles of Ramadan as I have worked with the Muslim community for so long, and it makes me think about how they must feel at Eid. You really do have to have everything taken away from you before you start to appreciate it. And we didn't have everything taken away from us, we still had food and drink every day, but we had enough taken away from us to hopefully appreciate it when we got it back.

I wonder if this is really the beginning of the end of lockdown, and in some ways, I feel torn. My life has been speeding up a bit again over the last couple of weeks and next week I start training again, which I look forward to, but it does start to put the pressure on. Yesterday I did my rehearsal for the Association of Project Management Conference next week, and I am also delivering to a new client and doing my first full half-day session next week. We have set up a studio in the utility room so that we can try out using a microphone and sound bar, to avoid wearing headphones and be closer to the router, and it works well. It allows me to stand up and deliver training rather than sit at a desk, so I feel a bit more comfortable and in control. Really, why would I go back into an office or travel around the world? The client that I am delivering to on Thursday is in Strasbourg, which used to take me ten hours to get to for a day!

The news is bad from the US. Riots have started in Minneapolis, following the death of George Floyd, an unarmed 46-year-old black man who died in police custody. Floyd was accused of using a fake bank note to pay for something in a store and was arrested. A white officer knelt on his neck, allegedly for over eight minutes, whilst he was filmed gasping and saying, "I can't breathe." The police were forced to flee from the burning Minneapolis Third Police Precinct late Thursday when the rioters broke in and set fire to the building. They then ran through the corridors with baseball bats, axes, and torches. The news footage showed the uncontrollable fire with flames billowing out of the building, just hours after prosecutors warned: "There is evidence that does not support criminal charges," in the case of the four cops who were accused of killing Floyd.

Donald Trump puts out a crazy Tweet threatening that 'when the looting starts, the shooting starts', which later gets hidden by a warning that it violated Twitter's rules about glorifying violence. This morning there were extraordinary scenes as a CNN television crew were arrested as they reported on the unrest and a CNN reporter was handcuffed and led away.

The mayor had to issue a curfew from 8.00 p.m. at night until 8.00 a.m. in the morning to curb the chaos. The National Guard were bought in but could not control it.

The officer, Derek Chauvin, who kept his knee on Floyd's neck was arrested today and charged with murder – absolutely right, it was brutal. And quite rightly; this is not going to go away quietly

The day flies past again and just as we think our luck is on the upturn with business, one of our biggest partner clients writes to us. They had cancelled all training up until June and rebooked it from September, but now they were cancelling it all until December. No surprise really as they are in the aviation business, but we had been working so hard to get new business in, so to lose that amount was a big blow. I pick myself up again, I cannot control this, it is just symptomatic of what businesses are going through. I have to reground myself and push on through. I try to stay positive for the team call and thankfully some of the team also have some good news with bookings about to be confirmed, so all is not totally lost.

Today we see Rishi Sunak taking the briefing, which can only mean news about the furlough scheme. He is accompanied by Steve Powys and Sunak looks cool, calm, and collected. As always, he is sincere, authentic and humble in the way he speaks. He discusses the figures and is totally believable when he expresses his remorse for the sad deaths of today.

He goes on to tell us that today's figures confirm that we are past the peak. We can start to open offices and schools (or dust-off school uniforms as he puts it!) Businesses will need to become Covid-secure and we will need to stay alert and adapt emergency programmes that we needed to get through the crisis.

He mentions all the loans, grants and payment schemes that the Government have used to support people and reminds us that no British Government, Labour or Conservative, have ever done anything like this. There is no denying that they have been incredibly generous in doing this. However, he warns us that the furlough scheme cannot continue indefinitely. It will stay open until October and then they will ask companies to contribute. He believes it is right, in the final stage of the eight-month scheme, to ask employers to contribute so has decided to ask employers to only contribute a modest payment. June and July remain the same. In August we will only be asked to pay for NI contributions. By September employers will have had sufficient time to make changes to their workplaces and so in September employers will contribute 10% and October 20%. Then the scheme will close. From the 1st July employers will have the maximum flexibility for their staff. Therefore, we can bring people back for a few days a month and have furlough for the rest.

For the self-employed – he confirms the scheme will be extended for applications in August for a second and final grant covering three months. The value of the final grant will be 70% up to a total of £6,000 over the three months. He assures us that they will develop new measures and kickstart our economy. LJ will be grateful of that as he still is not getting work through.

Steve Powys takes us through today's figures and the latest figures are 4,043,686 infected. There were 131,458 tests yesterday and increasing every day. There has been an increase of 2,095 cases since yesterday. The daily admissions to hospital are on a steady decline and yesterday 552 people were admitted into hospital. Sadly, another increase of 324 fatalities.

Its Friday night and it's girls' quiz night and we giggle our way through the quiz. It takes my mind off the money I lost today from cancelled bookings. That's the thing, when you gamble you have to be prepared to lose.

TOTAL DEATHS – 38,161

Saturday, 30th May

And that is it, another month done! Hard to believe and I wake up thinking about how far we have all come, and how much I have personally achieved. Before the group workout I do a good half an hour in the gym and am really pleased with my progress. I review my other goals, some have been completely nailed, others are almost there, and some are well in progress. I start to think about resetting goals for the next twelve weeks, that would take me to the beginning of September.

I don't want to work today apart from a rehearsal on my speech for the conference on Tuesday, so I get in my car, put the roof down and go out. Yes OUT! Driving my car is a complete treat, which I thoroughly enjoy, and I head for the garden centre. The simple act of wandering around and shopping is just so liberating that I keep smiling. It was well organised with social distancing and protection and I revelled in choosing some new plants. I take a little drive on the way home to give the car a blow along the motorway and even though I am out for less than an hour and a half I feel completely energised. I don't think Keith was feeling quite the same way when I dragged him out to help me dig the holes to bed my new plants in! After a few hours' gardening I then have a lovely relax in the helicopter chair reading.

During the day I hear snippets of news – scientists saying it is too early to break lockdown and having big concerns, a post on Facebook showing the daily deaths starting with Spain only having two, and with us way at the top, with far more than any country, at 324 yesterday. A UK government adviser, John Edmunds, a professor of infectious disease modelling at the London School of Hygiene and Tropical Medicine, said he wanted the level of new cases to 'bc driven down further' before larger gatherings are allowed as the Government has said it wants to do. It feels crazy that we are easing the lockdown, and many are suggesting it is just to gain political brownie points rather than the right thing to do. Certainly, when I was out I felt that everything was back to normal with far more cars than I have seen in a long time and the weather is just beautiful again, so I am sure that the beaches will be packed. I see pictures of crowded beaches at Durdle Door on the Jurassic Coast, and Bournemouth beach, and there is no space to move at all. My short trip out was the first time in three weeks but as I drive past the parks there are many people in large groups not socially distancing. Apparently, in the United States, pool parties over Memorial Day weekend may have caused further outbreaks.

The briefing is taken by Oliver Dowden, Digital, Culture, Media, and Sport Secretary – a new face.

He tells us the death toll since yesterday is 215, which is the lowest Saturday total since lockdown began, but it is still a lot of people and for every family a tragedy.

He then goes on to talk about sport and I can feel the nation's excitement. He says that football, tennis, horse racing, Formula 1, cricket, golf, rugby, snooker and others will all be returning to our screens shortly with horse racing being the first next week. He tells us that much of the media attention has focused on football, because it has a 'special place in our national life'. Not mine! So, he wants to ensure that remaining Premier League games will be broadcast free-to-air, and that the financial benefits of returning will be shared throughout football. He confirms that a third of the matches will be free-to-view including Liverpool versus Everton, and the BBC will be showing live free to air Premier League football for the first time ever. This will encourage people to watch safely from home. But that won't happen; the minute they open pubs people will come together to watch them. I am filled with a sense of impending doom.

He also gives credit to the momentum that has built up behind women's sport after the Football, Cricket and Netball World Cups, and says he will be working hard with the Sports Minister to ensure that progress was not lost. I think of the ECB, who I have worked so closely with for many years, and how well the Women's cricket team had done last year. It is devastating for them.

He confirms that they are relaxing rules on exercise further so that from Monday people will be able to exercise with up to five others from different households as long as they socially distance. That means teams can train together and do conditioning and fitness session that don't involve contact.

Deputy Chief Medical Officer, Professor Van-Tam says he believes this is also a very dangerous moment and says that we shouldn't 'tear the pants out of it'. An interesting analogy! He reminds us how quickly the disease could spread. Absolutely agree, and if you think of the fact that nearly 2,500 people have tested positive for the virus today, taking the total cases to 272,000, it means that there is still a huge amount of people out there who could be infected.

The riots in Minneapolis continue for the fourth night in a row and security forces are overwhelmed. The Governor says the situation is no longer about the death of Georg Floyd. The damage in Minneapolis is massive.

Apparently, they thought that after the police officer was arrested the violence might die down, but fever is high as the protestors shouted: “I can’t breathe,” trashed shops and police cars. Keisha Lance Bottoms, the Mayor of Atlanta, pleaded for it to stop by saying: “We are better than this.” The protestors are demanding accountability and they come out to clear up some of the mess, but the racial tension might mean another night of rioting.

I feel a mixture of emotions, glad that the issue is being taken seriously, disgusted that it took the death of George Floyd to provoke action and concern that the riots are getting worth.

TOTAL DEATHS – 38,376

Sunday, 30th May

Even though it is Sunday I am up early to go for a walk date with Trudy on Southampton Common. The weather is stunningly beautiful again. As I walk to the common, I take heed of government advice not to step off the kerb to avoid joggers – it seems it is more likely I could get run over than get COVID-19! Trudy is waiting at the common for me. Even though it is only the second time we have met we have a fantastic conversation and find lots in common, including a couple of projects we might be able to work on. I feel it is serendipity and we have been brought together for a reason. She also coaches me as I walk and helps me to think through a couple of key situations I am battling with. It is so refreshing to be coached by someone else and I am very thoughtful when I get home and cook my customary weekend poached eggs.

I do a bit of work and decide to have a couple of hours reading in my helicopter chair.

First, I flick through the news on my phone and read an account in the *Guardian* of someone who applied for the Track and Trace job. It was a shocking tale of how they had been taken on and assured they would be given training and how the training didn't happen, how they spent hours online waiting for someone to come and to talk to them in chat rooms, were asked to train other members when they hadn't even had their own training and how people kept assuring them they were being paid so not to worry. His guilt at being paid for just sitting there and playing online games and watching Netflix whilst they waited for someone to come and tell them what to do ate away at him and he resigned. It certainly felt genuine in the way it was written, but if that is true that is really concerning as we are putting all our eggs in the track-and-trace basket.

Another article says that there is significant challenge at the moment to the quarantine ruling and whether this will be applied, with many saying that it will kill travel and it is not enforceable. Border Force has said it would not be possible and people with electronic passports would just be waved through. Greece has banned travellers from the UK visiting (as well as Italy and Spain) and I wonder how many other countries will soon ban us.

And then an interesting article (albeit in the *Daily Mail*) that Boris has told Dominic Cummings he is on his last chance after the recent debacle – he has apparently told his chief aide he cannot afford another media storm. Boris has been paying a heavy price for the fiasco and it is reported that he is 'very miffed' with how the fallout was handled – that sounds like words Boris would say!

Confirmed cases around the world have now exceeded six million according to John Hopkins University

Donald Trump is under massive criticism for not spending time on the pandemic, getting rid of the WHO, and spending time on a public spat on Twitter condemning China over Hong Kong. He calls protestors in Minneapolis thugs and even re-tweets a video in which a supporter says: "The only good Democrat is a dead Democrat." However, apart from a brief tweet he has remained silent on the pandemic! Unbelievable; he is really a law unto himself.

I listen to the briefing by Robert Jenrick, Jenny Harries, and Dame Louise Casey from the homeless.

The figures have risen today again with a further 113 people confirmed dead, although the reporting could be low. There were 1,936 new cases confirmed on Saturday, which is the first time in ages that the figure has dipped below 2,000. This takes the total confirmed cases to 274,762. In the last twenty-four hours 115, 725 tests have been done and they now have capacity for 200,000.

Jenrick pays massive tribute to the people who have been shielding throughout the crisis and reminds them of the help that is available. This leads to him setting out next steps for the shielded. He says: "Now we have passed the peak the risk to those shielding is lower and want to give them the advice to make the best decisions."

First steps, they have updated the shielded guidance, so from tomorrow people who are shielding can safely spend time outdoors, however, only in England. They can meet with one person from their household, or if they live alone, with one member of another household. I guess that is some small relief to grandparents who live alone.

Dame Louise Casey is there to give an update on rough sleepers. Jenrick goes on to say that the goal has always been that as few people as possible return to the streets. But now he says that we know who the rough sleepers are and where they are and can individually help them. He announces 6,000 new supported homes can be made available for people and he confirms the Government have put £33 million to fast track this effort. 3,300 of these homes will become available in the next year. Dame Casey spends time talking about the unprecedented support and gives thanks to all partners for their help. For the first time ever, they have all rough sleepers inside and now the job is to be able to keep them inside and get them all the help that they need. She calls it a small but incredible silver lining in the dark cloud that is COVID-19. Whilst I agree, I feel angry that we needed this to happen for the Government to step in and help the homeless.

TOTAL DEATHS – 38,489

Monday, 1st June
Official Lockdown, Week Eleven

I wake up today feeling really out of sorts, I could pretend I don't, but I do. I slept badly due to the heat and was woken at 5.00 a.m. by some noisy crows in the garden, so when the alarm went at 6.00 a.m. the temptation to stay in bed was strong. Thankfully, I had a PT session booked with Olivia or I may not have bothered for the first time since lockdown. I try to work out what is going on with me; I think probably it is internal stress coming out as I feel irritable and emotional. Losing the £40,000 on Friday was incredibly disappointing and I feel as if it is one step forward and three steps back. Once again, the responsibility eats at me – I so want to bring the team through this and to come out the other side even stronger but I am beginning to wonder if, after twenty-five years, I am running out of energy. I do my PT session and take a breath. Time to dig deep and pull on all the techniques I have learnt. A slight irony is that I am talking about mental health at the conference tomorrow and my own has taken such a dive today.

I turn on the television as I get dressed and Piers is back and looking as if he might spontaneously combust. Still unable to interview any government ministers, as they are on day thirty-five of the boycott on the programme, he has to resort to either commenting on interviews that are on the BBC or inviting random people for interviews. Today he is resurrecting the Dominic Cummings affair as he missed it during his week off last week and shouting down people trying to protect him. Whilst I agree that Cummings broke the rules, my feeling is that we have bigger things to worry about now and as Boris clearly isn't going to fire him, we have to move on. I am sure his day will come but wasting energy on a witch hunt is not helping us to get over the virus.

But there is really distressing news from the US – the protests over the death last Monday of George Floyd have spread uncontrollably, to almost 40 cities, starting with peaceful protests and ending in riots. His lawyer has now said that it should be pre-meditated murder although the police officer was only arrested for third-degree murder. At least five people have died so far in the protests, one in Minneapolis, one in Detroit, two in Indianapolis and one in Chicago on Sunday. There are riots and looting in places that you just couldn't imagine, such as LA, on Rodeo Drive. Violence has broken out everywhere across the country including places like Melrose, Santa Monica, and Washington of course, outside of the White House. The protests often have started peacefully and then turned nasty. At one point on Friday President Trump was actually taken into a bunker. The streets are so dangerous that TV reporters have been told not to go out on the streets as it is not safe.

So far there have been 4,000 arrests and now most major cities are having problems, with still no call for unity from Trump. He hasn't come out and made a public address from the White House yet and I wonder how he will ever get control of it. His Tweet last week about 'looting and shooting' inflamed people massively.

In London people marched in unity on the US Embassy and I hope that it doesn't turn into riots. Police arrest 23 people after alleged assaults. Chants of, "I can't breathe," rallied around London. Thousands had earlier gathered at Trafalgar Square before making their way to the gates of Downing Street and then down the river to the US Embassy. I remember the riots in the UK about five years ago and it was terrifying. It is bad enough having the virus and lockdown but the impact of this is inconceivable, like a crisis within a crisis within a crisis. To say nothing of the fact that the 1,000s of protestors are not socially distancing. I 100% agree with the cause and am glad this has happened as finally this might be the time for the world to truly look at white privilege and equality for the black community.

In the UK it is 'return to education' day and people are really torn about children going back to school today. Certain schools have opened and apparently at least 50% of people have said that they won't be sending their children back. Those that are opening have taken into account a lot of measures, putting children in little bubbles to reduce contact, staggering drop-off and break times, and encouraging learning outside where possible. I can imagine that it is causing some conflict within families. I am not sure I would want to send my children back to school.

Elly calls and although I thought my emotions were under control the sound of her voice makes me emotional again. I really cannot wait to see my children and even though I am waiting another two weeks it will be worth the wait. LJ messages me too, he tells me how proud he is of me and once again I blink away tears. For goodness sake, if the people listening to my presentation tomorrow on mental health could see me today, they wouldn't bother turning up. Or would they? Perhaps that is just authenticity – mental health isn't a constant and I remind myself it is OK to have wobbles, particularly if it means that tomorrow I will be back on the proverbial horse.

Matt Hancock is taking the briefing and tells us he is doing it differently today and going through the slides himself first rather than leaving it to the scientists. Is this an economy in the amount of people doing the briefing?

The first slide up indicates testing completed – 128,437 tests meaning a total of 4.4 million tests. Of course, testing capacity stands at a higher level at 206,000 and tests are available for people if we go online. He wants to highlight this as it is so important. There are 1,570 cases confirmed as of yesterday, the lowest number since the 25th March. So continual downward progress – we are getting the virus under control – admissions to hospital have gone down from a peak of over 3,000 to 479 and the number of people on ventilators is the lowest since late March. Sadly, an additional 111 died yesterday making a total of 39,043. My ears prick up. That doesn't tally with my numbers and I check yesterday's figures again, yes, they said it was 38,489 so something isn't right.

Hancock thanks everyone, and at the beginning of Pride month, he thanks all people of any diversity for what they do to support people during the virus. It lacks sincerity and comes across as perfunctory.

The first question from the public is about the impending recession and Hancock says they take it really seriously. He reminds us of all the support that they put out into the businesses to try and keep things up and running. But he counters, it is true that the economy will need to change, and he says the Chancellor and Prime Minister have been working incredibly hard to get this right – we will be hearing more apparently.

The BBC's Hugh Pym asks a question about Test and Trace and notes that he has heard newly employed team members saying they had very little to do. Hancock says it is up and running and has been very successful. He adds that a piece of good news is that as the rate of cases comes down there are fewer cases to track. He tells Pym: "We have more capacity than we need – this is a good thing," and says he would rather err on the side of having too many contact tracers.

Professor John Newton, National Testing Co-ordinator, adds that it is important to build a system for whatever comes in the future. Aah, that is what he is here for.

Next question is from Tom Clark from ITV, who asks how many of the 9,000 people infected since the Test and Trace service began last week have now been contacted and their contacts traced. Hancock hesitates and says he does not have the figures. Oops, there we go again, nothing to offer, but he adds he is confident that the vast majority of recent cases will have been identified and tracked.

Newton rushes to his aid and says he understands that people are keen to see the figures and promises that they will be published soon. He also insists the Test and Trace service is operating 'pretty much' as clinicians hoped and says he is 'pleased' by the response so far. He adds that they would like to do a bit more work before they publish them.

Hancock is also asked if the Government would reimpose some of the blanket lockdown measures if infection rates went up again, and he confirms that he is prepared to reintroduce either national or local measures.

It is a much briefer conference than usual.

Tonight, is the last of the *Killing Eve* series. In my humble opinion it did not live up to expectations after Series 1 or 2, but I wonder if I paid full attention to it; I find I am less and less interested in television.

TOTAL DEATHS – 39,043

Tuesday, 2nd June

I wake up early and get up quickly. My mood feels lifted today thank goodness. Today is the APM Conference and I am excited to be doing what I love. I go for a walk to get my adrenalin up and mentally rehearse as I power-walk. I am looking forward to presenting today and really hope that I can reach some people and let them know that mental health is a subject that people shouldn't feel ashamed to talk about, particularly men – the suicide rate in men under 45 is tragically high.

I come home and realise with excitement that I can get myself dressed in my work clothes today, which means doing my hair properly and putting on make-up! It is amazing how small things like that can lift you.

I set up my makeshift presentation booth. The router is in the laundry room, which used to be my study in the front of the house but I have worked out that I can fit in two of our Emerge banners that I can stand in front of and prop the microphone on a couple of boxes. The acoustics are not bad and generally the presentation goes well (more of that later!).

I go back to my desk afterwards and some interesting news comes through that under new legislation police in

England can order people to leave a property if they are not complying with the new coronavirus laws – it is now a crime to stay at someone else's home overnight and have sex (the news reports this quite specifically), or to hold gatherings of two or more people indoors or more than six people outdoors (thankfully no mention of sex with these groups!) However, officers can fine rule-breakers and arrest them if they do not co-operate, according to the laws that came into force to coincide with lockdown restrictions being eased. I know of several people who have now started 'staying over' with boyfriends and I have visions of them being dragged out of bed in the middle of the night and marched to their cars! However, the chair of the National Police Chiefs' Council (NPCC), Martin Hewitt, said that it was key that people took personal responsibility and added that officers would use common sense and discretion and only fine or arrest people as a last resort. Well, that should scare them all into behaving themselves!

The situation in America has worsened and protests are now happening in all 50 states. One person was shot. George Floyd's family are begging for peace. I watch George Floyd's brother appealing for calm. He tells the crowd that George had loved his town and would hate to see it like this. Whilst Derek Chauvin has been charged with murder and manslaughter, the other three police officers involved are still being investigated. I watch the whole video and I am sickened to my stomach by the police actions, and the expressions on their faces, whilst they pinned Floyd down is vile. There are curfews in many states now from 6.00 p.m. to 6.00 a.m and whilst some protests are peaceful others are still setting fire and looting. People in the US are looking to the White House and not getting any answers. There will be a music industry blackout to take place in protest over the death.

Trump has now come into the community and participated in some bizarre photo opportunities. Did he rally the country? Did he instil peace and calmness? No, in one of his dreadful press conferences he spoke from the Rose Garden and said: "If a city or state refuses to take the actions necessary to defend the life and property of their residents, then I will deploy the United States military and quickly solve the problem for them." Unbelievable. He then got his people to start to move protestors using tear gas and rubber bullets so that he could walk to the church across the street for a photo opportunity. This caused outrage in the religious community as apparently Trump does not even belong to a congregation, rarely attends a service and has often said that he does not like to ask God for forgiveness.

Rabbi Jack Moline, President of the Interfaith Alliance, said: "Seeing President Trump standing in front of St John's Episcopal Church whilst holding a Bible in response to calls for racial justice right after using military force to clear peaceful protestors is one of the most flagrant misuses of religion that I have ever seen."

It's another 'brief' briefing from Hancock today. We hear that 135,643 tests were carried out in the twenty-four hours to 9.00 a.m. on Tuesday and that there is still spare capacity as they can meet the demand for over 200,000. I can't help feeling that it is easy to say that, as 200,000 was the figure that was promised to us.

Yesterday there were 436 new hospital admissions, which is the lowest figure since 20th March, so apparently we are making progress. I think of how many families would still be terrified about those people going in. It is easy to say we are making progress but not for those loved ones.

Another 324 deaths recorded and we are almost at 40,000, although other sources suggest that the real figure could be nearer to 50,000. Once again Hancock says: "We mourn each one of these." Statements like this really jar with me as clearly he doesn't mourn each one and I would rather he didn't say it.

Hancock goes on to talk about racial injustice and the anger people are experiencing. He tells us that black lives matter and thanks the BAME staff in the NHS who have been on the front line during the COVID-19 pandemic.

He is also questioned on the effect on BAME communities and Hancock says there is 'much more work that needs to be done' on the issue and the Government is looking further at what steps it can take. Apparently, they are up to twice as likely to die from COVID-19.

And just to demonstrate further government commitment they are scrapping weekend briefings due to low viewing figures – what about me? I watch them.

TOTAL DEATHS – 39,369

Wednesday, 3rd June

This morning I have a call at 8.30 a.m. and a training session to deliver from 10.00–11.30 a.m. so I am glad that I set up the 'training room' last night. The laundry room was pretty good for the presentation yesterday, so I am going to try a longer session today.

As I prepare I reflect on my conference presentation – ironically, it was the most stressful presentation I have ever done, starting with finding my slides had de-formatted when the cover slide was added. Then, when I went to set up the room, I found that I had the wrong pull-up banners, so Keith had to rush into the office and bring the right ones home.

I got ready for my 12.15 p.m. presentation slot, did my technical run-through with thirty minutes to spare, and was told to be logged in at 12.14 p.m. ready to start, so I relaxed with a cup of tea.

At 12.02 p.m. I got a call to see they had changed the time of my session and not told the host, so it should start at midday – two minutes ago! So, I just had to stand up and go!

The laundry room was hot, so I had the window open and at one point the cat jumped in and got tangled in the blinds behind me! After fourteen minutes I got a phone call to say my connection had just dropped out! After three minutes of faffing with their technical guy I get back in, although I am now not even sure if people can hear me! I tell people it was done deliberately to show how stress can impact on us! Fortunately, I finish, we didn't lose any of the 400-plus delegates, we had some good questions, and my host tells me it was a really excellent presentation. The joy of virtual presentations! I shake off yesterday's emotional rollercoaster and get focused on today.

Boris is in for a bit of a beating at Prime Minister's Question Time with Sir Keir Starmer urging him to get a grip and saying there is a suspicion the PM was 'winging it' over his easing of the lockdown.

Apparently, McDonald's were swamped as they opened yesterday, and Ikea stores saw massive queues whilst the country's largest coronavirus testing centres stood idle. The queues in Southampton, along the M27 to turn off to the nearest McDonald's, were ridiculous although I expect Ronald was thrilled!

My day goes well today; a good call with a client and some confirmed work, a great virtual training session in my new laundry training studio, a promising call with a client and then a very upbeat call with the team. There are lots of sales calls going on and a little confirmed work for August and September. I feel grateful for the energy my team have put into this and there is a lot of banter on the call.

And then, would you believe, Boris is on our screens to take the briefing. He first tells us that it was 'inevitable' that there would be 'many, many job losses' this year because of the impact of coronavirus on the economy. Technically, we have not in the UK, reached the official benchmark for a recession (i.e. two successive quarters where there is negative growth) but the economy is already shrinking considerably. There are some forecasts that say we are facing the deepest recession for three-hundred years and Johnson admitted this when he said it was inevitable that the job losses will happen. He follows that by saying the Government would be as 'activist and interventionist' as possible in helping people during the next phase of the crisis.

He tells us that we have made progress on controlling the spread of the disease due to the NHS Test and Trace service and the new regime at the borders from Monday, although Professor Chris Whitty, the Government's Chief Medical Adviser, said it would take 'quite some time' before the new Test and Trace service was working at full capacity. I wonder what the briefings would be like if Whitty was allowed to do them on his own.

Boris announces that sadly 359 people have died during the last 24 hours. The figures show that 1,871 cases were confirmed today, which means that 279,856 cases have been confirmed in total.

In a surprise turn, Sir Patrick Vallance refuses to explicitly back the Government's decision to impose quarantine on new arrivals to the UK from next week and implies that scientists are sceptical about the policy generally.

Johnson dodges a question about whether Britons will be able to take a foreign holiday this summer by saying: "I'm not going to give advice on individuals' travel arrangements, but you know what the Foreign Office guidance is – everybody at the moment should avoid non-essential travel." He did admit that the UK was talking to other European countries about setting up 'air corridors' that could allow them to bypass the quarantine rules. Priti Patel is being asked to publish the scientific advice behind the decision to quarantine people for fourteen days, months after the pandemic began.

I work late this evening getting ready for an early training course tomorrow morning, and we watch a really bad film! I watch the news and think again about the situation in America. My friend Lauren in America messages me to say it is like a war zone in LA. There is so much to take in and learn.

TOTAL DEATHS – 39,728

Thursday, 3rd June

I feel like my life is racing past. It is Thursday again and the weeks are flashing by. I hope I am going to get to see Sarah this weekend and the thought of going for a walk with her gets me excited. I get up early today as I need to be logged in at 7.30 a.m. and ready to start training. This course is all about change and very apt for the current climate, but it will be my first experience of a long virtual session! At least it is worth putting on a dress and doing my hair today.

I turn on *GMB* and OMG, the biggest row I have ever seen is being played out over breakfast tables around the country. Piers Morgan is interviewing Rudy Giuliani, Trump's lawyer and the ex-Mayor of New York. What starts as a strong exchange deteriorates into a childish slanging match and ends up with a deeply personal and bitter on-air row over the US President's handling of the George Floyd protests.

Morgan calls Giuliani 'unhinged' after he lashes out at him for 'misinterpreting on purpose' a recent tweet by the US President concerning the unrest. The tweet in question, published eight days ago was that 'when the looting starts, the shooting starts' as protests started in all states of America over the murder of Floyd. Piers insists that this phrase has its origins in the civil rights era and is linked to racism. Twitter later hid the post behind a warning that it 'glorifies violence'.

Piers asked Rudy what had happened to him and adds: "When I used to interview you, you were an intelligent, reasonable man and you've gone completely mad and you sound abusive." He also said, "You're so wound up in your support for Trump you can't see the wood for the trees." He honestly looked like he was going to spontaneously combust.

Giuliani hit back, accusing Morgan of being a 'failed journalist' and saying: "You misinterpreted him. You're misinterpreting him on purpose".

The two men then begin shouting over each other with Morgan calling Giuliani 'mad' and 'unhinged' over his 'abusive' comments, and Giuliani branding the *GMB* host a 'disgrace' and a 'liar'.

Guiliani meanwhile pushes back saying: "Everyone in America knows you're a failed journalist, so stop trying to recreate your career."

I am trying but I really cannot find any words!

The riots continue in the US and yesterday the UK experienced mass peaceful protests in London. Apart from scuffles outside Downing Street the biggest danger came from the fact that large crowds were not social distancing. The news reports that new charges have been announced against all the sacked police officers attending the scene where George Floyd was murdered. The charge against Derek Chauvin has been escalated to second degree murder and the other three officers, Thomas Lane, J. Alexander Kueng and Tou Thao, face counts of aiding and abetting murder. Whilst this is a significant step for the family, they still want the charges against Chauvin increased to first degree murder. People everywhere are trying to educate themselves on what racism really is and how they can support and stand by black people and this is not going away. I could probably write a whole other book on this but I need to stay focused on the pandemic. However, I seriously think that 2020 will not only be known for the coronavirus but also the year that changed racism forever.

I start the training session and it goes well; my first half-a-day session with a team of IT Managers in Strasbourg. Technology holds up and we get lots of interaction – I am beginning to feel like a pro at this now. It is more exhausting than usual training but luckily we had no dropouts and I felt pretty pleased by the end of it.

At 5.00 p.m. Transport Secretary Grant Shapps takes the briefing with Sir Peter Hendy, Chair of Network Rail, who says very little. He goes through the figures and the number of tests *posted* out (he emphasises *posted*), has reached past the £5 million mark with a record 220,057 carried out, or *posted* out yesterday and 281,681 cases in total with an increase of 1,808 cases since yesterday. The daily figure for deaths is 176 – the lowest working weekday total, with a daily average of 229 down from a peak of over 900 daily.

He talks about the importance of avoiding a second infection spike and that transport needs to be adjusted for social distancing. He also mentions the work done on cycle lanes and he celebrates the lack of overcrowding.

He announces what they will do to make it safer and what we must do.

1. If you can work from home you should continue to do so.

2. If you can't work from home avoid public transport.

3. If you have to use it, avoid rush hour.

On the 15th June face coverings will become mandatory on public transport. Not necessarily surgical masks, you can make your own. This will apply to trains, buses, air travel and ferries. He tells us that will provide limited protection for other people. The words 'horse' and 'stable door' come to mind. Apparently, you could be refused travel if you don't comply. Front-line staff in contact with passengers will also wear face coverings. Shapps advocates buying bikes or scooters and they are introducing a £50 voucher to fix your bike! There has apparently been quite an increase in cycling!

I feel like I need wine and a session in the hot tub as today has been exhausting, but it has been good to get back to training again.

TOTAL DEATHS – 39,904

Friday, 5th June

I get up at 6.30 a.m. and do a gym session as I missed yesterday. I am feeling a bit more energised today, so I push it quite hard. I am at my desk and starting work by 8.15 a.m. I am also being interviewed for a podcast show this morning, so it feels quite hectic. And in between I need to get a mailshot out and do my emails from yesterday. I also have a call with the team and a company about a joint-venture arrangement and a coaching session before we hit the virtual pub at 4.30 p.m. I glance around the house, there is washing and ironing to do and the floor needs cleaning but there is no urgency. There never is, no one is going to see it so what does it matter? Gemma has sent the monthly figures to me and I take a deep breath as I settle down to read them with a coffee. I can see that we lost just shy of £14,000 last month. It's not great but it could have been worse. We still have a long way to go before we are in the clear, but I feel I have made the right choice in keeping the business going.

I have *GMB* on as I work and Kate Garraway has joined her fellow presenters remotely for a discussion. As she talks tears roll down my cheeks. She gives an emotional update on her husband, Derek, who has been in a coma for almost ten weeks after contracting coronavirus. She holds herself so well as she tells people that it is a miracle he is still alive. She pays tribute to the amazing NHS staff who have battled his coronavirus and talks about the most extraordinary battle he has been through, and is still going through, and tells fellow hosts Ben Shephard and Ranvir Singh that she is so grateful that he is still here. She says that he is very sick, and she is praying and hoping. The virus has affected him from the 'top of his head to the tips of his toes and whilst free of COVID-19, it has wreaked havoc on his body and it is not known if he can recover from that. So terribly sad and really rams home the consequences.

The riots are still continuing in America and the whole world is standing by the Black Lives Matter campaign. I have been spending the last few days learning more about white privilege, reading and listening to podcasts to try and educate myself. I have never considered myself to be a racist but the more I read and learn, the more there is to learn. One of the most powerful things I read is about a man who tells the story of deciding when it was the right time to tell his child that one day they will experience racism of some kind. Did he tell her when she was old enough to understand and ruin her innocence by telling her that one day someone would do or say something because of the colour of her skin or does he wait until it happens and then support her? That is something that I never had to consider whilst my children were young; they just had the fairy-tale childhood that they deserved, and all black children should have that too. Will life after Floyd be different or will it never truly change? I just hope that no more lives are lost.

The podcast I record is about this book and it allows me to ask for help – to see if anyone who is an editor, PR expert or publisher wants to help with the project. It will be interesting to see if they do; I have already got someone willing to help with the jacket.

I rush from call to call and before I know it, that's it, another week in the bag. It all feels so normal now and I realise that on Monday I will have been in isolation for twelve weeks. Unbelievable, three months of the year gone in a flash.

At 5.00 p.m. Matt Hancock appears for a very brief and lonely briefing. He goes straight into the slides. He tells us that the R value for the UK is estimated to now be between 0.7 and 0.9 according to SAGE, it is not going down much. The ONS survey estimates the number of new infections stands at 39,000 per week, which is roughly 5,600 per day. Lower than last week.

He tells us that 7,080 people remain in hospital with COVID-19, down from 8,285 last week, he says, but sadly a further 357 people died following a positive test, showing we have so much more to do. He goes on to say that all hospital staff, visitors and outpatients must wear face coverings from the 15th June.

He finishes by urging Britons to avoid the mass protests over the weekend 'for the safety of your loved ones' adding that he understands why people are appalled at the death of George Floyd but warns of how much of a threat coronavirus poses in the UK.

I silently add my own pleas.

TOTAL DEATHS – 40,261

Saturday, 6th June

Today is the best day of the last twelve weeks. Today I saw Sarah. The whole day is pretty amazing as it starts with a workout with my daughter, then I drive my car (and it feels so good!) to Bournemouth and we go for a long walk and talk about everything. She really is my soulmate and whenever we are together I feel complete; she is truly the most special person I have ever met. We stop for a coffee at a takeaway shop and then go back and sit in the garden and carry on talking. We talk about her mother's death and she says she is really struggling to believe it is real. I guess that is because she hasn't had a funeral and hasn't had the closure that you need. It takes every ounce of will power for us not to hug or get close to each other, but I just cannot risk infecting her.

The only disappointment is that the photo book I had made for her hasn't arrived yet, but soon after I leave it does, so I come back. I sit on her doorstep and she sits in the hall and opens the package. When she sees the front page with a beautiful picture of her mother, and Bob with her son, Thomas, titled *Sarah's Family Memories*, she is so emotional and as she looks through the pictures of her as a child with her father, pictures of her mother, and of

Thomas she sobs. But it is good for her to sob, she needs to grieve, and I sob too. I will never forget that moment, of her sitting on her hall floor and me sitting on the doorstep remembering her mum and dad, not able to hold each other and open a bottle of wine as we normally would but trying to comfort each other with looks and words. This is the reality of the virus and so many people around the world will be feeling this way; no closure, terrible memories of the end, it is just too tragic. But she tells me her tears are happy tears and I can see already how much she is treasuring the book, all her memories in one place. On Monday she has her scans to see if the cancer has spread. It is always an anxious time and she won't get the news until a while later, so we always hold our breath and wait to hear that Small and Stable (as we named the two spots of cancer) are still small and stable.

I get home and watch the news, which shows that the R rate only just remains on the right side of 1 – above 1, and the number of cases increases. Apparently, in some parts of the country it is nearer 1, which raises the questions about local lockdowns. Lifting the lockdown is dependent on the R rate coming down and we now know that the R number remains unchanged. I look at a map and we are 0.97 in the South. That makes me think of the number of people on the beaches in the South last weekend and what that means. Apparently, the overall incidents are much lower in the South, but the R is much higher than other areas. Some health experts feel that change is required, and that we probably shouldn't relax any more restrictions yet, as although overall the COVID-19 figures are improving it is still not enough. SAGE actually are disputing the rate and saying it is above 1 in the North West and this could mean the virus would spread even faster. I hear on the radio that there will be more protests over George Floyd today and my heart sinks.

There is no briefing today, so I check the internet for figures. Another 204 people have died with coronavirus in the UK, according to the latest Department of Health figures. The data came alongside an indication that hospital deaths from COVID-19[3] in England are down. There were 218,187 tests carried out, according to the latest daily figures, with 1,557 positive. Public Health England (PHE) said that 75 more people had died in hospital, the lowest number since the 25th and the second lowest since the 25th March, just after lockdown began.

I decide to brave Sainsburys and am rewarded with many delights that we haven't eaten in months. I search the bookcase for cookery books and head to the kitchen with Nigella to become a domestic goddess with my hoard of food. I am a messy cook and I like to blitz the kitchen and mess everything up and then let Keith clean it. Keith surveys the kitchen in horror but for the first time in months I actually feel happy.

TOTAL DEATHS – 40,465

Sunday, 7th June

This morning I am walking (or limping) round my six-mile trek to the common and back. My second to little toe has a slight infection and for a small piece of bodily equipment it certainly can inflict pain!

To take my mind off it I am thinking about the words and phrases that have become part of our vocabulary over the last three months, some may have existed before but we didn't use them, or use them in this context, but now they are a major part of our everyday vocabulary.

- Unprecedented.
- Lockdown.
- Underlying conditions.
- Keeping the R down.
- Face covering.
- The WHO (not the rock band or doctor).
- PPE.
- Social Distancing.

- Black Lives Matter.
- White privilege.
- Taking the knee.

The last one has been the symbol of the riots following the murder of George Floyd. 'Taking the knee' is now being used as a symbol of respect to show solidarity and in some instances, police facing riot lines have adopted this. American football teams, who were originally banned from doing this and threatened with disciplinary action, are now being allowed to.

The protests are continuing all over the world, with more protests in London after a reasonably peaceful demonstration in central London yesterday. The news shows thousands of protestors streaming through the streets of London, but amongst the peace are some clashes. At one point a mounted police officer swerves into traffic lights and her horse bolts through the crowds trampling another person. Miraculously, it found its way back to the stables. Dame Cressida Dick, Commissioner of the Metropolitan Police Service (MPS), has urged protestors to find another way to make their views heard, but it shows no sign of abating and 27 police officers have been injured in the protests. However, demonstrators have said that they have seen officers acting very aggressively.

The pictures that I see show people making little or no attempt to social distance, with megaphones being passed around from person to person, so even with the R under 1, if you have thousands of people around the chances of people infecting are really high – particularly if they are not already demonstrating symptoms.

There is no briefing again today as it is the weekend and the decision to pause the briefings at weekends has been met with anger and confusion from the public. The Government has said it was because of poor TV viewing figures. However, I feel we still need the leadership and the updates – I mean, it is not as if the virus is not happening at weekends. Following criticism of Boris Johnson's absence at the briefings Downing Street have now committed to him taking one of the five nightly sessions.

There is news from a scientist who advises the Government on coronavirus and he says he wishes the UK had entered lockdown earlier. In his view the delay cost a lot of lives.

Professor John Edmunds says that the problem was that data was quite poor in March making it 'very hard' to do so. So, how come other countries knew to make the decisions? I just don't understand why we waited so long.

The only figures I can find today are from the Department of Health and Social Care who say that a further 77 people have died in the UK after contracting COVID-19. This is one of the lowest since the lockdown began but there is usually a delay in reporting deaths over the weekend. As of 9.00 a.m. today, 286,194 people in the country have tested positive for coronavirus.

TOTAL DEATHS – 40,542

Monday, 8th June
Official Lockdown, Week Twelve

This morning I get up very early as I am conducting a seminar for a school in South Africa organised by my friend Anthea. They are an amazing group of dedicated women and it is very exciting hearing their plans for mentoring. I work with them to define the scheme and to look at what can be done to ensure the girls at the school get the best help available. It is a small thing but I am keen to find anything I can do to support the changes that the world is now trying to make to eliminate racism.

According to the news, Boris Johnson has ordered ministers to swiftly ease the lockdown and this week will unveil plans to enable pubs, restaurants and cafes to open to try and avoid the potential loss of three million jobs. He will be setting out a roadmap to show how this is going to happen. It is all too fast for me; I need to see the result of the riots in two weeks before they ease anything else and I think he should announce this to let people know that further large gatherings could mean a slowing down of easing lockdown. I am fully in support of the Black Lives Matter campaign and will do everything in my power to support this cause. I am delighted that they are getting coverage, but I am nervous that the amount of people there might have caused more infections.

My toe and foot are badly swollen today and I fear the infection is getting worse. I phone the doctor to try and get an appointment but they suggest I go directly to the walk-in centre. The service is incredible; they take my temperature at the door, usher me in and I barely sit down when I am asked to go through to the treatment room. I tell the nurse how excited I am to have a trip out and see some new people and she looks at me as if I am a very sad person! She immediately prescribes antibiotics and says that it was a good thing I had come in so soon as the infection was starting to creep up into my foot. She dresses the toe and I am literally out and back in the car within five minutes. But I have to elevate the foot for a while, so I collect my laptop and head for the sofa and switch on the TV whilst I work.

The news today is full of the protests that happened at the weekend. Thousands gathered outside the US embassy in South London in solidarity with the US. Crowds gathered in Parliament Square and were also joined by Stormzy, the rapper. The statue of Winston Churchill was covered in graffiti with crowds writing 'is a racist' under his name. There were tussles as police held back demonstrators near the Foreign Office and 12 arrests were made and 8 officers injured. Boris Johnson announced that protests were 'subverted by thuggery' and Priti Patel called the hooliganism of the people attending the protests 'utterly indefensible'. She rejected claims the Government doesn't understand racial inequality by telling them that she was called a 'p**i' as a child in the playground.

In Bristol, ten thousand people descended on the city yesterday and tore down the statue of Edward Colston, dragged it through the streets to the harbour and threw it into the water after symbolically kneeling on his neck. Colston was famous in Bristol with many buildings, schools and roads being named after him. He was a member of the Royal African Company, described as a philanthropist but a renowned slave trader. His company transported about 80,000 men, women and children from Africa to the Americas and his statue was thrown into the river at the place where his boats sailed from. When he died in 1721 he bequeathed his wealth to charities, which is why he can still be seen on Bristol's streets, memorials and buildings. I have visited Bristol on many occasions but I had no idea that the statues and buildings actively celebrated a slave trader. How must it have affected African people to walk past these every day? As I am having to work from the sofa I put on the television and watch *13th*, a film exploring the history of racial inequality, which focuses on the fact that American prisons are disproportionately filled with African Americans. I feel sick to my stomach as I watch the programme; it is more than uncomfortable viewing.

The news this evening shows today's preparations are in place for George Floyd's funeral and aside from the walk-by in Houston, where thousands of mourners pay their respects at the Fountain of Praise, memorials have been built for George Floyd around the world, with portraits, roses, candles, flowers and murals.

It really has been the most extraordinary ten days, however, since the protests changes have started to be made, as the world has really stood up to be counted. I sincerely hope that the changes continue and that this really makes a difference. It is a start but is it enough?

Matt Hancock takes the briefing at 5.00 p.m. and he is joined by David Pearson, the newly appointed chair of the Social Care Sector COVID-19 Support Taskforce. Still no scientists joining him – I will watch this carefully to see if any of them return to the briefings or whether the Government have totally decided to ignore the science.

Matt Hancock suggests that he is pleased with the news today and is able to tell us that Covid is retreating in all counties. Data shows that the R rate is below 1 in all regions. People dying in care homes are falling and only 55 people have died today. Still tragic for those families but apparently the lowest since pre-lockdown. There were 1,205 new cases diagnosed today.

The antibiotics kick in leaving me sick and dizzy, so I head to bed early.

TOTAL DEATHS – 40,597

Tuesday, 8th June

Despite my toe I still get up early to do a virtual session with Olivia in the gym. The antibiotics are working fast so it doesn't look quite so swollen. We work on upper arms and do the best we can do.

Piers is engaged in a verbal battle with Nigel Farage this morning and I have to admit that I am on Piers side on this topic. Farage is arguing about the felling of the statue and how it was not democratic and spouting off about the removal of Hitler's statues in Germany. You cannot compare #BLM to Hitler. In other news, the Government have shelved plans to get all Primary pupils back to school before the end of term but missing six months of schooling is serious. And hearing they may not even open in September must be truly bad news for parents.

I decide to see how we are doing on coronavirus cases in Hampshire. The latest number of cases of COVID-19 has been confirmed as 4,269 in Hampshire and 200 on the Isle of Wight. The figure is up by 4 from Friday's total of 4,265 cases so far in Hampshire. It looks like Southampton have had just under 600 cases and only 13 deaths. Somehow that makes me feel a little safer – I had been concerned being at the hospital yesterday but with a population of 255,000 the chance of infection is low.

Alok Sharma, the Business Secretary, takes the briefing with Sarah Albon, the Chief Executive of the Health and Safety Executive.

In response to a question pointing out that in recent days scientists have not been there, a spokesman for No. 10 said it was wrong to say that scientists were no longer appearing at the daily government press conference. However, the move has coincided with government policy increasingly diverging from the scientific advice. For example, Sir Patrick Vallance has refused to publicly back the quarantine policy and Professor Chris Whitty has refused to agree to lower the coronavirus threat level, which was supposed to be a precondition for lockdown measures being eased. These are being eased regardless. Leading scientists have warned that ministers need to rebuild the trust of the public for the way they have handled the coronavirus outbreak and compensate people for lost earnings when they were asked to self-isolate to prevent a resurgence of the pandemic. According to the Guardian, another independent group of scientists has said that the testing and contact-tracing system is not fit for purpose and will not be able to keep coronavirus in check, as in other countries.

Alok announces that the death toll has risen today, by a shocking amount, 286. Compared to yesterday's 55 it again shows that it is too early to start believing it is anywhere near over.

Alok Sharma confirms that non-essential shops in England can open from Monday (I sincerely hope that means TK Maxx!) He says that this move will allow high streets up and down the country to 'spring back to life'. Northwest England, and the deaths in care homes, has driven up the number of excess fatalities since the UK went into lockdown. The UK now has a death toll believed to be greater than anywhere else except the US.

The opening of schools has not gone as Boris Johnson planned with only one in four children returning to school in England last week. The intention had been for a phased reopening of schools to allow parents back to work to boost the economy. Gavin Williamson, the Education Secretary for England, confirmed that primary schools will not have to take any more pupils before the end of the summer term. He told MPs earlier today that it would take a year or more to repair the damage done to pupils' education by the time spent in lockdown. Particular concern is about under-privileged children, for who school is respite from their home situation.

Tonight, I have a call with a fabulous lady, Aarti Palmer who has volunteered to design a jacket for the book. That makes it all a bit real. She asks a very good question – what is my timeline and when do I propose to stop writing? That gets me thinking; in my naivety, I originally thought that by now the would all be over and I would be writing about the fabulous street parties we were having to celebrate, as they did after the war. Clearly that is not going to happen, and I have to stop somewhere. I commit to stop writing in a month or so, whatever point we are at.

TOTAL DEATHS – 40,883

Wednesday, 10th June

My foot is getting fatter – it is so swollen that it looks like a pufferfish! I am praying that the antibiotics kick in today so that the swelling goes down, and so grateful that I don't have to wear shoes. Lockdown does have some benefits!

The next two days are busy delivering two virtual learning sessions a day including a new client, so I have to be really focused on ensuring I get delivery right. Sometimes it is so hard to keep motivated, but I just have to keep trying. I have to be honest, the tedium of working from home is getting to me a little now. Apart from the days when I am running training, just sitting in my office and looking at the screen all day is starting to get particularly boring. I recognise that it is because I am not taking a break or a lunch hour now – my schedule has increased with calls and coaching sessions so I have almost returned to back-to-back meetings again, just in a different way. I must try and find a way to take some more breaks – I am having Friday off this week but already someone has booked in a call for 2.00 p.m. as they know that I won't actually be going anywhere! If all goes to plan I will see LJ and Elly at the weekend and I am beyond excited. I decide to spend Friday giving the house a good spring clean, not that they will be in the house, but it has given me a reason to do it!

I do as much exercise as I can with my uncooperative foot and wash my hair. Only thirteen days till I get my hair cut and coloured and I cannot wait. Piers is actually hosting some interesting debates this morning, one on the readiness of schools to receive people and the consequences for under-privileged children, and another on the Black Lives Matter list of statues around the country that they say should be removed. He facilitates this really well and it is a fascinating subject. Do we delete all history, i.e. Churchill, Nelson, James 1 due to their connections to slavery? I need to think about this some more. I can completely understand how it must affect the black community looking at these statues, but shamefully, there is so much of it in our history. I wonder if there is a way that this history can be preserved to show the lessons we have learnt in a way that does not impact on minorities and without making these people look as if they have been immortalised.

We also hear that zoos and animal parks can now reopen. That is good as many of them were looking at potential closure, and last night I heard that theme parks were reopening and I wondered about zoos. I feel totally confused now about lockdown and what we can and cannot do. Shops are opening and they are talking about cinemas and other attractions, but do we really know it is safe? The scientists seem to have abandoned us and we have very little clear direction. We can protest in masses but only meet in groups of six outside.

I set up the training room (i.e. move out the laundry and iron!) ready for the first session at 10.00 a.m. The session is on managing your team effectively during lockdown and a subject I am very familiar with, but it is followed quite quickly with a Senior Leadership Team session with a new client and then a team meeting at 4.00 p.m., so not much time in between to do anything.

What a ridiculously busy day – I deliver the two virtual sessions and get a couple of documents out before the meeting with the team at 4.00 p.m. I am exhausted when I finally come away from the computer at 5.30 p.m. and then watch the briefing.

Well, surprise, surprise, we have Boris tonight and even more surprising is that he is joined by Whitty and Vallance – so they are all still friends!

The PM begins again by outlining the Government's five tests and reminds us that they are designed to ensure any changes to lockdown are 'careful, proportionate and safe'. He adds that we must do everything in our power to avoid a second peak. Again, the words 'horse' and 'bolted' are on the tip of my tongue.

He continues to announce that the death rate and number of positive cases both continue to fall. However, a further 245 people have died since yesterday, which is a lot more than on Monday.

Then, with a flourish he tells us that the UK has met all the Governments five tests and 'we can proceed with the following further adjustments'. We now can have support bubbles. Those people who live alone will be able to go and stay at someone's house from Saturday and act as if they live in the same household. But they are only allowed one support bubble. This will be wonderful news for single grandparents who are dying to see their children and grandchildren. I decide to stretch the rules this weekend. My daughter lives with her boyfriend but to visit me she really needs to stay over so I will be her support bubble and not feel too guilty about it! Obviously if anyone in the 'bubble' develops symptoms everyone will have to isolate.

He reminds us that if those who do not qualify do start meeting inside people's homes they will be breaking the law, but I am willing to risk it.

Boris says that we will continue to remain cautious and measure the impact and will apply the brakes if required. He says that the rate of infection is not quite low enough yet and that is why the Government cannot bring all the primary schools back before the summer.

I finally sit down to dinner, only to be reminded that I have a networking event at 8.00 p.m. However, despite being exhausted it is run by my amazing walking buddy, Trudy, and I leave feeling energised and positive. By 9.30 p.m. I am barely able to keep my eyes open and head for bed.

TOTAL DEATHS – 41,128

Thursday, 11th June

Another early start to work with my team of leaders in Strasbourg today on change. I set up the laundry room/ training room and get ready to work. I have no idea why I am exhausted but once again the week is spinning past and my days are jam-packed with calls and delivery. However, my diary is much clearer next week so that may be a little easier to get back into the marketing. We absolutely need to.

The Prime Minister has announced that Professor Ferguson's claim that delaying lockdown for a week doubled the death toll is premature. A paper written by the academic team at Imperial College led to the Government announcing the lockdown but one of the scientists, who was advising the Government at the time, has made a damning testimony that enforcing lockdown one week earlier could have saved 20,000 lives. The revelation by Professor Neil Ferguson at the House of Commons Science Committee had left Boris facing repeated questions at PM's Question Time yesterday. The case is helped by Sir Chris Whitty who, when asked about his regrets about the handling of the crisis so far said, " I think there's a long list of things that we need to look at very seriously." Very different from the speech Nicola Sturgeon made, labelling the deaths of care home residents due to coronavirus 'tragic' and saying every death from the virus is a matter of 'deep personal regret'.

The news is all over this, and quite rightly so; I have been thinking for a long time about whether we should have locked down earlier and I remember back to the week we came back from France. France had locked down the night before we left and it was a further ten days before Boris announced lockdown. I remember when he said not to go to pubs on the Friday night and I thought to myself that was an invitation for everyone to go for one last time – an opportunity where he should have been more directive and wasn't. The same with allowing the sporting events to go ahead that week. I feel sure that if I had lost a loved one I would be wondering if they would have survived if we had locked down earlier. Along with the questions of the handling of the care homes, the PPE and the tracing it has become clear that they have a lot to answer for. It seems we may have made the classic mistake of 'hoping for the best' rather than 'preparing for the worst'.

I hit the ground running at 7.30 a.m. ready to start my first session and by 3.00 p.m. I am absolutely exhausted; these sessions take so much more out of me than normal training sessions although I guess with time I will get used to it. However, my last session had 30 people and I managed to get lots of interaction, so I must be getting the hang of it!

Matt Hancock takes the briefing today and is joined by Baroness Dido Harding. The Baroness chairs the coronavirus Track and Trace service. He is going to need her tonight as it has emerged that several thousand people who tested positive could not be reached by the system. Brace yourself Madam!

Apparently, a total of 31,794 contacts were identified with 8,177 of the 26,985 contacted and told to self-isolate after testing positive for the virus.

Hancock says that the latest figures show the number of coronavirus patients to die in the UK has risen by 151 today. The youngest person to die was just aged 26. I think of the poor grieving family. I also saw an article today that showed the lungs of a young woman affected by coronavirus and they looked horrendous. I think of my lungs and once again remained convinced they were damaged when I had swine flu.

Hancock tells us that virus is 'in retreat and the Government's plan is working' – I wonder how the grieving family of the 26-year-old feel about that? He then talks about Test and Trace. He says it is like the Government's 'radar' and that it shows where the virus is. He states that people have a role to play and that if they have symptoms, they should get a test and participate in Test and Trace and insists it is people's 'civic duty to comply'. He goes on to say that the figures will show why Test and Trace will be world-class and says it is a service for the public and works best with the cooperation of the public.

Questions from the public start with whether there will be any more public support for people told to self-isolate by Test and Trace and whether all workers at a firm will have to self-isolate if a colleague tests positive. I can relate to that with a small office; if one of us was to get it we would no doubt all get it and it could wipe us out. Hancock replies and says there is a support package in place for people who need to self-isolate. Really? I haven't heard of anything. So, are they saying that if I couldn't work for two weeks they would pay my daily rate?

Someone boldly says that this is not yet a world-class system and challenges that it is too early to relax lockdown.

Hancock says that the Prime Minister had promised there would be a world-class system and we will have one. He then neatly dodges a question about the app by saying they will introduce it when is right to do so.

Well that told us absolutely nothing apart from Test and Trace is not really fit for purpose yet.

Friday, 12th June

I have decided to take today off. I have been feeling a bit overwhelmed this week and whilst the training was really good and I thoroughly enjoyed it, learning and delivering so many new sessions was quite exhausting. Plus, I have the children coming to visit this weekend and I want to clear some stuff up so that I can totally relax. I also have a big decision to make about whether to make a member of staff redundant and I want to give it due time and consideration whilst I have head space. This is the terrible part of the consequences of the pandemic, but economically, as I look forward, I have to think about the company as a whole and until business really picks up we are haemorrhaging money on a monthly basis.

Also, today should have been the day we started our annual Isle of Wight Festival weekend with the girls. This morning we would have been packing clothes, food and alcohol (well mainly alcohol and a little food) and heading over for a weekend of non-stop talking, silliness, music, drinking and dancing. This is the saddest I have been about anything that has been cancelled this year, as it is a tradition we have had for almost twenty years, and the line-up this year was insane. An email pings into my inbox from the festival and I feel better when I read it – they have kept exactly the same line-up for next year and added a few more, so at least we have that to look forward to. Hopefully, this weekend there will be some highlights on the television to remind me, but I feel grateful that I have our family BBQ to prepare for and lots to do.

Some news catches my eye; we know that the Government will have to have an inquiry into how the pandemic was handled but relatives of 450 people who have died are demanding an urgent review of steps needed in order to prevent more deaths. It had to happen and quite rightly so. Apparently, there is a group called the COVID-19 Bereaved Families for Justice UK Group and they say that waiting for ministers to launch a full inquiry will cost lives. It is no wonder, when a recent report reveals it is not known how many of the 25,000 people discharged from hospitals into care homes at the peak of the outbreak were infected.

The debate continues about whether schools will go back in September with academies now calling for a relaxation of the two-metre social distancing to one-metre as they say that two metres makes it absolutely impossible for more than half of children to go back. September seems such a long way away and surely by then we will have eliminated this, or am I just being unduly optimistic?

The day passes quickly with calls and chores, even though it is a day off the emails keep coming and there are some urgent things to deal with that I need to attend to.

I tune into the briefing at 5.00 p.m. and tonight it is Grant Shapps, joined by Professor Stephen Powis and Peter Hendy. He hits the ground running with the news that the R rate remains unchanged from last week at between 0.7 and 0.9, which, he tells us, is stable.

As of the 12th June there were a further 1,541 cases confirmed positive. He says that the number of people testing positive is falling and the number of patients in hospital with coronavirus is broadly continuing to fall across the regions plus the seven-day rolling average of deaths continues to fall. The death toll rises by 202 today.

Shapps tells us that from Monday, if we don't wear face coverings, we could be refused travel and could be fined. He tells us that if we can work from home that we should continue to do so and if we can't, we should try to avoid public transport or use it at quieter

A great question is asked about student nurses who came into the front line after the Government called for support and whether they are being asked to carry out duties beyond their level of competence. I think this is something that should be fully explored but Shapps simply says that people should be working in areas in which they are and feel competent. That is ridiculous, how could they possibly be competent, no one has had to deal with this before. But age and general experience must be really important.

Shapps is questioned on whether Chief Nursing Officer Ruth May is either unwilling or unable to attend these press conferences anymore because she won't defend Dominic Cummings. Shapps denies this and says she has attended many times and he has noticed one of her tweets is pinned on the No. 10 Twitter feed. What a strange response.

And then it is time for our Friday night girls' call and we have a great time catching up – Lauren in LA tells us what is happening with Black Lives Matter protests, and Claire, who is in the TV industry, gives us an insight into what they are trying to do to be able to start filming again. These sessions make my week and allow me to feel connected; thank God for Zoom, I truly don't know what I would do without it.

TOTAL DEATHS – 41,481

Saturday, 13th June

My eyes fly open at 7.00 a.m. and I remember it is Saturday and I can get ready to see my children tomorrow. I go straight to the kitchen to start cooking and happily begin chopping veg. By 8.00 a.m. I have made roasted pepper couscous, aubergine, mushroom and sweet potato salad, coleslaw and a lemon cheesecake. I pause at 9.00 a.m. to do my virtual group workout and Elly joins from Lincoln. The minute she is finished she is going to jump in the car and drive down to surprise her best friend for her birthday and then I will pick her up around 9.00 p.m. I spend the rest of the day scrubbing the house from top to bottom and disinfecting and steaming everything.

Despite warnings from the Government to avoid crowds, the protests continue in London and this time it starts to get nasty. In Parliament Square bottles and smoke bombs are thrown at police and the crowd turn on journalists. The groups include some far-right activists who claimed they were protecting statues from anti-racism activists. Hundreds of mostly white men end up near the Cenotaph War Memorial in Whitehall and the statue of Winston Churchill, which has been boarded up. Some protestors manage to break metal barriers. The Metropolitan Police had placed restrictions on several groups, including insisting on a 5.00 p.m. curfew, but several groups remained on the streets of central London after the official cut off. Scotland Yard said they had arrested five people for offences including violent disorder, assault on police, possession of an offensive weapon, being drunk and disorderly and possessing Class A drugs.

Underground and mainline stations were temporarily closed due to the protests but later reopened. Large groups of right-wing protestors then moved to Trafalgar Square where fireworks were thrown across the crowds.

I check the figures for today and there are another 181 deaths sadly, so we are creeping up to near 42,000, I long for the day they tell us there are no deaths to report. There is no briefing today as they have stopped the weekend briefings.

Boris Johnson tweeted: "Racist thuggery has no place on our streets. Anyone attacking the police will be met with full force of the law. These marches and protests have been subverted by violence and breach current guidelines. Racism has no part in the UK and we must work together to make that a reality."

Home Secretary Priti Patel said the desecration of the memorial was utterly shameful.

BBC News reports that the effect of the lockdown to date has been pretty devastating with figures showing that the UK economy shrank by more than a fifth in April, which is the largest monthly contraction ever recorded. And that was in the first full month of lockdown. Apparently, this slump of 20.4% in economic growth is three times larger than the whole of the financial crisis twelve years ago. The ONS says it has affected almost all areas of economic activity – with house building and car manufacturing particularly badly hit. So, it is official. We are on our way to a recession, which is defined as two consecutive quarters of negative growth. The only glimmer of good news is that analysts say that April was likely to have been the worst month. This economic uncertainty has led to calls for trade talks with the EU following Brexit to be extended beyond the end of this year, although the Government are still saying there will be no delay and Michael Gove stating that he had 'formally confirmed' to the EU that there will be no delay. Great, we just start to recover from COVID-19 and then they will hit us with Brexit.

Meanwhile, our dear Queen celebrates her ninety-fourth birthday at Windsor Castle where she has been isolating since the beginning of lockdown. Traditionally, there would be a big Trooping the Colour parade, which would be held at Buckingham Palace and would be televised, but this year was a very low-key affair with a military ceremony at the castle's ground with no other Royal Family members in attendance. Just her and Phillip in a little gazebo watching the pomp and ceremony! Of course, she would follow the lockdown rules, but did anyone tell her she could have had four more people? Apparently, it is only the second time in the history of her reign that the parade has been cancelled.

We go to pick up Elly from seeing her best friend –.it is so wonderful to see her and we stay and have a drink, sitting round their pool, and it feels like the world is getting back to normal.

TOTAL DEATHS – 41,662

Sunday, 14th June

Today I get to see LJ and Sophie as well, and also their father, Barry, and his partner, Janine, are coming. OK, that is a gathering of seven but we have plenty of garden space to sit in! I am up early and in the gym, and by 9.45 a.m., when Elly emerges from her lie-in, I am well prepared. The weather is not being particularly kind but apparently it is going to clear up this afternoon, so we cross our fingers, put up our big parasol and open all the bi-folding doors from the dining room. So, even if we do need to eat inside, that would, in theory, still make us in the garden!

I shower and dress and even put jewellery on today. It really feels like the beginning again but I know it isn't. I know that the virus is still out there and in theory could spike at any time. But with shops opening tomorrow, and talk of pubs starting to open, it feels so hopeful. I still am worried about the future, but I feel grateful we have survived and are all healthy.

Some people clearly thought that lockdown was over on Saturday as two 'quarantine raves' took place in Manchester last night with images and pictures showing thousands gathering in a park – according to police 6,000. One man dies from a suspected overdose, three people were stabbed, and a woman was allegedly raped.

As I survey the food I have prepared, and our beautiful house and garden, I once again feel incredibly thankful. This period has taught me so much in many ways and I am incredibly lucky to have what I have, and I think of all the people who have had to survive lockdown, in desperate situations with little money, no outdoor space and with people they don't want to be with.

My guests arrive and we have the most amazing day. We crack open the champagne, but I can't hug my son; it is just too much to bear to see him and not hold him. We sit outside on the decking and have nibbles whilst I cook on the barbeque and everything feels like it always was. We catch up on our stories and how it has been for everyone and the champagne leads to a jug of Pimm's, my first this year, followed by pink gin and tonic and after the food-fest we end up playing games in the garden. Hula Hooping, bean bag throwing, archery and even netball. It is truly the most magical day and we sit outside until nearly 8.00 p.m. laughing, and then it is time for them to go home. I will never forget today, amongst the sadness, the pain and tragedy there is some magic.

But not for everyone. The death rate rises by 36. No celebration there; still terribly sad – a whole lot of families coping with bereavement, but it is at least on the downward trend. I want to hear that there are no deaths. And no cases.

TOTAL DEATHS – 41,698

Monday, 15th June
Official Lockdown, Week Thirteen

I have a hangover! A real full-on head and stomach hangover. I get up at 6.30 a.m. ready to do my PT session and for the first twenty minutes I am convinced I will throw up. Ironically, with a little mind over matter, I do a good session and get my heart rate nearly up to 130 bpm and sweat like never before. Kill or cure?

I get ready for work knowing that today will be difficult. I have to put a member of staff at risk of redundancy. I have always been quite an emotional person, so this really hits me and even though I try to concentrate on my work, I just keep thinking about him and his situation.

The day passes in a blur or calls and emails and I only stop for five minutes to wave a sad goodbye to Elly as she starts to make her way up to Lincoln. I am so sad to see her go but so grateful for the time we had together. I miss her and LJ living so close to me and I feel a bit sad and lost today.

The high street opened today and was absolutely packed with queues outside of all stores. The European Health Authority told the Guardian we shouldn't be easing lockdown any further until the Test and Trace service is up and running effectively, but the Government insists that there were 20,000-plus people trained on testing and that it is safe to.

At 2.00 p.m. I make the call to my staff member and he is unsurprisingly shocked and upset. It wasn't that he couldn't see it coming; I think everyone is prepared for the inevitable at the moment, but even thinking you are prepared doesn't always prepare you.

At 5.00 p.m. Dominic Raab begins today's briefing setting out the latest coronavirus figures. There are currently 395 people in critical care and 38 deaths were recorded up to 5.00 p.m. yesterday. Overall, a total of 6,866,481 tests have been carried out and 296,857 cases have been confirmed positive.

As always, he talks about the evolving science, which they are using to make any policy calls. Just a thought, Dominic, we don't call it evolving science, we call it utter confusion, lack of direction and mixed messages.

An interesting question – he is asked why there are no scientists with him during the briefing, and he tells us that scientists and the Chief Medical Officer will continue to come but, "I think it is true to say that as we go down the roadmap and start to talk about the changes we are making whether to businesses or to schools or in other areas we will also bring other independent experts along." Hmm, really?

At 8.00 p.m. I watch the ITV Corona Question Time, which starts by showing us that Northern Ireland is opening hotels, bars and restaurants from the 3rd July and the unsurprising news that 2.3 million children have done barely any work through lockdown.

A question from someone who is due to get married on the 5th September, what restrictions will be in place? I am sure many brides-to-be held their breath waiting for the answer. The response? The positive answer is just to keep on planning. Professor Karol Sikora, presenting, says it looks good for September, so he advises people to 'carry on planning and be optimistic'. A later guest contradicts this statement and says they don't think that we will be anywhere near ready to have public gatherings by then.

There is a question about support bubbles – "If you live alone and another person is shielding can you see each other?" The response is that technically social bubbles do not apply to people who are shielding, however, if you both have been shielding for more than two weeks, and if you can get together without touching or being in contact with other people, then do it!"

A question about barbeques; if people come to the garden of your house, can you give them food? Apparently, yes you can, but they need to bring their own cutlery, plates and even chairs! They would have had a fit if they could have seen the party that Elly was at, on Saturday night and certainly during my BBQ, they didn't bring their own cutlery! I honestly don't think that is happening anywhere!'

I fall asleep on the sofa as I try to type; it's been an exhausting day.

TOTAL DEATHS – 41,736

Tuesday, 16th June

I wake up to the news that stats are out that the number of UK workers on payrolls fell by 600,000 over the last three months in lockdown. If I didn't feel bad enough about making someone redundant already, I do now.

The news is full of unemployment figures and other depressing facts including New Zealand announcing two new cases of the virus. They had been free for over forty-five days, so this is disappointing, particularly as those cases came from the UK. The online debate is still around whether the economy is more important than saving lives and are we easing too quickly. The general opinion is that the public is now totally confused about what they can and can't do any more.

Piers Morgan is getting behind England Striker, Marcus Rashford, who is fighting for free school meal vouchers during the summer, but the Government confirms it is not going to provide them. Piers urges viewers to get behind the Twitter campaign and get it turned around today, but the Department of Education said it would not reverse its decision. Rashford was drawing on his own experience of relying on free school meals and food banks growing up.

Incredibly, there is to be a big Trump Campaign Rally in

Tulsa, Oklahoma, the first in three months since coronavirus hit, and unbelievably there have been more than one million ticket requests for the indoor rally. I find this hard to take in – even if they had a thousand people there, how can you go from not being able to meet in groups of more than six to a massive rally like that? If that happened in the UK it would then open the floodgates for cries around big concerts to be reinstated. But there has been a U-turn on wearing masks and everyone will be receiving temperature checks and hand sanitiser. Considering people lining up to get in will face temperatures of up to thirty-five degrees and will be standing around I would imagine that by the time they get to the door the temperature checks will be pretty much redundant.

And then it is time for the briefing and tonight we get Boris. But before the briefing the news comes through that Boris has done a U-turn on free school meals after Rashford's campaigning. Great work that man and no doubt Piers will be smug tomorrow.

Boris is joined by Sir Patrick Vallance and Peter Horby, Professor of Emerging Infectious Diseases and Global Health at University of Oxford – a bit of a newbie. And even more intriguing is the fact that Boris says that he will let Vallance and Horby do most of the talking as they have some news! What an anticipation frame to start with.

Boris announces the death toll for today and as expected it has risen since the weekend and this time it has gone up to 233 deaths. Boris does the normal blah blah, following the plan talk; he says he is pleased shops are opening and more pupils returning to school. He is still doing everything in his power to get life back to normal but will proceed carefully – including his review of the 2 metre social-distancing rule.

He reminds us of his global effort to find a long-term solution, and how it is continuing, and that a big breakthrough has been made by a team of scientists. Backed by government funding, they have led the first robust clinical trial in the world proven to have reduced the risk of death. OK, let's hear it!

Described by scientists as a major breakthrough, a cheap steroid has become the first life-saving treatment in the COVID-19 pandemic, raising hopes for the most seriously ill. The drug, dexamethasone, is cheap, available from any pharmacy and can be obtained anywhere in the world. The drug has been trialled on some of the sickest patients, i.e. those on ventilators, and was responsible for the survival of one in eight of the sickest patients. Called the Recovery Trial, it was the biggest, randomised, controlled trial of coronavirus treatments in the world. Peter Horby says that it is the only drug so far shown to reduce mortality and it reduces it significantly, which is why it is being cited as a major breakthrough. Horby continues by saying it is not a drug that would be used on patients who do not have breathing difficulties but if they do it has significant benefits. And it is ridiculously cheap. To use on eight patients in this category it would cost £40 and save one life out of the eight. Ironically, it has been around for many years. However, if there was a second wave it would not stop people getting the illness, and if there was a second wave, there would still be a need for social distancing.

"The Chief Medical Officer will issue guidance soon saying this should be used for clinical practice," Horby says. He also says, "doctors should be able to use the drug this evening. It is in the cupboard, and they know how it works."

Boris is challenged by a journalist who reminds him that he said twelve weeks ago we would be almost through this and it doesn't feel like we are anywhere near. Boris says he had told the country they would 'turn the tide' in twelve weeks and thinks he has done this. He replies with one of his strange analogies – he says they have 'flattened the sombrero' or whatever he said they would do. This was something he said as the pandemic was taking hold describing the need to flatten the curve of the disease. This statement feels a little inappropriate and is challenged by a journalist. I am sure that the families of the deceased will not be thrilled to hear that analogy. He follows by saying that 'they have turned the tide on it. They have not yet finally defeated it. But people are resolved to defeat it'. He adds that we are seeing the first 'chink of light' in the fight against coronavirus with drugs such as dexamethasone.

Finally, there is a question about whether Boris will be talking to President Macron about travel corridors.

Johnson replies that he will be talking to Macron about all sorts of things, including this, when they meet later this week. And he says they will be talking to Spain too about this. I wonder if he will be talking in Spanish?

I decide it is time to have some escapism and that normally means Daniel Craig. Quantum of Solace it is then.

TOTAL DEATHS – 41,969

Wednesday, 17th June

I wake up and decide to spend a few minutes setting my 'state'. Today needs to be a productive and positive day so I decide to go for a long walk and get my day planned. When I can get in the zone it is amazing what I can achieve, so during the hour tramping around the woods I get a good strong focus and by 8.15 a.m. I am at my desk with my plan, a big jug of water, a cup of tea and I am quickly in my flow.

As I work I listen to the news and as predicted Piers is quite smug about Marcus Rashford's campaign (and rightly so), it is a great thing he has done. A lot of news is around dexamethasone, which is a totally amazing breakthrough. Sir Patrick Vallance hailed the treatment as 'a ground-breaking development in our fight against the disease'. The real excitement is that it is so readily available and so inexpensive. Chris Witty adds that 'this is the most important trial result for COVID-19 so far'. Significant reduction in mortality in those requiring oxygen or ventilation from a safe and well-known drug. I feel hugely relieved but sad for those families who have lost loved ones that might have been saved if this had been discovered earlier.

I check in today on travelling to see if anything is shifting. Greece is hoping to kick-start its vital tourism sector after three months in lockdown. Passengers arriving from an airport deemed high risk by the European Union Aviation Safety Agency (EASA) are tested for a high temperature and quarantined for up to fourteen days if necessary. British people are still barred from flying in. I can't really imagine any country wanting us to fly in!

There are still ongoing negotiations between Portugal and Britain on an 'air bridge' that would mean we could dodge the quarantine upon returning home – with Prime Minister António Costa saying discussions are going well. So, some hope there!

I haven't really thought much about Mauritius recently – I don't expect we will get there, and there would no doubt be a quarantine if we did, but we are still waiting for a couple of weeks to see what happens.

Once again, the news is looking at whether there will be a second wave and Sir John Bell, Regius Professor of Medicine at the University of Oxford, tells the community that with lockdown restrictions easing it is likely that the UK will see a return of the COVID-19 epidemic. However, if we had used dexamethasone right from the beginning of the pandemic, we apparently could have saved 4,000 - 5,000 deaths.

By lunchtime I have completed the three tasks that I set myself and get ready to do a podcast for a colleague in Toulouse. I take the team call and tell them about the redundancy – I can see it makes some of them are nervous and so I try and reassure them that there will be no other redundancies. However, in this climate there are no guarantees.

The briefing is held tonight by Oliver Dowden the Secretary of State for Digital, Culture, Media and Sport. First the figures; 184 people have sadly died today.

Dowden suggests that the Government might be planning a bailout for theatres as they were likely to remain shut for some time, admitting that indoor venues providing live entertainment were even more constrained by social distancing than outside arenas. He admits that they had set the challenging target of the 4th July for a further relaxation of the lockdown in England before stating that this would be exceptionally difficult. He is continuing discussions with the Government to see how they can support the theatres.

Dowden is asked whether he had asked experts to advise him on what could be done to pilot ideas that might allow live performances to continue in theatres and other arts venues. He responded by saying:

> *"We do need greater flexibility to overcome some of the very specific and practical obstacles to the return of live performance. So that's why over the next week we will be convening experts in a targeted way, bringing together our leading performers in theatres, choirs and orchestras with medical experts and advisers, and the idea is that they will work together in detail to develop that roadmap, which is so badly needed to perform safely, with a particular focus on piloting innovative ideas that may permit live performances."*

He is challenged on whether the UK was late in going into lockdown and he rejects the claim that the UK was particularly late in implementing the lockdown. Asked about claims that locking down late led to an extra 20,000 or more deaths, he reinforces the fact that ministers were informed by scientific advice in doing so and they did so at a relatively similar stage in the progression of the disease as other countries did do.

It's a short briefing tonight, with very little to report.

TOTAL DEATHS – 42,153

Thursday, 17th June

Today I have an 8.00 a.m. call so the alarm goes off at 6.00 a.m. – it is a rest day today for exercise but for the first time ever I switch off the alarm and go back to sleep for another hour. When it goes off again I really don't want to get up. I don't know what is wrong with me. As I shower and get dressed I feel sluggish and my head is heavy, my sinuses feel a bit blocked. Maybe I have a cold coming on?

Not only am I not feeling great physically, I am feeling really aimless about the lockdown now. When I spoke to the team yesterday I talked about bringing a member back from furlough at the beginning of July and how we might be back at work, but I still feel unsure about what is changing in the rules. However, I have a positive call with one of the team to discuss when she could come back and I guess we just have to keep hoping for the best.

There is news that the much-anticipated 'NHS Contact Tracing' app may not be ready for national rollout until winter and a health minister has told MPs "it isn't a priority for us." Lord Bethell, the minister who is in charge of the NHS app, claimed the delay was in part caused by a fear of 'freaking out' the public by using technological means to tell them they might be ill. I am even more confused;

I thought this was up and running and that everyone was trained. I Google NHS Test and Trace and it suggests it is all working; very confusing and disappointing as this was really our 'get out of jail' card.

We also have to contend with having the US pouring cold water on our dexamethasone 'breakthrough', calling for the full results of the trial to be published and warning of potential side effects. They clearly hadn't read the fact that the drug has been used for authorities for many years without side effects. Germany's health ministry, meanwhile, said there was no need to stockpile the drug.

Last night saw the start of the Premier League with support for Black Lives Matter visible on shirts and stands. Both teams and referees 'took a knee' and there was a minute's silence for the victims of the pandemic. Seats were covered and the crowd noise was artificial but after a 100-day absence many people were happy to see it back. Manchester City triumphed over Arsenal with a 3–0 win, and Aston Villa and Sheffield United played a draw.

Aviation is still taking a hit with our holiday looking less and less likely this year – Qantas has cancelled all international flights until late October, apart from to New Zealand, as they want to keep their borders closed to prevent the spread of the virus into next year. It joins a growing list of carriers impacted by the virus.

And then some very sad news comes in – Dame Vera Lynn has died at the age of 103. I am so glad that she managed to come back into the public eye and become the oldest artist to get a Top 40 album during the pandemic when she re-entered the charts and beat her own record. God bless her for all her contributions to the war and also the pandemic.

And a glimmer of good news – the Bank of England is going to pump an extra £10 billion into the UK economy to help fight the impact of the coronavirus downturn. They said that there was growing evidence that the hit to the economy would be 'less severe' than initially feared. The Bank said more recent indicators of economic activity suggest that the economy was starting to bounce back. However, it warned that the outlook remained uncertain.

I finally make some traction on my to-do list this afternoon and when 5.00 p.m. comes I have cleared enough outstanding work to have a day on marketing tomorrow, which feels positive.

At 5.00 p.m. Matt Hancock appears again with the sad news that we lost another 135 people today – still a high number. There have been a further 1,218 positive tests for COVID-19.

He skims over testing mentioning there has been a total of 7,259,555 – these figures seem meaningless now. The majority of the briefing is about the fact that the Government has confirmed that they are ditching the 'Track and Trace' app. Apparently, Apple are all to blame for the fact this has been dubbed a 'shambles' by critics due to ongoing delays, but testing on the Isle of Wight showed that the app works well on Android devices but Apple software prevents iPhones being used effectively for contact tracing unless you are using Apple's own technology! Is it just me or does anyone else think they might have tested this before releasing it? So now Hancock tells us they have agreed to join forces with Google and Apple to 'bring the best bits of both systems together and bring together some of the best minds to find a solution to this global challenge'. However, when pushed he refused to put a date on the release of the app and then says the most extraordinary thing: "But I am confident we will get there -- we will put that cherry on Dido's cake." Apparently, he was referring to Baroness Dido Harding!

The vaccine is discussed and lucky us oldies (i.e. those of us over 50), front-line workers and vulnerable people will be first in line if and when a vaccine is available. I won't hold my breath for that one, even though Hancock has told Downing Street that AstraZeneca has already started manufacturing a vaccine being produced at University of Oxford and if it is approved it will allow officials to 'build up a stockpile'.

TOTAL DEATHS – 42,288

Friday, 18th June

Today I am back firing on all cylinders – yesterday we had a few 'planes landing at work'! When we discuss sales, we often talk about the fact it is great to have a lot of planes circling, but we need to land them and get purchase orders. So, yesterday the team sent me several emails with plane analogies such as 'you are cleared for landing, runway 26 left!' detailing confirmed sales. Whilst it is mainly from September onwards, we managed to get some in for July and August, so I am feeling a bit more positive about the future. It still isn't enough for me to keep all the team but there is some light there. My nausea from yesterday has dissipated and my head feels clear, so I get up at 6.00 a.m. and go to the gym. I suddenly realise that Asda is open at 7.00 a.m. and decide to go and do the shopping, so I whip down the road and am second in the queue at 7.00 a.m. I am back by 8.00 a.m. and after dumping the shopping go back in the gym; my energy knows no boundaries today!

No Piers Morgan today on *GMB* and it is actually quite interesting to hear other news being reported again today; for months it has been solely coronavirus and now there is other news coming through including tributes to Dame Vera Lynn. Piers has been taking quite a bashing from Twitter this week. Monday marked the fiftieth day since the last government minister agreed to appear for an interview on *GMB*. Since then, they have only agreed to be interviewed by Sky and BBC. Pretty disgusting as, regardless of how they feel about presenters, we have a right to hear from them. But Piers has still been regularly attacking politicians on the morning show and has really turned his attention on to Boris Johnson and Matt Hancock. Recently, Piers has been replaying old footage from recent interviews and dissecting them, blasting Hancock for the Government's overall handling of the coronavirus pandemic – quite rightly in some respects, but his behaviour was inappropriate. But a lot of viewers took to Twitter suggesting it was a 'character assassination' and ranting that his behaviour was disgraceful and calling it 'lazy reporting'.

We are starting to discuss bringing some of our staff back from furlough and it is beginning to look quite complicated as they are allowed to work part-time or shifts now. I wonder how this will be policed. The furlough scheme has currently cost the public £19.6 billion so far. Staff are currently not allowed to provide services for the organisation whilst on furlough, but research has found that 35% of UK employees have been asked to work by their boss whilst on the scheme. This is considered to be an act of fraud under the rules of the scheme, which begs the question that if they know this, what are they doing about it?

Staff are allowed to undertake training, volunteer for another organisation or even work for another employer, but the research from Crossland Employment Solicitors across 2,000 employees revealed that a third of furloughed members were asked to continue to do their job as normal whilst 29% were asked to do administrative tasks. Apparently, these were both large firms and SMEs in sectors including PR, IT and manufacturing. I find this quite shocking – we have absolutely kept to the rules, even though there were times when we were quite desperate from support from our furloughed team members. It was also discovered that one in five have been asked to cover a colleague's job or work for a linked firm. This could mean that the taxpayers are potentially footing a massive bill, millions of pounds in fraudulent furlough wage claims. The Government does say that an employer could get a hefty fine and be asked to pay past payments back, have any future payments withheld or even face prison sentences. Apparently, employers have got a thirty-day window to confess to 'furlough fraud' and staff who think their organisation is flouting the system have been encouraged to get in touch. I hope they do as this money will mean we are depriving public services of essential funding. I am currently putting the plan together for our two furloughed staff and the plan will be to bring them back for 20% of the time but to also have a significant training plan for them to bring them up to speed when they are ready.

Closely following this is the news that the UK's debt is now worth more than its economy after the Government borrowed a record amount in May. The £55.2 billion figure is five times higher than they borrowed at the same time last year and the highest since records began in 1992. Ouch! No doubt they will really be rushing us back to work to get the economy going.

And just on cue, news comes through that the UK's coronavirus alert level has been downgraded from four to three. According to the Government guidelines this means it is now considered to be 'in general circulation' and there could be a 'gradual relaxation of restrictions'.

Education Secretary, Gavin Williamson, takes the briefing and starts by reminding the public that even though the alert level has been lowered there is still a threat of continuing infections as the virus is still circulating. There have been 173 deaths today, which means that the average number of deaths per week in the UK is now over six times lower than it was in April.

Williamson goes on to say that all children will return to school by September, which is part of how the UK will 'rebuild and recover' after COVID-19. He added that the Government recognises the 'important role schools play in keeping children safe'. There will be an ambitious £1 billion catch-up fund to make this happen.

We have the girls' Friday night call at six-thirty, and as always it is a great giggle, and then it's in the hot tub to finish another working week. It has been a strange and difficult week; quite a rollercoaster of emotions so I am glad to see this one off.

TOTAL DEATHS – 42,261

Saturday, 6th June

With another week in the bag and another week closer to a sense of normality (even though I still can't get a sense of what that normality will look like) I am pleased it is the weekend but I am feeling a slight anti-climax. I think maybe I thought that it would be like the announcements at the end of the war whereby suddenly the Government would declare that the pandemic is over and we would all rush out on the streets whooping and hugging each other and celebrating. Of course, that was never going to happen but I think I have been so caught-up with what has happened on a daily basis that I hadn't really processed that 'the end' was going to be a long drawn-out process. With hairdressers opening next week, the shops open now, talk of pubs and restaurants opening in two weeks and flights starting in July, I guess that really this is the beginning of the end. For now. However, drinks and meals will all be ordered on apps and pubs will be patrolled to ensure that social distancing is happening and potentially use the app to book a trip to the toilet!

Certainly, it is my feeling that we are getting back to normal; yesterday the team talked about coming back to work. It won't be difficult for us with only six of us as we all have our own offices and sit two metres apart anyway, but we still need to ensure that we have complied with government guidelines. Apart from the morale issue, we don't have to go back, we could continue to work from home, but everyone wanted to come back. Personally, I would like a mix; going in to have meetings and to do training but working from home when I need to focus. I don't want to lose my exercise routine, which I have thoroughly enjoyed, and the drive to the office can often take forty minutes each way, which is an hour and a half that I lose each day. I think it will be September before we are fully all back in the office and maybe visiting clients and I am definitely taking two weeks off in August, even if I go somewhere in the UK, so I think that will be our target. Ironically, yesterday Keith managed to find a Wi-Fi booster that actually works, so after twelve weeks of the signal not reaching the study, we now have a great signal. Typical!

I do my PT session and then prepare for our BBQ tonight. It is only the four of us, my hairdresser Kate and her partner and us, but I still love pottering around the kitchen, it gives me such a sense of normality and I am really excited to see Kate. It's getting hard to remember what freedom was like; I think of all the things that we used to do that we may be able to do in the next three months and it is the weirdest feeling. How on earth do people cope who have been kept captive for many years when they suddenly get their freedom back?

My son messages me to say that he and his fiancée have had a test today and both of them were negative, so he didn't need to worry about hugging me last weekend. It hadn't occurred to me at all during the week to even think about it but now that he has told me I feel reassured. Sophie works as a midwife, so has been out and about throughout the entire lockdown and I know it had worried her that she might get symptoms and pass it on.

The death toll today has increased by 128, which once again, sad as it is, is the lowest Saturday. The South West is the only region to report no deaths at all this week.

We have a wonderful night, sitting in the garden until 11.00 p.m., drinking Pimm's followed by red wine and eating barbecue food whilst we catch up. I will remember evenings like this forever, not yet the new normal but not feeling like lockdown.

TOTAL DEATHS – 42,589

Sunday, 21st June

I have decided that alcohol and I are not getting along lately. I have the worst night's sleep and when the alarm goes off at 7.00 a.m. I am groggy. Even though it is Sunday I am going on one of my long walks with Trudy. She really has been one of the amazing things to come out of lockdown and I think we will continue to be friends. I drive to Shawford and we have an energising walk through the countryside until we arrive at St Catherine's Hill. The steps are cut into the side of the hill and it is a steep climb, but this is a good test of my fitness and I march up it despite my lungs crying out half way up, and when I get to the top it feels amazing. Trudy is an incredible woman, and on each walk we get to know each other better, and coach each other. She takes me through a little tour of the forest, a cutting that seems to be full of amazing energy and we sit on a log and drink some coffee she has brought in her rucksack. We walk 10 kilometres; it is a great Sunday morning and I just feel very grateful for everything I have.

Better news comes in from Spain – UK tourists can visit without needing to quarantine. This gives fresh hope to people wanting a holiday this year (including us!). We have a couple of friends with villas in Spain, so maybe if we can't go anywhere else, we could use one of those. I check on Mauritius and the lockdown has been lifted as they only had 10 deaths, but the borders are not reopened yet. It is so massive that we won't need to self-isolate after a holiday; that will make a real difference.

I read about whether we should be expecting a second wave. Many countries, particularly those who have had large epidemics, fear the second wave but there are mixed views as to what this might look like. In 1918 the second wave of the Spanish flu was more deadly than the first. Is it inevitable? And when it comes should we expect the worst? I read an article that describes it as waves in the sea. The number of infections goes up and then comes back down again. Each cycle is one 'wave' of coronavirus, but there is no formal definition, and it is not particularly scientific. Apparently, to say that one wave has ended would need the virus to have been brought under control and that cases would have needed to fall substantially, and therefore for a second wave to start there would need to be a sustained rise in infections. At the moment this might not apply to New Zealand, which has its first cases after twenty-four days without coronavirus, and Beijing, which is facing an outbreak after fifty days clear, however, some scientists think that Iran may be starting to meet the criteria for a second wave. They have seen a rapid surge in recent weeks after relaxing restrictions in mid-April and have now reported new infections averaging more than 3,000 a day in the first week of June, which is a 50% increase on the previous seven days.

The big question is, will the UK get a second wave and apparently is it all down to the decisions we make now? In fact, it appears there is huge uncertainty and great fear. There is definitely potential, as the virus is still around and it is equally deadly as it was at the beginning of 2020, it is not like the strength of the virus has diminished. Only 5% of people in the UK have been infected at this point and we still have no idea whether they would be immune now. If all measures were lifted, we could be back to where we were at the beginning of March. It definitely means that we cannot just lift everything and go back to normal. It really is so difficult – it is critical to business that we do not have a second wave, but we have to restart the economy now and I am not sure how long people's patience will continue with the lockdown anyway. If only we had a crystal ball.

There were 43 deaths today, which is low but again it is a weekend and it will no doubt increase in the next few days.

I try sitting in the garden but the wind and cloud make it just too chilly. It is such a shame as apparently the rest of the week is going to be boiling and I have a full-on week's work plus three days of virtual exhibitions. The long-range weather forecast taunts me with five days of pure sun symbols and next weekend cloud again. No doubt this means that the tourists will be flocking to the beach again this week.

TOTAL DEATHS – 42,632

Monday, 22nd June
Official Lockdown, Week Fourteen

I can barely wake myself up this morning, I feel like I have sleeping sickness! But I manage to get myself in the gym for 7.00 a.m. and do a good hard session, which makes me feel energised.

Piers is back doing an interview on Black Lives Matter, and whether the song, 'Swing Low Sweet Chariot' should be banned from rugby matches due to its slavery roots. It is an interesting debate, looking at the potential of removing anything that relates to slavery and insults black heritage. The debate moves on to songs and why the 'N' word is used in rap songs. Quite rightly, we have been educated that it is offensive, but a story emerges that some girls were suspended from school for singing along to a Kanye West song, which was peppered with the word, and why, if it is so offensive, do rappers include it in their songs? There was no conclusion but an interesting debate – is this the right focus for Black Lives Matter?

For some reason I am pretty unsettled today and find it hard to focus on work. We have a couple of calls and I try and get some documents out and then my daughter asks for a call and suddenly I realise why I have been unsettled. In my heart I knew something was going on. She excitedly announces that she is *pregnant*! I am so excited; I have been dying for this to happen but never wanted to put pressure on her, so whilst we have talked about it a lot, I had never got my hopes up. But the problem is, I can't tell anybody, not even Keith as Elly doesn't want anyone to know until she tells Barry and LJ, and she doesn't want to do that until she knows the pregnancy has settled. But she had to tell me as it would impact on going to Mauritius – she would be too nervous to go in July or August, which I completely understand. To be honest, I had given up all hope of us going this year, so at least we now know, and maybe Keith and I can go somewhere else. I hug my secret to myself and we message a little, both still in joyous disbelief. Only two weeks ago, when she had visited, we had been laughing and joking about it and discussing what I would be called as a grandmother – no Nan, or Gran for me, Elly had already decided I would be GG! I desperately want to tell Sarah, but I want to keep my promise. And then Sarah messages to say her cancer scans were all good and Small and Stable were still small and stable, which is great news. Maybe now I can relax!

In the news we hear that the death toll in the US has reached over 120,000, which means that more Americans have now died from COVID-19 than were killed in World War 1. After weeks of the cases in the US declining, cases are rising again with record increases in at least 12 states as they try to reopen the economy.

We hear that Boris might be doing a briefing on Tuesday about relaxing lockdown rules even further – again it feels so fast and strange, I don't know what to make of it all. Apparently, he will be taking the distancing down to one metre and we can expect a 'raft' of announcements to come over the next two weeks. The 'bubble' debate will also be continuing with anticipation about what changes Boris will make. If he says we can expand to two households in our social bubbles will people be forced to choose which set of grandparents to see? Or is he going to include all households with two people in them as some papers have reported? Or will people from multiple households be allowed to 'bubble up' but with an overall cap on numbers? It all starts to sound so complicated and I fear that people will not understand the new rules and just meet anyone they like. I know that lockdown is coming to an end and pieces to the jigsaw are being put back, and I don't know why; I just don't feel ready yet, it is just a gut instinct thing. I would have thought I would have been raring to get out and back to normality, but I don't.

However, at the briefing this evening Matt Hancock tells us that a month ago one person in 400 people had coronavirus and now it is one person in 1,700. That is quite a difference. For the first time since the peak the number of cases confirmed is less than 1,000, and yesterday there were only 15 deaths, the lowest since mid-March, which is why the Government can relax the lockdown further. This means that people who have been shielding can start meeting others in groups of six outdoors from the 6th July and from the 1st August they will not have to shield at all. That is going to be quite a shock for them to come out of lockdown having seen no one for nearly 4 months.

Travel corridors have also been being debated and we will hear before the 22nd June with Matt Hancock telling us he has been working over the weekend on this. Well done Matt! He says that plans will be published in good time based on epidemiological advice. Today we have heard that Spain, and potentially Portugal and Greece, are allowing Brits to travel to the country without quarantining upon arrival. I can't lie I will be interested in this as I so want to book a holiday.

Well that was an interesting day! Elly messages to say that it is funny they will be having a clichéd lockdown baby – so long as they don't call it Covid!

TOTAL DEATHS – 42,652

Tuesday, 22nd June

I wake up early this morning and my waking thoughts are of yesterday's news. I leap out of bed so I can do a long walk and process everything. My head is full of prams and baby clothes although I have promised not to buy anything yet. I still can't quite believe that it has happened and I know that she and Ernie will make the most wonderful parents. It makes me think about work again; as I didn't expect this to happen for a couple of years I was hoping to have my business under control so that I could be a very active support for her, but this was a lot sooner than I had expected. I think hard about what I can do to adjust my work life so that I can be ready to help. Elly lives in Lincoln, which is over three and a half hours away from me, so I have to find a way to be available. I walk fast for about six miles and get my head ready for a focused and busy day.

The debate over children returning to school continues and Dr Jenny Harries has said that many children, who are not at school because they are shielding, would be better off in classrooms. She told the Downing Street press conference last night that children with asthma, which is under control, should be in school. Her argument was that they are at very low risk from COVID-19 but at a very significant risk of getting left behind in their education, which would be far worse in the long term.

I settle down to work and have a good call with a client. An email pings in from one of my staff with another 'plane' landing, which is great news. Boris takes me by surprise by doing a briefing to the commons today at 12.30 p.m. I was waiting for the 5.00 p.m. briefing but suddenly the BBC alert comes up and I abandon my emails and tune in. He is bouncy and loud; his overgrown fluffy hair almost covering his eyes.

He talks about the figures and how new infections are declining every day. As always there is a lot of talk about what the Government has done and achieved during the pandemic and how 'together we have saved our hospitals from being overwhelmed'. He says, "This pandemic has inflicted permanent scars and we mourn everyone whom we have lost."

He then goes through the figures – how the rolling death toll was 943 on the 14th April, 476 on the 11th May and yesterday 130, which shows that there is progress being made. He says that a total of over 8 million tests have been conducted and adds: "We remain vigilant but we do not currently believe that there is a risk of a rolling wave. We are meeting the five tests and the chief medical officers have downgraded the UK level from four to three meaning we no longer face the virus spreading exponentially, but it is still out there."

He addresses the speaker to say that the two metre distancing rule will be eased by the 4th July to help the hospitality industry. He adds, "Where we can keep two metres apart we should, but where not possible, one metre but still taking steps to reduce transmissions, particularly for workers and customers. Avoiding face-to-face seating, improving ventilation, closing non-essential spaces, having screens where appropriate."

The speech continues with a flourish: "There is only one certainty – the fewer social contacts you have the safer you will be." He says he cannot lift all the restrictions at once and has to make difficult judgements and weigh up issues against the evidence. He adds that they need to trust the British public to be vigilant. And here it is – the big one! "We will ask people to follow guidance rather than legislation. From the 4th July, two households can meet inside or outside; it doesn't always have to be the same households. But we are not recommending meetings of multiple households indoors. Outside the guidance remains that people from several households can meet in groups of six."

He continues to say that they will also reopen restaurants and pubs. All hospitality indoors will be limited to table service and guidance will be issued on limiting interactions. He says they will work with the sector to make it manageable. This is met with cheers from the benches.

He says that they will open hairdressers (and references his own hair needing a cut) and says he will also open other salons as well as nail bars as soon as they can (a cheer from me there!). He goes on to tell us that from the 4th July people will be able to stay in self-contained accommodation including campsites. Most leisure facilities will reopen if they can do safely, including outdoor gyms, playgrounds, outdoor attractions, etc. However, close proximity venues such as nightclubs, indoor gyms, swimming pools, spas, theatres, bowling alleys and water parks remain closed, but there will be taskforces with sectors to help them to reopen. He references that they will also work with choirs, orchestras and theatres to allow them to open as soon as possible, but no mention of the music industry – so still no hope for LJ.

Places of worship will also be open for individual prayer and services including weddings with a maximum of 30 people with social distancing. Now that could be interesting – does it mean that you can have a wedding with 30 people but only an outdoor reception with 6?

Wraparound care for school age children will restart over the summer. Primary and secondary schools will reopen in September and those children who can go to school beforehand should go now.

No doubt this will confuse the country about who can and who can't meet – from this it sounds like we still can't hug our grans, but we can take them on the Nemesis ride at Alton Towers!

Time for his big finish and another Churchill moment:

> *"After the toughest restrictions in peace-time history, our long, national hibernation begins to end. But the virus has not gone away, and we will continue to monitor it with our Test and Trace service. I have to be clear, there will be flare-ups for which local measures will be needed and we will not hesitate to put back restrictions locally or nationally if required."*

> *"I urge everyone to follow the normal rules, wash your hands, keep your distance and wear masks on public transport, and I trust in the common sense and community spirit of the people to see us through to victory. Stay alert and control the virus."*

Speech over. Now for the opposition. I hold my breath.

Kier Starmer stands up and we wait for his criticism. He thanks Boris for the pre-sight of his statement and adds his condolences regarding the Reading attack. He refers to the speech Boris has just made and says they will scrutinise this in more detail but overall welcome the changes, and says the Government is doing the right thing and they will support them. Sounds a bit too good to be true to me.

He asks about the two-metre rule and whether SAGE has approved it and what assessment has been made of the R rate? He also asks about additional powers for local councils should a second wave or spike appear. What enforceable measures will the Prime Minister put in place to give people confidence to return to work? He references the small businesses who have put money and time into enforcing the two-metre rule and how this change will affect them. He questions how quickly we can get children back to school. He counters with the fact that concerns over Track and Trace remain and it is important that the Government clarifies when the full system will be working.

Boris responds by saying that the Chief Medical Officer has been 'intimately involved' in all of this.

So, all playing nicely in the Commons today – both parties clearly want to kick-start the economy.

I work through the afternoon and have a few meetings; it is incredibly hot and I feel lucky that my office is cool and has French doors to let the breeze in, but I am still not feeling well on and off.

At 5.00 p.m. Boris appears on our screens again and takes what will now be the 92nd and final, regularly-scheduled, Downing Street update. He tells us that the Government is winding down these press conferences as they have less to say. They will still publish the slides though! Great – he announces the biggest, most confusing and dangerous changes yet and then they abandon us to work it out. I wonder what I will do in between 5.00 and 6.00 p.m. with no briefing to write about – it has become part of my life for the last ninety-two days.

Also, along for the farewell gig are Professor Chris Whitty and Sir Patrick Vallance. Today's figures show that there have been 306,210 recorded cases. The death toll today is 171.

It might be my imagination but Vallance looks like a really worried man. I think Boris has just opened the floodgates and now he's cancelled the daily briefings there's no one to hold him to account. I think it's clear the scientists and health organisations are not behind him.

Whitty confirms this when he says people should continue to stay two metres away from others where possible and that the new 'one-metre-plus' rule did not invalidate this original advice. And he says that he expects coronavirus to continue to pose a significant risk for another year. He is questioned on when life might return to normal and he says:

> *"I would be surprised and delighted if we weren't in this current situation through the winter and into next spring. I think then let's regroup and work out where we are."*

> *"I expect there to be a significant amount of coronavirus circulating at least into that time and I think it is going to be quite optimistic for science to come fully to the rescue over that kind of timeframe. But I have an absolute confidence in the capacity of science to overcome infectious diseases – it has done that repeatedly and it will do that for this virus, whether that is by drugs, vaccines or indeed other things that may come into play."*

> *"For medium to long-term, I'm optimistic. But for the short- to medium-term, until this time next year, certainly I think we should be planning for this, for what I consider to be the long-haul into 2021."*

That doesn't sound like the words of someone who is celebrating today's announcements.

TOTAL DEATHS – 42,927

Wednesday, 24th June

I wake up early ready to hit the gym and exercise. I keep wondering if I should just give in and have a lie-in but I just don't feel the same if I don't exercise and I always feel great afterwards when my heartbeat is up and my limbs are being stretched. As I work out, I think about last night's announcements and I still feel really concerned about the speed of the easing of lockdown.

Piers has the same feeling – for once we are on the same page, and he conducts an interesting debate this morning about whether we are ready for this level of easing the lockdown and why places such as gyms were not included. It is a good point as people in gyms have to sign in and so if anyone contracts the virus it is really easy to trace who has been in the gym at the same time with them. And people who are in gyms are far more likely to keep to social distancing than people in pubs who, in theory, have to remain seated but after a few pints will need to be contained. When Piers listens to people the interviews are really worth watching, but I guess that is because it is not a government minister that he is looking to catch out, or anything controversial.

Apparently, health leaders are calling for an urgent review to determine whether the UK is properly prepared for the 'real risk' of a second wave of coronavirus infections. The presidents of the Royal Colleges of Surgeons, Nursing, Physicians and GPs signed an open letter urging the Government to examine 'areas of weakness where action is needed urgently to prevent further loss of life'.

I also can't stop thinking about something that Chris Whitty said last night, which really resonated with me, that the Government's Test and Trace service could make an important contribution and he was worried about people not complying with it. If people don't report symptoms and get a test, and if people then are contacted by NHS Test and Trace and don't engage properly with that process then they won't isolate, which is the real risk.

We finally make a decision about the holiday and decide that we won't be able to go to Mauritius as a family group. However, we still want to spend time together to celebrate the three birthdays, so we have the idea of going to Cornwall for a week in September. Elly had attended university in Falmouth, which she absolutely loved, so we decide that we would go the week of LJs thirtieth birthday. I get straight online and find the most beautiful house that we can rent – this should mean that even if restrictions come back, we might be OK, and I book in quickly. With the relaxation in the rules it is likely that everyone will start booking holidays in the UK and this is just perfect; walking distance of our favourite beach and all the restaurants, which I hope will be open by September. It is so hard not telling LJ about the baby as I know he will be thrilled, but by the time we go to Falmouth it will all be out in the open and we can enjoy the conversations.

We have a team meeting at 4.00 p.m. but I have started to feel unwell, hot and dizzy and nauseous. I had a headache first thing this morning but have just felt worse as the day went on. My throat is sore, but I am not coughing. I spray some air freshener and I can still smell it, so I am not concerned that it is COVID-19, but I have just been so well over the last three months that this feels strange. I make it through the meeting but by 6.00 p.m. I hit the sofa and watch the news.

With no briefing today I search the internet for today's figures and 154 fatalities were reported and 653 new cases over the last twenty-four hours, which is the first day it has dipped below 1,000.

TOTAL DEATHS – 43,018

Thursday, 24th June

It's Thursday already and I am speaking at another conference today. This time it is the Association for Coaching on the topic of Coaching Culture and why it doesn't work. I have already written a book on this and is a subject I feel very passionate about. Fortunately, this time the presentation was filmed in advance so all I need to do is be present for two live Q and A sessions, so a lot less stressful. I still don't feel great this morning and under normal circumstances I would be concerned but as I just have to walk to my study and sit in my chair, I know I will be able to make it through the day.

It is nice to do something different. I am definitely getting bored with being in the same place every day. I always have plenty of work to do to find new clients, but sometimes it is hard to get motivated without some variety. Yesterday we talked about going back to the workplace and the team are really keen to go back. With Dawn returning on the 1st July we talk about how safe it feels and if I am honest there is very little risk in our office. I am going to set a goal for the 1st August, which is another five weeks. We might go into the office for some meetings before that, but Dawn is tasked with ensuring that we are following guidelines as soon as she returns from furlough. We also need to set up a proper virtual studio for the Zoom calls.

In the news and social media, people are still questioning the decision to ease the lockdown so quickly, and yesterday, just a day after Johnson declared the winding down of 'our great national hibernation' (oh please doesn't this demean the thousands of deaths?) he was grilled by Sir Kier Starmer on the UK's tracing app and enforcement of local lockdowns amidst the scientist's warnings. The PM was accused of dodging the question as he faced Starmer in the Commons at lunchtime. Nicola Sturgeon announced Scotland's own easing of lockdown and reopening beer gardens and shops on the 6th July. Still much more caution in Scotland.

A glimmer of hope from University of Oxford as volunteers have started being immunised with a new UK COVID-19 vaccine. Around 300 people will be vaccinated over the next few weeks at Imperial College in a trial led by Professor Robin Shattock. They have already tested animals and the results suggest the vaccine is safe and triggers an effective immune response. If it is successful it could be distributed in the UK and overseas in early 2021. Still a long way to go, but the virus still really frightens me, particularly as news suggests that thousands of coronavirus patients could face long term effects from being ill with it. Some research from the Chartered Society of Physiotherapy suggests that patients who were hospitalised are likely to need ongoing rehabilitation for lung problems, breathlessness, fatigue and other lingering symptoms. Some experts also suggest that the virus could cause impairment to the brain and an increased risk of Alzheimer's. Some figures are muted that suggest potentially 29,845 of the 50,000 or so survivors may need some level of rehabilitation on discharge, whereas some NHS guidance suggests that around 30% of survivors may be left with damaged and scarred lung tissue. I am absolutely convinced that my lung damage was a result of swine flu now, and I was only ill for five days, so I have had a glimpse of what the future could be like for the COVID-19 survivors.

The weather is steaming hot with temperatures set to soar to 34 degrees, and the Covidiots flock to the coast. In Bournemouth, a major incident is declared and a multi-agency response activated to co-ordinate resources. Officials say that the beach is stretched to the absolute hilt, with gridlocked roads, fights, and dispersal issues being handed out on the sardine-packed beach. Yesterday 33 tonnes of rubbish along the coastline had to be removed. And as most public toilets are closed, it doesn't bear thinking about.

But when you hear the news from Europe it makes this even more worrying; they have seen an increase in weekly cases for the first time in months as restrictions are eased, and in 11 countries the WHO has stated accelerated transmission has led to 'very significant' resurgences. If left unchecked, Dr Hans Kluge warned health systems would be 'pushed to the brink'. He stated: "In several countries across Europe, this risk has now become a reality – 30 countries have seen increases in new cumulative cases over the past two weeks."

The US are at least demonstrating a modicum of sense as Disney announces it will not be reopening its Disneyland California theme park on the 17th July as planned. They will now wait for approval from government officials.

My day is all about the coaching conference and a podcast I am recording, and I don't even see the sun. I am just glad that my office is cool and I can open the doors and let the breeze flow through. The question sessions are really good fun with people dialling in from Canada, the Middle East, the US and Europe. I love talking about coaching and there are some great questions and wonderful comments. I have missed these types of sessions.

The latest figures from the Department of Health show a further 149 people have died with coronavirus in the UK across all settings with only a small drop today of 5 fewer deaths compared with yesterday, but actually, an increase from the 137 announced a week ago. Plus, another 1,118 people have tested positive for the virus from 167,023 tests. But looking at the crazy scenes on Bournemouth beach again today, I feel sure we can expect a massive increase in cases in the next month.

And in politics, Sir Kier Starmer has sacked Rebecca Long-Bailey for sharing an article containing an 'anti-Semitic conspiracy theory'. She had retweeted an interview with actor and Labour supporter, Maxine Peake. The Shadow Education Secretary, who had previously, unsuccessfully, run for party leadership, had defended herself saying that she had not meant to endorse all parts of the article but Sir Keir was clear that he had to restore trust with the Jewish community and asked her to step down. Hear, hear! The anti-Semitism displayed by Corbyn was disgusting, so it is good to see clear and unbiased leadership from the top of the Labour party for a change.

By the evening I am feeling a bit better but still completely wiped out.

TOTAL DEATHS – 43,230

Friday, 25th June

I am up early and feeling much more with-it today. I have my day planned out with calls and meetings and my daughter's friends are dropping round for lunch in the garden, so I want to make sure I have some time free. So, I get up and six and go straight in the gym, and at seven rush off to the supermarket to get some shopping. I prefer to shop whilst it is quiet, and I am out and back before eight.

I realise I just feel all out of sorts and I need to work out why. I have a long chat with Sarah whilst I shop. I think I feel totally unsure about the future of the country – yesterday's scenes were so worrying, as if it were all over and we were back to normal. Police were attacked in Brixton at parties and the massive fights in many seaside resorts feel like just the beginning. The news also comes through that Liverpool won the Premiership last night and the scenes in the city were insane – people hugging each other, fireworks and a packed city centre to celebrate with all social distancing forgotten. It makes me anxious and I wonder whether it is just me that is feeling this way. If I were Prime Minister I think that I would put us all back into lockdown today – we have clearly proven that we can't be trusted so why not take a stronger stance until the R rate is even lower down? It feels like the Government has abandoned us at the moment. Hancock has said that he 'could' close the beaches. *Could*? Just do it right now before another crazy day of tourists descend and spread the virus further. Everyone is talking about Super Saturday, the 4th July, when they will all return to the pubs and restaurants and I don't know who is checking and helping to control everything. There has been no guidance since Tuesday when Boris made the announcements, and we don't know when we will get anymore briefings.

I try to put some words on how I am feeling; aimless, unfocused, lacking in direction and structure. I feel like I am working each day to do what I need to do but it doesn't feel as if I am being strategic enough; I feel quite transactional and it doesn't feel right. I think I need to go back to where I started at lockdown and spend some time setting some more goals and making some decisions. I also think I am totally bored going just from the bedroom to the office to the lounge – this week I haven't had time to go outside at all apart from one walk and I think I need to do something different, so this weekend I am going to make some decisions and spend some time thinking and getting refocused so I have a plan.

I start with a change of scenery this morning and take my work out in the garden whilst it is cool – by 11.00 a.m. the sun will have come round and it will be too hot to work at the garden table, but for now the breeze feels good and the change of scenery is nice. It helps a lot, and the day is actually quite productive with calls and a lovely lunch with Georgia and Millie. I haven't had a lunch break for weeks – another bad habit slipping back. There is no reason to eat at my desk but I have got back to the position where I don't feel I have enough time, and as I sit in the sun with them today, enjoying a chat and a salad, I realise that I am not practising what I preach.

I spend the rest of the afternoon working on my research for the Black Lives Matter inclusivity workshop. I find it such a fascinating subject and I am learning so much, but it is also unnerving because it could be so easy to get this wrong. I have been training people in unconscious bias and anti-harassment for so many years that I am very familiar with legislation and examples, some from my own experience of being bullied or sexually harassed or discriminated, but with BLM everything is different. The first session will be with a Board and I want to ensure that I compel them to action.

We go to the virtual pub at 4.30 p.m. and have a good chat about the future. The team is very cohesive now and we start to get excited about Dawn and Lucy coming back and being all in one place again. Afterwards, it feels time for a drink and a session in the hot tub so without the briefing I check on today's figures. It is not good news; we have had the highest daily increase in fatalities in ten days, back up by 186. This is the highest number of deaths since the 16th June when 233 were recorded, and higher than last Friday. It should be going down each day now. It comes as the Government warns it may tighten lockdown again due to the beachgoers sparking fears of a second wave.

I have a large drink.

Saturday, 26th June

So today I wake up feeling a bit better, not completely myself – just a bit heady with a sore throat, but my nausea has gone and my energy is back so I start on my plan to get myself back to full energy and productivity. I manage to sleep until 8.00 a.m. and do a workout at 9.00 a.m. in the gym.

I take this time to work out what is going on with my feelings and realise it is a lot to do with control. When this first happened, I took control and felt that I had some direction and there was point to what I was doing. However, now I feel as if I am just drifting with no destination or endpoint, which is not true. I do have goals and a destination but maybe I am losing sight of them and need to refresh them. I also realise I am not getting enough variety and I need to take charge of that. Now that we are allowed to go out and do things, I need to have them arranged and planned in my diary so that I have things to look forward to. I develop a new list of goals and targets. I also have to think about this book. It is now at 150,000 words. The average novel is between 50,000 and 80,000 so it is going to get too unwieldy. I have to start the editing process, but more importantly I have to make a decision about when to stop. And with no clear end of lockdown in sight, I can't go on forever. I make a decision that from now on I will write just once a week on Saturday. That will also take a lot of pressure off me as I have been writing for between one and two hours every day since the pandemic started. It will be hard not writing every day, but I have to have an end date and also, I need to do a lot of editing. I also decide that the book will finish at the beginning of August. We have agreed that we will all go back into the office on Monday, 3rd August, so that feels like a fitting date. I know that it will be months or even a year before the pandemic really plays out, maybe there is a follow up book or two to be written – by someone else!

The big news today is that blanket restrictions on non-essential overseas travel will be relaxed in the UK from the 6th July and we will be allowed to travel to certain European countries without quarantining on return. It is thought that this will be to Spain, France, Greece, Italy, the Netherlands, Finland, Belgium, Turkey, Germany and Norway with a list being published next week. I am not sure what this means about long-haul holidays.

Today 78 deaths were recorded in England.

NHS England revealed the latest victims were aged between 56 and 97 – with 2 having no underlying health conditions. As of 9.00 a.m., 27th June, there have been 9,067,577 tests, with 155,359 tests on the 26th June. 310,250 people have tested positive. That still seems a huge amount.

TOTAL DEATHS – 43,492

Saturday, 4th July
Official Lockdown, Week Fifteen

Well, it has been an interesting week and as today signals officially the 110th day of lockdown and the 4th July, Independence Day in the US, and potentially a day that will be remembered in the UK as Independence Day, as lockdown is eased and pubs, restaurants and hairdressers reopen.

The week has been a good one generally; once again the same old routine and lots of exercising, working, and trying to bring in sales. I have got over my previous feelings of negativity and loss of energy and am recognising the issue. It was the feeling that I am not living every day to the max, just passing time. That is what had been dragging my mood down. Resetting goals daily had helped with this.

On Monday' travel companies said that holiday bookings have 'exploded' once the Government announced current restrictions will be eased and blanket restrictions on non-essential overseas travel will be relaxed. It took them until Friday to announce the countries that we could visit, and whilst Mauritius was on the list, the flights will not start until the 1st September, so we definitely won't be going.

But we book for next year in July and our money is safe, so whilst disappointed, we are happy. But I did get a date in the diary to go up to stay with Elly in Lincoln and to see LJ, and a few parties with friends in, and Sarah and I have rebooked Juicy Oasis for May next year.

On Sunday, the death rate increased by 36, one of the lowest rises since lockdown and on Monday, 25, but towards the end of the week it was back up to 175.

Most of the week was focused on the lockdown easing and Super Saturday – would the pubs be overwhelmed? Police were concerned about whether they would have enough resources to cope with the celebrations. And then the worrying news comes through that Leicester has to lock down again due to a surge in cases. They are told they need to remain restricted for another two weeks; devasting news for all the shops and hairdressers who had worked so hard to be ready to open up. In total, Leicester has had 2,987 positive cases with 866 in the two weeks to the 23rd June. It is also feared that Doncaster could be at risk of local lockdown.

Boris sets out an ambitious economic recovery plan and says he will use this moment to fix longstanding economic problems and promises a £5 billion new deal to build homes and infrastructure – more money that the taxpayers will need to repay.

Wednesday is a big day, as millions of furloughed workers can start returning to their jobs part-time. We excitedly welcome back Dawn and Lucy – the Government is still paying 80% of their wages but it is the first step towards winding the scheme down. Having Dawn and Lucy returning two days a week will really help us to get back on our feet. We agree to make the 3rd August our goal for returning to the office and Dawn started to work on the legal requirements.

As each week passes we get more information about the dangers that coronavirus can trigger a huge range of neurological problems – it is apparently not just a respiratory disease, it can cause strokes, delirium, anxiety, confusion, fatigue and more. I watch an interview with someone who talks about the lingering cognitive impact of the disease, problems with memory, tiredness and staying focused, so the worrying thing is that for those people who have recovered, there could be a long road to full recovery.

On Friday I take a day off. I need a break and I want to spend some time with Sarah, so I meet her in the New Forest and we walk for two hours. This time we can't resist hugging; I have missed her so much, and I discover her stepdaughter is expecting too! We walk for two hours, putting the world to rights in the early morning sunshine and it is so wonderful to talk to her about Elly's baby. Elly is at the six-week mark and had sent a note to say that at six weeks it was the size of a bee. I still can't believe that Sarah and I will become grandmothers in the same month.

Tonight, Boris does a briefing – nice to see some action at No. 10 again. He is flanked by Sir Patrick Vallance and Chris Whitty. He starts by telling us that since he last spoke to us we have continued to make progress.

SAGE tells us that the R rate remains between 0.7 and 0.9. He acknowledges that the amount of people dying remains too high and the picture is not universal, as there are areas such as Leicester where the virus is still more prevalent. Once again, he launches into some self-congratulatory bumbling about the great progress we have made and the fact that lockdown has saved many thousands of lives. Well, that remains to be seen when we have the investigation – so far, all the evidence points to the fact that many more lives could have been saved.

He recognises that coronavirus has had a devastating impact on our lives and economy and says he wants other restrictions to be quickly lifted. He talks of the task forces who are working on this and says a timetable will be set out next week with a goal of allowing as many people to live their lives in a way that is possible. He reminds us that he will only do what is safe, when the virus is under control. And sets out a five-stage plan for local lockdown and tells us he expects that these will continue for a long time.

1. Monitoring.
2. Engagement.
3. Testing.
4. Targeted restrictions.
5. Lockdown (as a last resort).

It will all be calibrated on the scientific evidence for each area and he will set this out in more detail soon. He ends by saying that he is looking forward to this weekend – there will be a moment of remembrance for people who have lost their lives on Saturday; on Sunday it is the birthday of the NHS so we can all come together and clap them. He urges us to support local business owners, restaurants, pubs, hairdressers and tourism as all these businesses have put in an heroic effort to work out how to trade safely. He also urges us to act responsibly and finishes by reminding us that he will not hesitate to put on the brakes again. Finally, he tells us to stay alert, control the virus, save lives and enjoy the summer. It sounds like he is abandoning us!

The first question from the public is around the decimation of the events industry and whether the Government will give any more support to the arts and entertainment and events industry. My ears prick up as I think of LJ. Boris says he has tried to support everyone to the tune of £120 billion – he knows that they are anxious about when they can get open and promises that next week he will be setting out a timetable for those industries. He says the crucial thing is we want life to get back to normal as soon as possible. Well, I shall await that announcement with interest, although I won't hold my breath.

Another question comes in around Super Saturday and whether the scientists agree with the lockdown easing, particularly as the fourteen-day travel quarantine has been seen as shambolic. Witty and Valance are professional and diplomatic, saying that there is no perfect time and it seems a reasonable package of risks at this particular time.

In total there have been under 500 deaths this week; still a massive amount of grieving families and we are a long way off this being over.

TOTAL DEATHS – 44,175

Saturday, 11th July
Official Lockdown, Week Sixteen

Another week has passed, and it feels like the world is gradually creaking into life again, or catapulting if you were in London and enjoying your first night out in four months. But not for Scotland and Wales, they will have to wait a bit longer.

People are on the move as police in Dorset, Devon and Cornwall reported gridlock on the roads on Saturday – including a high volume of caravan owners heading to the coast. For some reason I thought of the film *Jaws* and the scenes on the 4th July, even though the Chief of Police had insisted the beaches should be closed, and the consequences.

In the evening we stayed in as usual, but many others didn't and Facebook was awash with streets crammed with revellers – both in the UK and the US. Ministers tried a last-ditch cry for caution reminding people that the easing was not 'risk free' but many threw caution to the wind. For women, the excitement was about hairdressing visits, but for the men it was the pubs. In our town, Southampton, John Apter, the National Chair of the Police Federation said that it is 'crystal clear' that drunk people are unable to socially distance as they dealt with 'naked men, happy drunks, angry drunks, fights and more angry drunks'. Our friends from the North message to ask if we had anything to do with it!

The US sees a massive surge in cases following the 4th of July holiday, and Florida reported the most cases in a single day, surpassing 200,000.

On Sunday morning Keith walks with me – we intend to go to the common, have a coffee (a real one in an actual coffee shop) and walk back, but the café wasn't open. We end up walking seven miles to find one but the experience of sitting in a coffee shop and having a lovely latte was definitely worth it!

Today the news tells us that people are encouraged not to forget the NHS, and buildings and landmarks across the country are lit up blue to celebrate the NHS, including the Shard and the Royal Albert Hall. At 5.00 p.m. the country comes out again and joins together to clap to pay tribute to the NHS staff, it was their 72nd anniversary. All the Government leaders join in to clap with them. I can't help thinking they might have preferred it if people had stayed in last night rather than clapped. But even more so, I am sure that they would prefer a pay rise from the Government. Maybe we should all make a point when it comes to government pay-rise time of just giving the Government a clap?

On Monday we see the death toll slowing up again when only 16 people were confirmed to have died, although again it is likely to rise during the week. Scotland, Wales and Northern Ireland did not report a single new death related to COVID-19.

On Tuesday Boris is in a right shit storm. He has enraged care homes and the public by turning them all against him for criticising them and saying that 'too many care homes didn't really follow the procedures'. Piers Morgan quite rightly has a field day with this one saying it is absolutely disgusting that he would blame the care homes. Boris was responding to the head of NHS England's call for reform in social care. Mark Adams, who is the CEO of the charity Community Integrated Care, told the BBC the Prime Minister's comments were 'cowardly' and 'clumsy'. Piers interviews a woman who lost her father, and owners/ managers of care homes who are all similarly outraged by the fact and told stories of being forced to take back people who had been known to be on COVID-19 wards, who were refused tests and later went on to infect other people. It is estimated that half of the people who died from COVID-19 were in care homes and Shadow Minister for Care and Older People, Liz Kendall, told the BBC that care workers had been 'abandoned' by the Government, even saying that they had achieved a 'new low' in their attempt to shift responsibility.

Tuesday is an exciting day for me as I get to go out and deliver my workshop on 'Conscious Inclusion BLM'. I love driving to Brize Norton and feel entirely safe. We hold the workshop in a large space with chairs two metres apart and a cleaner swabbing down anything that is touched. It is so good to be back in the training room, and as I drive home I wonder whether it will ever be the same again for our industry.

On Wednesday I am back to my desk and watching *GMB* again early in the morning. Piers and Susanna are saying goodbye for the summer and conducting an interview with Kate Garraway who is coming back to the show. She looks broken but still smiling and full of love and possibility. As she talks about the journey that she and Derek have been through and tears roll down my cheeks. Piers and Susanna look teary eyed as they discuss it and I see a different side of Piers, genuinely caring and thoughtful. Ironically, I had watched him do an interview with Lorraine Kelly the other evening and seen this softer side. I think we are finally making our peace – I don't dislike him I just sometimes don't like his behaviour. I silently wish him a good holiday.

And then a final insult from the Government – there is talk that they will be removing free car parking charges for NHS staff, which was bought in at the beginning of the pandemic. Unbelievable, truly, after everything they have done for us.

And then a real surprise, we get hints through that Rishi Sunak is coming up with another package in a mini budget. His pockets have clearly deepened and we plunge further into national debt – probably around £190 billion now.

But the first item is a goodie – a holiday on Stamp Duty on house purchases up to £500,000 for nine months. This is amazing news for LJ if he can get his mortgage as it will save him around £7,000. He then tackles the furlough scheme and also offers firms a £1,000 bonus for every staff member kept on for three months when furlough ends in October. Diners get 50% off weekday dining out in August, and he also plans to cut VAT on food, accommodation and attractions from 20% to 5% from next Wednesday. The opposition snubbed it labelling it a 'meal deal'.

The Chancellor warns 'hardship lies ahead' but vows no one will be left 'without hope'. In a statement to MPs he says that details of how the package will be paid for (through borrowing and possible tax rises) are likely to be unveiled in the autumn budget. Not entirely true Rishi – whilst we appreciate what you are doing, for the music and entertainment business there is nothing to support them.

Suddenly, there is an unexpected briefing from Downing Street again at 5.00 p.m. Oliver Dowden has the pleasure of telling us the next steps of easing of the lockdown; indoor gyms, swimming pools and sports facilities will reopen from the 25th July to help people to get fit, with gyms giving out timed bookings. Beauticians are now allowed to open on Monday – seems a bit unfair that they only get four days to prepare when hairdressers had weeks. They are not allowed to do facial treatments but can do nails and pedicures. My feet breathe a sigh of relief as they are in desperate need of some love and hard skin removal!

On Friday the death rate is still higher than I would like to see and 48 deaths are reported. However, much as it may feel as if the world is recovering and we are getting back to normal, we still have a long, way to go.

Gemma sends the last month's figures over to me and the projections. It makes pretty unsettling reading. The losses are eyewatering. We do have bookings for September, October and November but still not enough to cover our overheads yet. I had said all along that if we weren't breaking even by September I would need to shut the business down, and we are hurtling towards that date. Will we be able to turn it around before then? We certainly have a mass of sales activity but those planes need to land fast. I try and shake off my sense of impending doom and think of the positives.

TOTAL DEATHS – 44,650

Sunday, 12th July

It is Sunday again and time for my long walk with Trudy, and this morning it is an absolute corker. The weather is stunning and we go back to the Meon Shore, parking close to the house where my children were brought up. We walk along the cliffs and watch the boats bobbing about in the sea and put the world to rights. It is amazing how much comes out of our Sunday morning walks and we casually coach each other as we clock up our best distance yet of over eight miles. The rest of the day is relaxed, sitting in the sun, cooking dinner for my stepson, Sam, who is staying with us this week and participating in our evening quiz. I am really getting used to having weekends off now.

On Monday the Government announces that the last remaining businesses, indoor pools, gyms and leisure centres will be able to open on the 25th July. Finally! There are still questions as to whether this is too early, despite the strict guidance in place to protect the safety of the workers and customers, but it is another step towards normality.

This week my work has very much been work catching up with marketing; no delivery and it feels ridiculously relaxed not to have to prepare anything or stress over any workshops. Apart from the amount of money that I am losing! So, I work hard to send out emails to clients and am rewarded with a few potential responses.

On Tuesday, the Government announced the compulsory wearing of face masks from the shops from the 24th July – with a £100 fine for anyone not wearing them. I can never understand why we wait for these things – are they saying it is not dangerous until then? Most people already have masks so why do they need to wait?

On Thursday morning my wonderful beautician says she can squeeze me in for a quick pedicure if I can get there at 9 am, so I get up early, work for a couple of hours and walk the 3.6 miles into town. It is so bizarre walking into Southampton; it has been four months since I have been into the centre and as I reach London Road it looks almost normal. Cafés starting to open, people walking to work; if it wasn't for the masks they were wearing it would all have looked as it was four months ago. As I get closer to the centre the first thing I notice are the homeless people sleeping back on the streets. I recognise some of them and I buy them a coffee and a sandwich. I am so sad that they are sleeping rough again. The next sad thing is Debenhams; the store that was the heart of Southampton, the store that had supplied me with so many evening dresses, sale shoes, and Christmas presents, has closed down, its windows mainly empty of displays of clothes and accessories, apart from a few naked mannequins lying face down, forgotten and lonely in the front of the store. It is heart-breaking to see such an institution closing down, one of the major casualties of the pandemic. I get to the salon and it is all very different. It is normally packed and bustling but now it is quiet, sparkling clean following a lockdown makeover, and with just three people having their nails done.

But the virus is never far from us and scientists throw out a grim warning that the UK could see about 120,000 deaths in a second wave of infections during the winter. This was their modelling of a 'reasonable' worst-case scenario and didn't take into account lockdowns, treatments or vaccines – but still terrifying. However, they tell us that the risk could be reduced if action is taken immediately.

Today was a big day of activities for the Queen, first she came out of isolation to knight the wonderful Captain Tom Moore, using her father's sword to bestow the honour on him. It's the first investiture for months and it is so wonderful that it happened to him. He looked so happy, surrounded by his family, he is such a legend. The Queen personally praised the 100-year-old veteran, telling him: "Thank you so much, an amazing amount of money you raised." Afterwards Sir Tom said: "Never ever did I imagine that I should get so close to the Queen and have such a kind message from her." The Queen revealed she had been to her granddaughters wedding saying, "My granddaughter got married this morning and both Philip and I managed to get there – very nice."

What a bizarre, surprise happening, with the first private wedding for a very long time as Princess Eugenie married Edoardo Mapelli Mozzi, a property developer. Prince Andrew was very much at the heart of the occasion, walking his daughter down the aisle, but was conspicuously absent from any official photos.

The decision to go ahead with the wedding privately will be seen as a clear show of support from his daughter and the Queen but in the light of Ghislaine Maxwell's arrest, the scandal is still firmly casting a shadow over the Royal Family.

And on Friday Boris pops up with a briefing and his plan to return England to 'normality' by Christmas. I listen to the news as I drive to Lincoln.

He starts by saying that ministers will be able to issue stay-at-home orders to tackle local outbreaks from Saturday, which would mean that they could close specific premises, shut outdoor spaces and cancel events. It is now up to employers to decide on whether staff should return to work in their offices from the 1st August. Also, now the remaining leisure settings including bowling, skating rinks, casinos and beauticians, can open from the 1st August. Sadly for LJ, nightclubs will stay closed but indoor performances to live audiences will also restart in August with larger gatherings in sports stadiums to be piloted in the Autumn. Wedding receptions for up to 30 people will also be allowed.

The drive up north feels amazing; it is so long since I have had the space to think on my own and I catch up on some phone calls. It is wonderful to see Lincoln and when I arrive Elly, Ernie and I sit in the early evening sun in the garden talking about babies and catching-up. These are the important things in life, and it is wonderful to be out and about. On Saturday morning we work out together in the garden, enjoy a late breakfast and then walk around the shops in Lincoln. The streets are buzzing with people and it is quite overwhelming – I have not been to a shopping centre since February and it is packed. We queue for every shop, antibac our hands until they start to dry out and buy very little, but we do a lot of baby clothes window shopping. Bliss! In the evening we go for Tapas – I wear a dress and heels and when we get to the restaurant it is packed solid. Everyone else is dressed up too. It is the first dinner I have had out for four months. It is incredible and we order a bottle of wine (and non-alcoholic beer for Elly of course) and laugh and order too many dishes. It feels so good.

The next morning, I leave Elly to relax whilst I have a power walk around Lincoln. It is the most stunning city and the cathedral shines brightly in the sun. Her house is just a few minutes' walk from the shops and as I walk along the streets with their delightful artisan shops, pubs and little restaurants I think about how beautiful it is for bringing up a baby. She can just stroll out of her door and walk along to every shop that she would need, and she already knows most of the shopkeepers. I know it is still early and it is still a few weeks to the crucial twelve-week point and we want to stay positive that everything is good when she goes for the scan, but she and her partner, Ernie, are so lovely together and will make the most wonderful parents. We have lunch in their local pub in their new outdoor area and it is the most delicious roast. It is incredible how you miss these things. Afterwards we walk down to the cathedral and for the first time I go in; it is open for quiet reflection and prayer and I want to go in and light a candle for Sarah's mother. The cathedral is extraordinary and as soon as I go inside I am overwhelmed with emotion. I think about the lovely weekend I am having and about all of the families who lost people who are still grieving and feel guilty and sad for them. Elly looks concerned when I emerge from the cathedral red-eyed and teary, but it is still very close to the surface for me when I think about the loss of life.

The death rate has, on average, been in the low 100s this week, but the toll is still creeping up and I think when they are readjusted the final figures might be nearer 60,000. Horribly, horribly sad.

TOTAL DEATHS – 45,300

Week commencing Monday, 20th July And I have lost count of what week in lockdown we are!

It all seems to have gone away! Apart from people wearing masks the world seems back to normal now. It's bizarre! The roads are busy as ever, the shops are full of people, the evening news is now full of other subjects, the Government have barely been seen. Everyone's hair is back to normal, nails are being done, my diary is getting full of dinners with friends, and people in care homes are beginning to be reunited with their loved ones. But it hasn't gone, it is still out there, the death rate is still increasing and the threat of local lockdowns, and even a second wave, is still out there. We have to remember that the NHS is still battling to save lives, people are still being admitted to hospital and there are countries out there with spiralling numbers of cases and deaths. The US is obviously the worst with over 143,000 deaths and approaching 4 million cases.

There is, of course, still the battle for the vaccines and research around the world is happening at breakneck speed, with every country wanting to be the first to break through. About 200 groups around the world are currently working on vaccines and 18 of these vaccines are now being tested on people in clinical trials. The first human trial data has shown positive signs with 8 of the first patients all producing antibodies that could potentially neutralise the virus.

The problem is that we still do not know how effective any of these vaccines might be, but it is pretty amazing that they are developing vaccines in months, which would normally take years, or even decades to develop. The view from the experts is that a vaccine is likely to become widely available by mid-2021, around twelve to eighteen months after COVID-19 emerged. I speak to a client in a big company who tells me that they have been told not to expect to return from home working until the end of 2021. A sobering thought.

However, the reaction is mixed with some people saying that they are not comfortable in taking a vaccine. I can see this is going to be a really big issue with people asking the question: "Is it about you, or about saving other people's lives?"

And suddenly my week is fantastic – I feel focused and alert, work is brilliant, and the 'planes' keep landing. Every day we get confirmation of another booking and by the end of the week we had booked a significant amount for September onwards. Not out of the woods yet but a hopeful beacon at the end of the tunnel for us all. The team are doing incredibly well and LJ has encouraging news. Just when he thought he might lose the house they were buying, his mortgage got approved in principle. Again, not out of the woods as apparently the underwriters are really scrutinising income at the moment and with his sector crashing, the last four months have not been good for fee earning, but we keep everything crossed. And Elly is delighted to hear that from Monday partners can attend the twelve-week scans, and with just a week to go before her scan, it means so much to her that Ernie will also be there.

The feeling of buoyancy turns into braveness and we book a holiday for August. The chosen destination is Greece – the beautiful island of Rhodes. Greece has only recorded 201 deaths and border control is strong. I coach someone who is working in Greece who tells me they took his temperature on landing and if anyone tests positive, they will contact them and test and trace everyone on the plane. We choose to fly BA as I have been receiving regular updates on the quality of cabin air and it is only a four-hour flight so we can easily wear masks the whole time. I find a great bargain for a beautiful hotel and before I know it, I have pressed 'book'. This feels so exciting. The idea of packing, sitting round a pool drinking cocktails and sight-seeing is utterly delicious, and we fly in three weeks. That will give me two weeks to quarantine if I need to before the busy month of September.

Thursday marks the date for the compulsory wearing of face masks but once again there has been confusion from the Government, who then reconfirmed that yes, if we are going in to buy a sandwich or a coffee we need to wear a face mask, unless we are going to eat it in the shop, in which case we don't need to wear a face mask. What if we go in, intending to eat and then can't find a seat and walk out – are we in trouble? It is already a requirement in Scotland but is not mandatory in Wales or Northern Ireland.

Today should have been the start of the Tokyo Olympics, which were cancelled due to the pandemic. It is very sad, as, for some athletes, today would have been the last chance to compete due to age, or finances, particularly if, as some are predicting, it is cancelled again next year. The economic impact on Japan could be crippling.

So finally, it is Friday and after the best week yet for business since lockdown, we have the best weekend since lockdown. On Friday our new neighbours come round for drinks and a BBQ. They moved in last November, but I was travelling so much that we didn't actually manage to get a date together and we had intended to meet once we got back from skiing, but it never happened. They are a lovely couple with a great sense of humour and we drink far too much red wine sitting in the garden. The end of the evening becomes a blur and I know I am going to have a hangover in the morning, but I don't care. It finally feels like we are living again. The next morning I wake up at 5.00 a.m. with a banging headache and stagger around the house looking for paracetamol, to no avail. I go back to bed and manage to drag myself out of bed at 9.00 a.m. to do a workout, go shopping and cook for my dinner party of eight on Saturday evening. Finally, my beautiful tree trunk table gets the loving attention it deserves. The rain pours but the bi-folding doors are all open to the garden, so technically, we are outside! I glance around at the table, my wonderful friends, laughing and enjoying the company, as we drink wine and catch up on the last four months – and my heart feels like it could burst. It is the closest thing to normality since March.

The next morning, I am up early to walk with Trudy and this time we tackle Farley Mount, near Winchester; a beautiful walk taking in the rolling fields and scenery. We have so much to talk about and we miss our turning, ending up walking for nearly 10 miles instead of the promised 9.7 kilometres on the map! We walk and talk for three hours and put the world to rights. Trudy asks such insightful questions, and by the time I get home I am bursting with ideas and motivation again. I wish my legs felt the energy, but they just wanted to collapse!

But my best weekend was not the best for everyone. The virus hasn't gone, cases are still being admitted into hospital and during the week lives were still being lost. Complacency is our enemy and I realise how easy it would be to carry on as normal now, to just erase all of this from our memories and pretend it never happened. That would be disastrous.

TOTAL DEATHS – 45,752

Week commencing Monday, 27th July

It has been quite a week this week and I am full of mixed emotions today. I wish that I could write good news about the pandemic, I wish that I could tell you that the virus was continuing to recede and that the ease out of lockdown has been a smooth and simple one, I wish I could say I was ending this book with the end of COVID-19, but I can't.

The week started with news from Spain that the virus was spreading again. A meeting had been held on Saturday afternoon, chaired by Hancock, to discuss whether the air bridge with Spain should be classed as unsafe. Spain had seen daily cases fall throughout May and June, but now it was on the rise again with a 75% increase over the previous forty-eight hours and currently seeing around 2,000 new cases daily. After the criticism levied at the Government about slow action in the early stages of the UK pandemic, it seems they were acting fast now. Whilst this clearly was an embarrassment for the ministers and anguish for holiday makers, the Government, (who had been notable for their absence recently) rapidly announced warnings against non-essential travel to mainland Spain, the Balearic and Canary Islands, and then suddenly announced that anyone returning from there had to quarantine for fourteen days. People had been flocking on holiday to Spain and were suddenly faced with no notice about the quarantine – it would have been impossible to get an earlier flight home.

Closer to home on Thursday the news became even more painful for No. 10 when the ONS officially confirmed that England has the worst excess death toll in Europe in the first half of the year.

This results in another massive U-turn in the North with Greater Manchester, and parts of East Lancashire and West Yorkshire, waking up to greater restrictions being imposed on Friday and people being told that they now cannot meet inside houses. Many of the areas have Muslim populations and it was the eve of Eid, the biggest celebration in the Muslim calendar that follows Ramadan. The Government clearly knew that this could cause mass spreading so they stopped it immediately.

Matt Hancock appears, taking the tone of an old school headmaster as he blames local spikes on people not following social distancing and that contact tracing indicated most transmissions were from people meeting in houses. Once again, there was mass confusion about who could meet who, in which bubble, in what place and several government ministers appearing on TV to clarify it, just seeming to make it worse!

On Friday, Boris appears from nowhere with an update – it has been two weeks since he hit the podium and he really should have appeared a lot sooner. As always, he starts by reminding everyone of the good stuff that they had done and their successes. He then dips quickly into the bad news and talks of the need to react. He tells us that the virus is rising since the first time in May and that the infections were signs that could not be ignored. He tries to reassure us by saying that we are in a far better position to keep the virus under control now. After reinforcing the move to reduce social distancing in the North West he also tells us that he will have to postpone the changes that were due to happen on the 1st August – indoor performances not resuming, pilots of larger crowds in sports venue cancelled and wedding receptions of up to 30 people not being permitted until at least the 15th August. This will be devastating for anyone who was getting married in August as they will now have paid for everything.

He tells us there will be a greater police presence to ensure face coverings – interestingly Keith came back from Tesco Express this afternoon to say no masks were being worn by shoppers or staff! So how they will actually police this is a mystery to me.

He finishes by telling us that this is how we will avoid a return to full national lockdown. Professor Whitty is stronger and he warns that the UK may have hit its limits on easing restrictions.

These depressing developments make me think about the book. I had said that I was going to finish the book on the 1st of August, and I will, but it seems that there is a long way to go yet for the pandemic. I wish I was finishing it on a happy ending, but I suspect that this could go on for many more months, and without question, into 2021.

Ironically, this has been the best week I have had since the Pandemic started so my feelings are very conflicted. We have had two really good work weeks, and we are preparing to go back to the office on Monday. The team are so excited to get back and on Thursday I had a team day with them in my garden, discussing how lockdown had been for us, noting learning points to take forward, games on the lawn, a lovely lunch, some visioning and setting plans for the future. Gemma delivered the figures to us, and whilst we had always known that July and August would not be good months, from September onwards it looks as if we could be breaking even again. It doesn't make up for the loss of the last five months, but it does mean that the business is viable again, and providing the economy keeps moving, our business will survive. It is a massive relief and we are all incredibly pleased. The team are so incredible, and I am so grateful for them

Just as people are leaving Elly messages me. She has had her scan – the heartbeat is strong, and everything looks good. Another massive relief and we can start to slowly tell people the news. She immediately posts cards to LJ, Barry and her grandmother with pictures of the scan in them, telling them not to open the envelope until we FaceTime, and finally on Saturday morning we get together on a Zoom call so she can reveal the news. It is wonderful watching their faces and seeing their excitement, but also a huge relief that I can finally tell Keith and stop worrying that I might let it slip! It is beginning to feel so real now – we are going to have a new arrival in February 2021.

With new life comes new hope, and this baby will always be a reminder of 2020, and how we should never take our health and liberty for granted. My greatest wish is that they will never experience anything like this in their lives and that the lessons that we have learnt now will be sufficient to protect our future generations from another pandemic.

TOTAL DEATHS – 46,119

Monday, 3rd August

It is Monday the 3rd August and I am back in the office. I sit at my desk looking around and the last five months seem to be like a dream; a long and exhausting nightmare that just kept recurring. But now that I am back in the office it all melts away. My energy surges, my motivation and focus are improved, and I feel unstoppable. Rob and Gemma are in the office, Dawn is on holiday, and we easily social distance as we work, but just hearing them around the office is such a buzz. My week is packed with calls and Zoom meetings, preparation for courses and sales activity, and it feels fantastic. It started when I woke up this morning, knowing that I could dress in something nice, wear shoes and drive my car. The simple things like packing up a lunch for work, listening to the radio in the car and knowing that I could go home at six and leave it behind just make such an incredible difference.

This pandemic has been the worst thing I have ever experienced in my life and there were times when it felt impossible to cope with, emotionally draining, sad beyond belief and devastating every time the news came on TV.

But it has also been strangely empowering, and as with so many things, now I can look back and see how it has also been an opportunity.

I reflect upon how my life has changed, and ironically, how much the enforced isolation has helped me to make the changes in my life and work that I had been unable to fathom out for so many years. Our company had always flirted with virtual learning but our lack of knowledge and busy schedules had meant we never investigated it effectively. In fact, we often used to think that when clients asked for virtual learning sessions they were potentially getting an inferior product. When we had no choice but to pivot and to truly explore it, we found a whole new world and were amazed at how effective it could be. This has now opened up a whole new offering for us and has also bought global opportunities.

But more importantly, my crazy whirlwind of a life, flying from country to country, travelling from one city to the next delivering full-day training courses and then managing my emails in the evening and catching up at weekends, seemed impossible to reverse. It felt like there was no way out; I needed to stop the craziness to be able to think and re-engineer the business, but the hamster wheel didn't have an off button, until the world stopped and I had to stop too. If the pandemic had been for a month or six weeks, I think I would have gone straight back to my previous life, but now, everything has changed. I don't want that life again and I don't need it. Yes, I want to travel but not every day of the week and every week of the month. I remember one night when I flew in from Toulouse on a Friday night arriving at 10.00 p.m. and Keith met me at a dingy airport hotel with another suitcase so that I could repack and fly out to Dubai the next day. It seemed easy at the time and when people used to ask how I did it I didn't understand what they meant. Now I do. Never again will I travel to London for a one hour meeting or drive all the way round the motorway to conduct one coaching session. When you can do it virtually why would you? And it feels great to have options. Over the last five months we have totally reshaped all of our offerings, reconnected with old clients and found new clients – it has been a time of discovery. I truly believe that everything happens for a reason and once I had recovered from the devastating blow and the shock of losing everything and started to see the opportunities, I saw the reason. I have learnt so many lessons about leadership – which is rich coming from someone who teaches it for a living but experiencing a change like this really forces you to dig deep. I have learnt the power of communication, the need for relentless optimism, the importance of showing tenacity to your team, being decisive and really leading from the front. More importantly, it has taught me to really trust in my team, allow them to shine and feel valued. In all the time I was travelling and working so hard I didn't have much time for meetings and checking in with the team, and as they were such a hard-working self-directed team I thought that was OK, but it wasn't. A mistake I won't make again.

Personally, it has also been a time of great change for me, which has been positive, and I know that I will take a lot of the lessons. I have never felt as healthy as I have done in the last five months and my fitness levels are off the scale. I have learnt the power of walking and how much work I can do when I walk – some of my best ideas came when I was clocking up the miles in the morning. I have taken much better care of myself, my eating, sleeping and generally taking time to relax – I have rediscovered weekends.

This period has also been really good for Keith and me – we have caught up on the backlog of jobs around the house, worked hard on the garden and discovered how much we enjoyed being together. We have also learnt to respect each other more.

At the moment, I feel as if I have my life back now – this weekend I will go out to dinner with Sarah on Friday night and then my friends and their children will come to stay on Saturday night and we will barbecue, go for walks and picnic. We have connected with so many friends in different ways during this period, which has been such fun. And in two weeks we will be flying to Greece for our holiday.

However, this could all change overnight. The virus is still out there. The danger is still all too real and the people that have always protected us are still putting their lives at risk on a daily basis. None of those people had the opportunity that I did, to stop, take stock, and revisit how they wanted to live their lives. They were too busy getting themselves ready to go out to work long shifts, in gruelling conditions. They didn't have long weekends in the sun, they didn't have time to make their gardens beautiful, they didn't have time to learn, to connect with friends and to decorate their houses. For many of them they didn't even see their children and loved ones in order to keep them safe. Whilst we were locked away in our beautiful prisons they were locked away in their own private hell. And for all of the people who lost loved ones and are still struggling to grieve, their experience was different.

I will always be grateful for the NHS heroes (apparently they don't like being called that but that is how I feel about them), and everything that they did, and how they suffered. I hope that this book serves as a record of their amazing sacrifices and raises some money to support the families of those workers who lost their lives in service.

May we never forget.

Golden Jubilee Bridge, London

Carnaby Street, London

EPILOGUE

It is the beginning of October, the leaves are starting to turn and the rain has set in; it is relentless. For the last six weeks life has been good. I have loved being back at work and bookings are continuing to improve – it looks as if we will survive. Lawrence and Sophie have finally moved into the house (thankfully) and have a beautiful Labradoodle puppy called Ziggy. Elly is enjoying a wonderful pregnancy, happy and healthy and glowing. We found out last week she is having a girl and there is much excitement in the family.

The changing seasons has always been my favourite part of living in the UK. Autumn is a time of year I normally love; the anticipation of Halloween, Bonfire Night and Christmas – my diary full of parties and engagements in the run up to Christmas. But this year is different.

It has started again. Well, when I say started, it never really went away, it just felt like it did for a while. In July, the Government seemed to disappear – we heard nothing, no briefings, little news, and things started to go back to normal. We shopped, we socialised, we went on holiday, we celebrated birthdays, and weddings even went ahead with 30 people. We went back to the workplace and businesses started up again, with less room to make profit but they were still trading. Even sport was starting to get ready with experimenting about bringing back spectators. And, of course, we all got those long-awaited hair appointments and beautician sessions.

It was different; we still had to queue and finally Boris got off the fence and issued a directive that we all had to wear masks in shops. But that was fine, no one minded wearing a mask if it meant we could go about our daily lives. There were still rules to follow, albeit people were confused. Well, some were confused, and some were just determined not to follow the rules. Beaches were packed, in London large groups congregated outside pubs and big barbecues were in full swing on parks and commons. And schools returned in September. Social media was full of heart-warming school uniform and 'first day' snaps. For a long time the news was about other things rather than the death rates and the R number.

But of course, it hadn't gone away, and it isn't going away until we get a vaccine. In the last few weeks it has got rapidly worse. The North has been badly hit by a resurgence of cases and some areas are even going back into lockdown. The R rate is rising rapidly. However, the Government have adjusted the total deaths to make it appear less people have died and stopped reporting the daily death rates.

At the end of September the Government issued a law called the 'Rule of Six, which stopped people from meeting in bigger groups than of six. Even if you went to a restaurant as a group of eight and had two separate tables booked, the venue could get fined for breaking the rule. This was serious and we now knew that we had to comply. Massive fines were issued to people having parties. The Nightingale Hospitals are standing by to reopen and many areas of the North are back to local lockdowns. Scotland, under Nicola Sturgeon's guidelines are under the strictest measures. Doctors are bracing themselves for the reopening of COVID-19 wards in just three weeks to combat the surge in cases.

The number of COVID-19 cases coming from schools quadrupled in a week. University students appear to be a breeding ground for the virus and the Prime Minister appeared to state that the UK has reached a 'perilous turning point' and set out a whole new raft of restrictions and fines. The restrictions are set to last for another six months, including restricting weddings again to 15 people, and shutting pubs at 10.00 p.m. at night. (Seriously, how is that going to help? They will all just congregate outside.) Many more countries are put on the quarantine list and workers are once again advised to work from home if they can. The planned return of spectators to sports venues is cancelled.

The country is split; those who want to comply with the rules and really see this off, and those that have had enough, disagree with the new legislation and even go as far as calling it a conspiracy and refusing to follow the rules, saying it takes their freedom away.

The talk is that this will continue to be the way of life until next summer when the heat comes again, or until we find a vaccine, if we find a vaccine. And if it comes to stronger restrictions, lockdown during winter is going to be very different. Long dark nights will make it very different from the beautiful summer that people enjoyed.

And just when America gets deep into the crazy throes of the election, with Trump and Biden entering into the biggest car crash of a face-to-face debate, Trump and Melania test positive for COVID-19. The world is torn as to whether he is really infected, or it is a sympathy vote and delaying tactics for the election, but he is then taken into hospital. Two days later he reappears from hospital and bizarrely does a drive past of his fans and then proceeds, in a grotesque Evita parody, to appear on the balcony of the White House declaring that COVID-19 was like the flu and urging Americans to 'learn to live with it' instead of closing down the country.

I can find no words to describe this latest insanity.

Saturday, 31st October
Halloween

The rumour mill is running at an all-time high and lockdown fever is everywhere – the air is thick with anticipation as we know that something is going to happen soon. The scientists' predictions tell us that the second wave could take us up to at least 80,000 deaths, if not more. A full lockdown has been muted but other people are suggesting we might just go into Tier 2 in the South. We should really have locked down six weeks ago like other countries but once again the Government's indecisiveness will probably cost thousands of lives. Is this the result of all the crazy rallies, packed beaches and partying at the end of the first lockdown?

I go to the supermarket to do the weekly shopping and it is mobbed; shoppers behaving like crazy locusts stripping the shelves bare as fast as the shelf stackers can fill them. I had planned to get just the essentials but decide to stock up on basics anyway while I am here. So, this is how mob mentality starts; I feel guilty that I joined them but relieved when I get home and know that we have enough food for a month if we do need to fully lock down.

The Prime Minister's briefing is scheduled for 4.30 p.m. and then moved until 5.30 p.m. and then 6.30 p.m. The usual shambles. By then the country pretty much knew what was coming as press speculation had been rife with most of the news being leaked before it started. Boris appears at the podium with Whitty and Vallance who take us through some broadly unreadable and poorly put together Excel slides. Boris then announces the full country lockdown from Thursday. Thursday? Not again – we announce a lockdown and then give the country four days to go crazy before it starts. Unbelievable. The full lockdown will be for a period of a month, and if, and only if, we get the R rate down, then maybe we will be allowed to see our families at Christmas. My Women's Business Group Network explodes with comments from people who have just reopened their business and will now have to shut again and possibly close permanently. The impact on the economy will be extreme, so Boris announces the extension of the furlough scheme. But this lockdown will be so different for people; dark nights, rain and little hope of it actually working. My heart tells me that many people will not comply.

So, we now live in this world full of uncertainty, ambiguity, fear over the economy and the future of our country. It is highly unlikely we will have any semblance of normality before Spring 2021.

And Christmas is probably cancelled.

But there's always Brexit to cheer us up!

TOTAL DEATHS (ADJUSTED) – 46,717

Monday, 30th November

Well, the last month has been incredible – starting with the US elections and the victory by Joe Biden and Kamala Harris on the 8th November. It was closer than we thought with many twists and turns. Trump threw a tantrum, declared the election was rigged, refused to accept the result and sent his lawyers into bat, but eventually he had to accept that the fat lady had sung and it was all over. For the sake of the US, but also for the UK, I am deeply relieved.

I thought that was actually the best news of the year since Elly announced she was pregnant, but then ... news comes through of a vaccine. And not just one; Pfizer/BioNTech, and Moderna, announce the RNA vaccine, which is 95% effective. We all celebrate, our first true glimmer of hope in the darkness. This is incredible news and not only this, they think that they might be able to get the regulations cleared to start vaccinating in December. This is amazing news. And then like buses, Gamaleya (Sputnik V) announce theirs at 92% effective. The scientists are even excited and whilst I am fully prepared for someone to come and rain on my parade and tell us the down side of the vaccine it doesn't happen. Everyone on the news is talking about it and as if that wasn't enough optimism, Oxford/AstraZeneca then announce that theirs is 90% effective. We now await with bated breath to hear from the regulators and pray that the Government will actually get their act together when it comes to administering this to millions of people.

And just when I thought the week couldn't get any better, news comes through of rising tensions in No. 10. Boris's love affair with Cummings seemed to come to an end after he discovered accusations that Cummings had briefed against him. He was asked to step down and Cummings was 'papped' leaving No. 10 with his box of belongings. The turmoil comes at a time when the death toll exceeded 50,000 and the Government were days away from a looming Brexit deal deadline.

Finally, Boris decides that all four countries need to align their rulings for Christmas and after much anticipation it is announced that all four countries were allowing a five-day period where families could get together from the 23rd to the 27th December. Only three households could come together (and related bubbles) but at least we could get together and see people. But we are told not to hug our grannies. Of course not, the risk is absolutely immense to the older generation.

After much speculation, on the 26th November, Boris announces the next steps that will happen when we are due to come out of lockdown on the 2nd December. But we are not coming out, we are moving to the Tiered system with the majority of the country being in Tier 2, which means no households can get together until the 23rd December, some areas of the north being in Tier 3, which is almost the same as lockdown is now, and just three areas, Cornwall, the Isle of Wight and the Isles of Scilly, being in the lowest tier.

And it is exactly as I feared. No one is taking any notice of the efforts of the NHS and what the staff are going through.

They are so bothered about having Christmas, refusing to have the vaccine, accusing the Government of conspiracy theories and moaning about not being able to go to the pub. No matter how much the NHS tell us how appalling it is in the hospitals, it still doesn't make them understand.

But the danger out there is clear and present, and as the UK enjoys its five day Christmas hiatus, drinking and eating and having fun, hospital staff will be working extra hours to keep people alive. Whilst we dress up in our Christmas outfits they will be donning cumbersome and uncomfortable PPE for another shift. Whilst we are snuggled up watching films, they will be watching people fighting for their lives on ventilators and praying they recover. Whilst we are playing games and enjoying being with our families they will be holding up phones for families to FaceTime to say goodbye to each other.

And they will be sobbing silently during and after their shifts. The 'lucky ones' will survive, and the 'not so lucky ones' will leave behind family members, children and loved ones.

How can we ever repay them?

May we always remember.

TOTAL DEATHS 57,000

ACKNOWLEDGEMENTS

My husband Keith for his tireless editing. Dawn Newson for her support in proofreading and formatting. Trudy Simmons for encouraging me to take this all the way. My publisher Sarah Houldcroft at Goldcrest books for her advice and guidance in getting me through the publishing maze. The fabulous Aarti Palmer for the jacket design. My son, Lawrence Jones for the cover drawing. Spiros Kurtidis for the amazing pictures of London in lockdown. Alexis Powell-Howard for suggesting the book title and all the wonderful people who donated to the Crowdfunder who are listed at the back of the book.

THANKS TO CROWDFUNDER SUPPORTERS

I have been so lucky to have some amazing companies and individuals support me on this journey. I would like to thank the following companies who donated to the Crowdfunder to make the book happen and who support the charity I have chosen.

100% of proceeds from the book sales will go to the Healthcare Workers Foundation Families Programme. This is providing support for the bereaved families of NHS workers who lost their lives due to Covid-19 such as legal advice, counselling, supporting children with education and finding jobs and respite. You can find out more about the charity here: www.healthcareworkersfoundation.org.

Big Yellow Storage

Big Yellow Self Storage is the most recognised self storage brand in the UK. The company provides secure and modern self storage for homes and businesses and currently has over 62,000 customers. Founded in 1998 it now operates from a platform of 103 principally freehold stores.

People use Big Yellow when they need to find some extra space - often at key events in their lives.

The security of customers' possessions is the Company's number one priority and its stores are purpose built, modern and located in safe and easily accessible locations.

The Big Yellow brand is based on its people and excellent customer service is at the heart of its business. Its store teams are highly trained to offer helpful advice to people needing storage, many of which might not have used the service before.

Contact:

www.bigyellow.co.uk

Crown Worldwide

We would also like to thank our friends at Crown Worldwide, Steve Hardie and Eileen Girling for their support.

Contact:

www.crownworldwide.com

Emerge Development Consultancy

Gillian Jones-Williams is the Managing Director of Emerge Development Consultancy, an international organisational change and development company that provides a full range of bespoke development interventions, training products and executive coaching. Emerge are delighted to not only contribute to the book but to support the Family Fund to work with the families providing mentors and helping the children from bereaved families to find work places and employment.

Contact:

www.emergeuk.com

info@emergeuk.com

01329 820580

Financial Services Compensation Scheme FSCS

2020 has been a year unlike any other for all of us: our colleagues, our friends, our families and our businesses and organisations. We've all had to adapt and evolve and at the (FSCS) we've had to deliver our trusted compensation service to customers entirely remotely so I'm hugely proud that in 2020 we made 36,981 decisions on claims, paying out £406.5m to help people get back on track. None of this would have been possible without our incredible colleagues and inspirational partners like Gillian Jones-Williams which is why we're delighted to be able to support the publication of Locked Down But Not Out.

Contact:

www.fscs.org.uk

020 7375 8130

Firesafe Solutions (UK) Ltd

Firesafe Solutions (UK) Ltd is an established nationwide Fire Consultancy working for a wide range of companies to help ensure they stay within the law in a cost-effective way.

We have a wide portfolio of clients ranging from NHS hospitals, care home groups, universities, pub chains, local authorities as well as small individual companies.

Our experience in the Licensing trade is truly vast and we currently work for some of the major pub chains in the country, assessing in the region of 2500 pubs and hotels a year.

The experience we now have in the industry allows us to speak with some authority on the subject of the legislation and Firesafe Solutions (UK) Ltd have (where it is appropriate) defended a number of clients from Fire Authority enforcement action with extremely positive outcomes.

We like to think Firesafe Solutions (UK) Ltd is somewhat unique. We are an established company with a good reputation who provide national consistent advice to clients with all types of commercial enterprises.

Contact:

www.firesafesolutions.co.uk

0845 456 5121

Hampshire Hypnotherapy and Counselling Centre Ltd

When you need a helping hand and are considering professional Hypnotherapy, Psychotherapy or Counselling you need to be sure you are getting the best therapy for you.

At the Hampshire Hypnotherapy & Counselling Centre Ltd, we offer you the best range of clinical Hypnosis,

Psychotherapy & Counselling available in Hampshire. We offer a free initial consultation to all of our hypnotherapy clients, to discuss how we can best serve you.

Our professionally trained therapists have the experience and expertise to help you to resolve any issues that are causing your symptoms. This quickly enables you to get on with living your life. You'll be free from the symptoms that have had such a negative effect on you until now. All of our therapists and counsellors are dedicated to helping you to overcome your symptoms... for good!

We can help with overcoming anxiety, stress, fears, phobias, addictions, weight Loss – Including the World-Renowned Virtual Gastric Band and much more.

We also offer a corporate mental health & wellbeing services to help your staff to get back to work and overcome any anxiety that may arise as a result of the Covid-19 lockdown.

Contact:

www.hantshypno.co.uk

0800 970 4776

info@hantshypno.co.uk

I would also like to thank the following individuals for their encouragement, advice and amazing contributions to the Crowdfunder campaign:

Theresa Agonmuo
Denise Aldridge
Lauren Alexandra
John Athanasiou
Rob Bartlett
Gemma Box
David Blackburn
Jennifer Bourne
Gemma Box
Karen Broadhurst
Sophie Brooks
Peter Burn
Rebecca Bush
Fran Butler
Julia Charlton
Sarah Christensen
Jenny Cridland
Emma Davies
Anna Derkacz
Anthea Eksteen
Jennifer Eldred
Claire Evans
Jackie Forbes
Louisa Fisher
Peter Foulkes
Eileen Girling
Gill Goodwin
Ro Gorell
Leah Greenbank
Mairead Grimley
Sarah Guilder
Steve Hardie
Cheryl Hathaway
Susan Heaton-Wright
Craig Herne
Steph Houghton
Bev Hurst
Annelies James-Ryan
Elly Jettson
Andrew Jones
Barry Jones
Lawrence Jones
Karina Langan
Suzie Lewis
Lesley Mann
Sarah Marsh
Lauren McKenna
Laura Meyer
Hayley McCabe
Steve Mustill-King
Dawn Newson
Reem Nouss
George Perris
Kate Preston
Tania Pugh
Rosie Ranganathan
Irene Reed
Helen Robinson
Andrew Sibbald
Trudy Simmons
Michael Smith
Justin Standfield
Hazel Tan
Carl Thomas-Bring
Anton Thomas-Bring
Teresa Thomas
Ken Way
Ben Wilberforce-Ritchie
Alison Wooden

ABOUT THE AUTHOR

Gillian Jones-Williams is Managing Director of Emerge Development Consultancy which she founded over 25 years ago. She is also mother to Lawrence (LJ) and Ellena and her stepson Sam.

Gillian partners with many organisations to implement culture change and has designed and delivered training programmes of varying sizes to many national organisations. She works in multinational cultures having facilitated events and coached executives in Europe, the Middle and Far East, the USA and Australia.

Gillian is a business writer and co-authored 50 Top Tools for Coaching which was first published by Kogan Page in

Autumn 2009 and is now on its 5th edition. She is also an expert in organisational culture change and her book 'How to Create a Coaching Culture Strategy' is in its 2nd Edition and on the CIPD list.

Gillian was named as one of the top 100 UK Female Entrepreneurs in the f:Entrepreneur #Ialso 2020 campaign in 2020.

In the last 5 years she has been specialising in championing Women's development, specialising in supporting women to achieve their goals, develop their confidence and reach more senior positions. In 2015 she developed the award winning Empowering Women's Programme RISE which is delivered in the UK and the Middle East.

She is a Master Executive Coach and motivational speaker.

You can contact Gillian on info@emergeuk.com

Printed in Great Britain
by Amazon

57531229R00291